"Consider yourselves lucky. If The Seagoing Hitchhiker's Handbook
had come out 15 years ago, there may never have been a Latitude 38.
We'd have been out there doing it.... It is one of the truly new and
different books we've seen in a long time.... This is the book we wish
we'd written."

> John Riise,
> Managing Editor
> Latitude 38 Magazine

"Greg Becker's Seagoing Hitchhiker's Handbook is an
encyclopedic guide to obtaining crewing positions aboard voyaging
sailboats that combines copious research with Becker's own first-hand
experience. In addition to useful lists of visa requirements, sailing
schools, and marinas located along the best-traveled cruising routes,
Becker also offers more subjective advice that aspiring crew would do
well to heed--advice about the social conventions in the typical
captain/crew relationship that to ignore could end in serious
complications.
"This is a useful guide for anyone seeking waterborne travel
across the world's oceans. With a few basic skills, the ability to sell
yourself and this book in hand, it can be done."

> Tim Murphy
> Associate editor,
> Cruising World Magazine

(over)

"There are many people, myself included, who have had some of their life's most fascinating adventures sailing other people's boats and living nearly expense free. The marriage of compatible, able-bodied crew and boat owners is one of the few that are ideal. Private sail and power boats are literally going everywhere in the world today. Owners often sit in ports waiting for crew so they can go on to the next exciting port. This book will offer would-be crew members the information to prepare for the tasks necessary on such voyages. It holds a wealth of valuable information."

Harry Munns
Executive Vice President,
American Sailing Association

"There is no shortage of tales about passages made solo or shorthanded due to a lack of crew. The Seagoing Hitchhiker's handbook should be a long step towards getting willing crew together with needed skippers. The book does an excellent job of detailing what it takes to be a crew member. In addition, the descriptions of routes and facilities at harbors around the world makes the book useful to anyone, skipper or crew, interested in cruising.

Lorin Weiss
Santana Magazine

$11.95 U.S.

The Seagoing Hitchhiker's Handbook:

Roaming the Earth on Other People's Yachts

By Greg Becker

Acknowledgments

As you can guess, any project of this scope takes a great deal of time and dedication. I would like to thank those friends and family members who helped me piece this thing together, especially in the editing and proofing stage. Those people include Doug Foote, Steve Coy, Bill Hines, Don Ashcraft, my brother Ron Becker and my father Don Becker. Without their help this book could not have been considered a success. I would also like to thank those people across the country who read and commented on this book and gave me their words of praise. Those people include Tim Murphy at Cruising World Magazine, Lauren Weiss at Santana, John Reiss at Latitude 38 and Harry Munns at the American Sailing Association. Your comments allowed me to gauge my audience and find my market. I would like to again give special thanks to Tim Murphy of Cruising World Magazine, Kim Hatch of Earth Technology, Captain Matthew Benjamin of the *Wild Oats* in Jamaica, Susan Foggett of Australia and my father for the special help throughout this project. I would also like to take this time to thank Jim Baldwin for allowing me to share the dream with his family and get this whole thing started. Of course, this book would not have been written if I didn't get constant support from my wife, Estela, who gave me encouragement and fulfilled all of the household tasks as I sat and typed away. This book is dedicated to her. There are many others who helped me launch this book, and I apologize if your name didn't appear in this limited space.

All Inquiries should be addressed to:
High Adventure Publishing
P.O. Box 3435
San Clemente, CA 92677

International Standard Book Number 0-0639712-0-4

TABLE OF CONTENTS

CHAPTER 1
INTRODUCTION

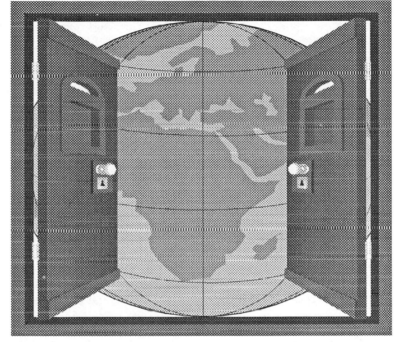

THE PURPOSE OF THIS BOOK

One February day in 1983 I was standing at the rail of the *Training Ship Golden Bear* as a midshipman of the California Maritime Academy, staring out across the Pacific wondering about my future. In the four years I had been at the books at the Academy, I hardly pondered my life beyond school. With the sound of Jimmy Buffett in my ears and the trades in my face, I found myself with mixed emotions about finishing my last annual three month training cruise and seeking out a job. Would I ever see the middle of the ocean again? In 1982 the maritime industry closed up and jobs on the freighters and tankers of the American shipping fleets were going away, leaving mediocre students like me looking to the shore for employment. I thought about something an older student had told me the year before on my previous cruise, and I was amused that a five minute conversation could influence how I was to think the following year.

He described a world which I had never heard of. A fraternity of spirited people intensely addicted to the finer things in life, people who do the things the entire world dreams about, living adventures in lands rich in culture and natural beauty. They surf the deserted tropical beach breaks, dive on long-lost shipwrecks, pulling up valuables and spearing the fish that look appetizing. With the sun overhead for the entire year, they never see the winter months. When the rainy season comes, they move to where it is dry and return a few months later. The freedom is absolute, the life is almost free, and the experiences are incomparable. This lost fraternity is the world of the cruising sailor, whose stories of the struggles they had to endure to attain the life they were living were almost as varied as their experiences since then. This student was able to sample their unique life of dreams, and he said it didn't cost him a dime.

He told me that it was possible to get on as a crew member if you were in the right place for imminent departures, and you could choose which yacht to go on if you had a needed skill. He said the three skills that were in demand were celestial navigation, cooking and engine repair. If you had one of these skills, you would find a yacht practically anywhere, if you possesed two of them, you would be in high demand.

That conversation influenced me to take up celestial navigation in the spring semester after the winter cruise, and on my final annual training cruise I borrowed a sextant and kept a plot from Cabo San Lucas to Tahiti.

Upon graduation, my worst fears were realized as I faced a life without employment. Devoid of money and in great debt from my student loans, I was forced to accept a job with the U.S. Navy in an old shipyard making barely enough to pay the rent. Then one day a wealthy land developer from Southern California called the academy looking for a recent engineering graduate who was adept in celestial navigation and knew how to scuba dive. The secretary gave him my name. That series of events led to my circumnavigation of the world on a 97-foot sailboat as I helped the family of Jim Baldwin sail their yacht 35,000 miles to 42 countries on six continents.

We went on safari in Africa, skied the Swiss Alps, filmed frenzied sharks with scuba tanks on our backs, surfed the giant surf of the remote islands of Indonesia, swam through shipwrecks in the Red Sea and navigated the muddy rivers to seek out the tribes of Asmat headhunters on the Irian Jayan coast of New Guinea. In short, I lived a life exactly as described by that student a couple of years earlier, a life I would never have realized if I hadn't struck up a conversation with him.

Over the last few years I have accumulated information that now makes up this book. I look forward to giving this opportunity to other spirited young men and women who have never heard of a life like this or simply don't know how to get going.

WHO THIS BOOK IS FOR

If you have ever been to Europe in the summertime, you will know of the multitudes of students and recent graduates from American high schools and universities traveling around, seeking worldly knowledge and looking for those experiences they are missing in their lives at home. The hostels and cheap hotels are crammed with them; the restaurants described in the latest edition of *Let's Go Europe* are full every night of the summer. Somehow it doesn't feel secure enough for them to break away from the pack and really find the out-of-the-way places and do the things not described in the guidebooks. I have linked up and traveled with dozens of them, and I've observed their eagerness to see the world, but their lack of guidance has kept them in what I call the 'circuit.' This circuit runs through the main arteries of the travel agent world. It tracks closely to the well-known attractions, encompasses the best sights and cultural centers along that route, and precious few wander far from that narrow path. My aim is to widen that track to encompass the places unknown.

If you find yourself with a bit of time off, from a few months to a few years, and you are looking for a vacation you will never forget, this book is for you. My target audience is:

1) Recent graduates with little money but lots of time;
2) Older people who are in the transition between jobs or have been laid off and need some time away from the western world and possibly an injection of self-esteem;
3) Retirees who lack the resources to buy their own yacht but wish to live that life nonetheless;
4) Those who are looking for the experience needed for a career as the captain or one of the crew of a yacht for charter

operation, for yacht deliveries worldwide, or for a private yacht; and

5) Adventurous watermen looking for uncrowded surfing, wind surfing, fishing and diving.

After the extensive research I did for this book I can truthfully say that a more complete worldwide guide for the cruising sailor does not exist. As a result, this book will provide an incomparable database for the cruising yacht owner, or a suplement to those guides in the yacht's library.

HOW TO USE THIS BOOK

First of all, it becomes obvious to all who glance within these pages that I have not included the maps that would make this book self-standing. The space involved in providing these maps would almost double the size of this book, or would necessitate the ommision of critical information, as this book covers the entire world. This is a reference book crammed with practical information for the seagoing hitchhiker and should be used in conjunction with a pocket world atlas. I recommend reading the first three chapters to gain insight on what is needed for a trip such as this and what you are likely to find. Use it to plan your method of departure and develop a plan that suits your needs, then do whatever research you feel is important to get you out on your first yacht. When you are ready to begin your voyage, read the applicable chapter that explains routes and that chapter explaining ports for the region you intend to depart from. Keep this book on hand for future reference when encountering new parts of the world. You will no doubt find this book invaluable when you are in remote reaches of the world, as there will be no other sources available to you. The information in this book would have made my journeys so much simpler had it been at my disposal.

THE SKILLS YOU WILL NEED

The three skills described to me by that midshipman so many years ago--celestial navigation, cooking and diesel engines--are still in demand today, but the emphasis has changed over the years. For example, the invention of the Global Positioning System has put the power of superior navigation in the palm of the inexperienced navigator and now precludes the necessity of learning celestial navigation. This is good news for you because not knowing this difficult task will no longer be a drawback. I have substituted a subject wider in scope but much easier to grasp: a good working knowledge of seamanship. Here is a brief description of the subjects you should try to learn prior to embarking on such a journey. Keep in mind that most yacht owners will take you aboard even if you have no experience at all, but it can't help to learn these beforehand.

SAILING

This is the most important for you to know before hitching a ride on a sailboat, but the essentials can be learned rather quickly on daysails or by taking a sailing course with a reputable organization. These classes are described in Chapter 3, *Training and Professional Opportunities*.

To become competent in sailing, you can learn the basics in a classroom or by reading books, and learn to handle small boats in the harbor, or you can throw yourself onto a large yacht with an experienced crew and get it by maximum exposure. Just remember that knowing how to sail a large yacht out at sea does not mean that you understand the basics that need to be understood for efficient sailing. Couple the experience you gain on a large yacht with some reading in the appropriate section of *Chapman's* or any other book on seamanship or sailing. There are many sailors out there who can handle their yachts perfectly well under normal circumstances but lack the fundamentals that are needed for maximizing speed on a crossing or for facing emergencies at sea.

KNOTS

Most people think that sailors are required to know several dozen knots, but in reality most only need to know a few and a sailor can really get by on one. Before you go to the docks looking for a daysail, learn how to tie a bowline. Without knowing how to tie this knot you are worthless on a sailboat, at least in the eyes of the observer. If you have no books on knot tying, go to the library and check one out. After you learn the bowline and can do it efficiently, learn the rolling hitch (a variation on the clove hitch), the square knot, the trucker's hitch, the sheet bend and the carrick bend. Nothing else is needed, so repel the impulse of trying to learn a dozen more, as they will certainly confuse you. Learn other knots as the months go by, after you have proven that the essential knots are forever locked into your skull.

COOKING

If you have the time, take a good class in basic cooking. Once you are proficient, get a book on cooking at sea and adapt your skills to preparing meals on a rolling yacht and serving fast meals. These books will show you how to plan the meals for a long trip, giving tips on how and where to provision and how to plan the meals for an extended voyage based upon the shelf life of certain foods. For example, if you can set up your sauces before the trip begins, prepare a pre-mixed blend of flour and other ingredients for fresh breads at sea, and mix up flavor packets for rice and other durable staples, you can whip out fabulous meals in any sea condition with minimal time in the galley underway.

ENGINES

I include in this topic a vast array of mechanical equipment including

GAS AND DIESEL ENGINES: for main propulsion and
    power generation;
STEERING GEAR: and the tiller controls, hydraulic and
    cable steering mechanisms, including installed back-ups;
ELECTRONIC EQUIPMENT: including radar, sonar, radios,
    antennas, navigation gear, and the controllers for
    steering gear;
AUXILIARY EQUIPMENT: Such as pumps, valves,
    compressors, filters, sewage treatment and discharge
    gear, anchor windlass and deck gear;
ELECTRIC MOTORS: and the drives for winches and furling
    gear.

If you have a good knowledge of mechanics and understand how things work, you can easily adapt that ability to the marine environment in a few hours of studying the owners' manuals of the equipment aboard and a few weeks of tearing into the gear itself. There are classes available to the general public in the repair of marine equipment. See chapter 3, *Training and Professional Opportunities.*

COASTAL NAVIGATION

This is a subject that is taught by the US Coast Guard regularly, but can be learned out at sea as readily with a patient navigator and a good book on the subject. It is essential that somebody on board knows the topic well, but it shouldn't be you. However, it is an excellent subject to understand if you plan to spend some time hitching around, and will only make you more marketable. Like sailing, it is not difficult to learn the basics.

WEATHER

Although the weather is very important to the mariner, it is not all that essential for you to know how to predict when looking for a ride on a yacht. This is a subject that is reserved for the captain. Most colleges teach this subject under the heading *Meteorology*, but it can be learned in books and then applied at sea easily enough. In order to use this book effectively, however, I have included the following passage to help in understanding why yachts sail in the directions that this book outlines.

The solar radiation that is absorbed on the surface of the earth is primarily done at or near the equator. The sun is more direct and is filtered out by a thinner layer of atmosphere than at the poles and with a shield of humid, tropical air the heat loss is blocked from radiating back out to space. Instead it is absorbed by the land and water, then that heat is transferred to the air in the form of water vapor and rises. Cooler air rushes to fill the vacuum and meets the same fate while the upper air is pushed by this high pressure of tropical contentment back towards the poles. This cycle is completed by the tropical humidity cooling and precipitation in the moderate climates and rushing back to the tropics to gather more heat. But as air sits or circulates above a spinning earth, it tends to want to stay stationary, resisting being dragged around the world with its rotation. To us this appears as an unreasonable wind to the west, but from the wind's point of view the earth has an unreasonable spin to the east. This is called the coreolis effect, or the curving of the air flow because of the twist imparted by the spin of the earth. Because of this, the winds just north of the equator have a predominately northeasterly breeze at the surface called the northeast trades while those just south carry the southeast trades. This is why most yachties propose sailing the world from east to west as it is unarguably more fun to sail along the equator and with the wind at your back. The same winds that travel aloft towards the poles from the equator eventually lose their heat and sink to a region of about $30°$ called the horse latitudes. This is a place where the wind predominantly comes straight down as it cools. The horse latitudes got their name in the eighteenth century from early sailors who, faced with the predicament of having too much weight to make way in the light winds, pitched their horses overboard to lighten load. As a result, the waters around $30°$ north and south were littered with the bloated corpses of horses. At the horse latitudes sits a high pressure ridge which initiates the northeasterlies and also the warm westerlies in the climates of both hemispheres. They pinwheel out from the high pressure region because of a strengthening Coreolis effect when in the vicinity of the equator.

BOAT HANDLING AND BOAT THEORY

You will probably not be asked to handle a yacht in the confines of a harbor upon your first few expeditions, so this subject will not be needed for a while. Watch the captain pull up to the dock and ask him questions, and do some supplemental reading on the topic to understand why the boat responds a certain way in a certain circumstance. Understanding the underlying reasons for the movement of a yacht will give you the knowledge you need which can only be obtained otherwise by blind experience.

PLANNING THE TRIP

WHAT TO TAKE

I would like to tell you a story about my first attempt to hitch my way across an ocean. I went down to the harbor in Long Beach to find a freighter crossing the Pacific, and found a Korean ship heading off to Australia. I talked to the chief engineer who decided to take me aboard and let me work my way across. My education on marine engines would have provided him with free experienced labor, and he felt sure that I could prove my worth. They were leaving the next day, so I went home and packed. I had about 200 dollars, no visas but a passport and a pack into which I threw what I felt I would need, including a trumpet and a loaded Derringer pistol. The captain of the ship called me the next morning and told me that their insurance prohibited them from accommodating me. I was pretty bummed out about my missed opportunity. Knowing what I know now, if I had gone on that trip, not only would I have been turned back at Australia at the shipping company's expense, but they would have jailed me for not having an Australian visa and for smuggling a loaded weapon. Even barring those disasters, I would have starved to death with my taking only 200 bucks. And I thought I was worldly!

In my experience I have always tried to carry as little as possible-- a day pack if I could help it. The reason for this is that a great deal of gear usually gets in the way, and I have found that even a big, half-full pack will inevitably get filled up, usually with junk I don't need. Get used to sending things home by surface mail (you are in no hurry). It is quite cheap and alleviates heavy, long term burdens. The object that necessitates a full pack is a sleeping bag, but in the tropics you could easily do without one. It is in your best interest not to take novels, especially during your first few crossings, and commit yourself to not reading any you might find on the yacht. I have found myself losing valuable time reading while I could have been learning piloting or practicing my celestial navigation. Force yourself to spend more time in the wheel house asking the captain about everything you observe, and read the reference books you find there. If you do find yourself too bored for comfort, most sailboats have many good books, and you have just found out why. Enough of what you should not take. This is what you should:

> A valid passport with visas for the destinations that require
> them;
> A personal hygiene kit;
> Some money;
> Simple navigation tools to show the captain you are serious;
> A pocket atlas of the world;
> A personal journal (very important);
> A sleeping sheet (like a sleeping bag, but light cotton, found
> in the tropics);

One pair of nice permanent press pants and a clean shirt only
   for special occasions;
A couple of credit cards if you have them;
A wind breaker;
Polarized sun glasses;
This book.

HOW MUCH WILL IT COST?

In my section *To Pay or Not To Pay,* I have brought up the subject
of paying for your passage. This factor will add some to your total, but
not a whole lot. Be prepared to spend a few weeks looking for your
first yacht. You may not have to spend more than ten dollars per day
for room and board in the ports of your search. Take enough to be able
to take the captain out for a beer occasionally, and in some places like
the Virgin Islands, where the best place to meet the crews is in the
dockside bar, be prepared to splurge a few times. In any case, the
amount you should take depends upon the way you like to live. In
Florida I met a Rastafarian from Jamaica named Rockers who asked
me for a ride to Bermuda. I struck up a conversation with him and
learned that he was planning a trip around the world and he was only
taking twenty dollars. I told him we had no vacancies on board, but I
wished him good luck. I ran into him in Bermuda and then again in
the Azores (he actually beat us to the Azores). He still had his twenty
dollars! I haven't seen him since, but I'll bet he made it. This story
shows why it is not all that important to carry a great supply of cash to
travel far, but you must decide how much you will need to be
comfortable.

For the time you spend on land, you could probably get away with
fifteen dollars a night comfortably, and at sea, nothing. In addition to
the amount you will spend for room and board, carry about $1500
extra to place in the strongbox of the host yacht (as outlined in the
section *The Skipper's Responsibilities* in chapter 2*).* This is mostly
optional, but in such places as the South Pacific, you are required to
post a bond of that amount anyway which is fully refundable when you
leave the country. This precludes the need for an ongoing airplane
ticket as required for all air travelers. The reason for this is to ensure
that you don't spend the rest of your life eating nuts and berries in your
own little cardboard home on the beach of their country. It might work
out best for you to plan a six-month trip and make it a personal

challenge to see how far and how long you could go on a given amount of money. It might surprise you. There are books describing short term employment around the world that show you how to work on a kibbutz in Israel or pick kiwi fruit in New Zealand, and although the pay is low, it could extend your trip for a few months. Another point to remember is that most American embassies will give you the amount for a plane ticket if you get into trouble, but they will require you to pay it back once you return home. In any case, even if you are one who likes a challenge, I wouldn't advise taking less than $1000 for any trip.

VACCINATIONS AND VISAS
One of the biggest uncertainties involved with international travel is the surprises lurking behind each immigration office door every time you enter a new country. The first thing you must realize is that the countries you enter are prepared to handle immigration matters as if you are a tourist entering for a predetermined amount of time and planning to leave the country by air. When deviating from the norm is when you must learn the details of the law and figure out how to get around them, or to take advantage of the leniencies.

When you have decided to leave the U.S. to fly abroad, one of the tasks you must do to make your journey possible is to visit the embassy of the country of your destination and find out all you can about their requirements for your visit. Since you will be planning to sail out of the country, you will not have the onward airline ticket you are usually required to possess and will be looked upon with skepticism by your travel agent, the person at the airline ticket booth and the immigration officer when you reach your destination. The travel agent is no problem because he or she has no legal requirements to make sure you have your papers in order. The immigration officer is no problem because you are already there and are almost guaranteed permission to stay. The person you will have to satisfy is the ticket agent who issues you your boarding pass. If a traveler reaches a foreign country by air and has no legal permission to be there, the airline has the legal responsibility of repatriating that person. Because of the number of foreign countries international airlines fly into, the ticket agent must act as the immigration officer for every country of destination. For this reason ticket agents must stay within the rules, sometimes under threat of termination. The responsibility then falls upon your shoulders to stay within their guidelines, or get special permission to sidestep their conservative rules. Either way, it usually requires a visit or phone call to the embassy. Note also that in many cases the airline information is stale, and even though you have the current facts, they cannot deviate from their written procedures to comply with what you need. Have the source of the information at hand.

I have devised a guide in this section based upon the information provided to me by the State Department for US citizens traveling abroad, current to 1993. It should be used as a guide to see the strictness of the different countries and to help in planning your route. When you have decided upon your first stop, call the embassy to find out the details, then take down the person's name. When you have done all that person has requested you to do, call the airline you plan to travel with and explain to them the details. Ask if there is anything else they will need, then ask for the name of the person with whom you are speaking. Explain to that person that your mode of travel is very unusual and you do not want to have any problems at the airport on the day of your departure. If you do encounter problems at the ticket counter, give them the name of the person who cleared your concerns by phone. It helps to get upset at this point. As long as you follow this path, you will be covered.

The table on pages 14-21 has some fields that must be explained up front:

TIME GRANTED FOR VISA: This entry represents the amount of time you will be able to stay in the country if you obtain a visa before you arrive. All N/A entries mean that you are not required to obtain a visa before you travel.

PASSPORT/VISA REQUIRED?: Is it required for you to obtain a passport or a visa before traveling? If a passport is not required, you will usually need a birth certificate. I recommend you always have a passport.

ONWARD TICKET REQUIRED?: Does the country need to see an onward ticket? This is the official stance of the country, but will not guarantee that the airline complies. Call both the embassy and the airline to cover yourself.

PROOF OF FUNDS REQUIRED?: Many countries require that you have a current bank statement showing a dollar amount totaling about

$1000 per month you intend to stay. For example, if you have $3000 in the bank, they might issue a visa for three months.

HOW LONG WITHOUT A VISA?: Some countries call the stamp in your passport that you receive at the airport a visa; some call it a visitor's permit. Whatever it is called, it will be issued in most countries without your having to obtain a visa ahead of time. There is always a time limit granted with the stamp.

CODE: What are the special requirements? Some countries will not allow you to enter if you have visited South Africa, Israel, or Libya previously. In Israel and South Africa, you are usually given a card to keep in your passport that has your visa stamp on it. When you leave the country they take the card and no records remain in your passport. I= Israel; SA= South Africa.

VACCINATIONS REQUIRED/RECOMMENDED: There are two parts of this entry, the first represents the required vaccinations for entering the country. Some are only required if coming in from an infected country: check with the embassy or call the Center for Disease Control automated traveler's hot line at (404) 332-4559. The field after the slash is what is recommended by the Center for Disease Control for your own protection. YF= yellow fever; Mal= malaria.

CONSULATE PHONE NUMBER: I have only included the numbers in Washington DC. and in some cases New York. The people there have the most reliable information.

COUNTRY	TIME GRANTED FOR VISA	PASSPORT AND VISA REQUIRED?	ONWARD TICKET REQUIRED?	PROOF OF FUNDS REQ'D?	HOW LONG W/O VISA?	CODE	VACCINATIONS REQUIRED/ RECOMMENDED	CONSULATE PHONE NUMBER
ALGERIA	90 DAYS	P,V	YES	YES	N/A	I,SA	YF/NONE	(202) 265-2800
ANTIGUA/ BARBUDA	N/A	NONE	YES	YES	6 MOS	NONE	YF/NONE	(202) 362-5122
ARGENTINA	N/A	P	CALL	CALL	3 MOS	NONE	NONE/MAL	(202) 939-6400
ARUBA	CALL	NONE	YES	YES	90 DAYS	NONE	NONE/NONE	(202) 244-6300
AUSTRALIA	6 MOS, M	P,V	YES	YES	N/A	NONE	YF/NONE	(800) 242-2878
BAHAMAS	N/A	NONE	YES	CALL	8 MOS	NONE	YF/NONE	(202) 319-2660
BARBADOS	N/A	NONE	YES	CALL	3 MOS	NONE	YF/NONE	(202) 939-9200
BELIZE	N/A	P	YES	YES	1 MO	NONE	YF/MAL	(202) 363-4505
BERMUDA	N/A	NONE	YES	CALL	21 DAYS	NONE	NONE/NONE	(202) 462-1340
BRAZIL	90 DAYS, M	P,V	YES	YES	N/A	NONE	YF/MAL	(202) 282-3133
CANADA	N/A	NONE	NO	NO	180 DAYS	NONE	NONE/NONE	(202) 682-1740
CAYMAN ISLANDS (BWI)	3 MOS	NONE	YES	YES	N/A	NONE	NONE/NONE	(202) 462-1340
CHILE	N/A	P	CALL	CALL	3 MOS+	NONE	NONE/NONE	(202) 785-3169
CHINA	CALL	P,V	CALL	CALL	N/A	R	YF/MAL	(202) 328-2517
COLOMBIA	N/A	P	YES	CALL	90 DAYS	NONE	YF/MAL	(202) 332-7476
COMOROS ISLANDS	CALL	P	YES	CALL	3 WKS	NONE	NONE/MAL	(212) 972-8010
COOK ISLANDS	CALL	P	YES	NO	31 DAYS	NONE	NONE/NONE	(808) 847-6377
COSTA RICA	N/A	P	YES	NO	90 DAYS	NONE	NONE/MAL	(202) 328-6628

COTE D'IVOIRE (IVORY COAST)	N/A	P	YES	YES	90 DAYS	NONE	YF/NONE	(202) 797-0300
CUBA	6 MOS	P,V	CALL	CALL	N/A	NONE	NONE/NONE	(202) 566-2701
CURACAU	CALL	NONE	YES	YES	90 DAYS	NONE	NONE/NONE	(202) 244-5300
CYPRUS	N/A	P	CALL	CALL	3 MOS	NONE	NONE/NONE	(202) 462-5772
CZECH AND SLOVAK	N/A	P	NO	NO	30 DAYS	NONE	NONE, NONE	(202) 363-6315
DJIBOUTI	30 DAYS +	P,V	YES	YES	N/A	NONE	YF/NONE	(202) 331-0270
DOMINICA	N/A	NONE	YES	NO	6 MOS	NONE	YF/NONE	(212) 599-8478
DOMINICAN REPUBLIC		NONE	NO	NO	60 DAYS	NONE	NONE/MAL	(202) 332-6280
ECUADOR	N/A	P	YES	CALL	3 MOS	NONE	YF/MAL	(202) 234-7166
EGYPT	3 MOS	P,V	CALL	CALL	48 HOURS	NONE	YF/MAL	(202) 234-3903
EL SALVADOR	3 MOS	P,V	CALL	CALL	N/A	NONE	YF/NAL	(202) 265-9671
ETHIOPIA	30 DAYS	P,V	CALL	CALL	N/A	NONE	YF/NAL	(202) 234-2281
FIJI	N/A	P	YES	YES	6 MOS	NONE	YF/NONE	(202) 337-8320
FRANCE, FRENCH GUIANA, REUNION IS.	N/A	P	CALL	CALL	3 MOS	NONE	NONE/NONE	(202) 944-6000
FRENCH POLYNESIA	CALL	P	CALL	CALL	1 MO	NONE	YF/NONE	
GALAPAGOS ISLANDS	CALL	P	YES	CALL	3 MOS	NONE	NONE/NONE	(202) 234-7166
GAMBIA	3 MOS	P,V	NO	NO	N/A	NONE	YF/NCNE	(202) 842-1356
GHANA	30 DAYS	P,V	YES	YES	N/A	NONE	YF/MAL	(202) 686-4602
GIBRALTAR	N/A	P	NO	NO	3 MOS	NONE	NONE/NONE	(202) 462-1340
GREECE	N/A	P	NO	NO	3 MOS	NONE	YF/NONE	(202) 232-8222

COUNTRY	TIME GRANTED FOR VISA	PASSPORT AND VISA REQUIRED?	ONWARD TICKET REQUIRED?	PROOF OF FUNDS REQ'D?	HOW LONG W/O VISA?	CODE	VACCINATIONS REQUIRED/ RECOMMENDED	CONSULATE PHONE NUMBER
GRENADA	CALL	NONE	NO	NO	6 MOS	NONE	YF/NONE	(202) 265-2561
GUATEMALA	3 MOS,M	NONE	NO	NO	30 DAYS	NONE	YF/MAL	(202) 745-4952
GUINEA	3 MOS	P,V	CALL	CALL	N/A	NONE	YF/MAL	(202) 483-9420
GUINEA-BASSAU	90 DAYS	P,V	CALL	Y	N/A	NONE	YF/MAL	(202) 872-4222
GUYANA	3 MOS	P,V	CALL	CALL	N/A	NONE	YF/MAL	(202) 265-6900
HAITI	CALL	P	CALL	CALL	CALL	NONE	YF/MAL	(202) 332-4090
HONDURAS	N/A	P	CALL	CALL	CALL	NONE	YF/MAL	(202) 638-4348
HONG KONG	N/A	P	Y	N	3 MOS	NONE	NONE/NONE	(202) 462-1340
INDIA	12 MOS	P,V	Y	Y	N/A	NONE	YF/MAL	(202) 939-9869
INDONESIA	N/A	P	Y	N	2 MOS	NONE	YF/MAL	(202) 775-5200
ISRAEL	N/A	P	Y	Y	3 MOS	NONE	NONE/NONE	(202) 364-5500
ITALY	CALL	P	N	N	3 MOS	NONE	NONE/NONE	(202) 328-5500
JAMAICA	N/A	NONE	Y	Y	6 MOS	NONE	YF/NONE	(202) 452-0660
JAPAN	N/A	P	N	N	90 DAYS	NONE	NONE/NONE	(202) 939-6800
KIRIBATI (GILBERT ISLANDS)	CALL	P,V	CALL	CALL	CALL	NONE	YF/NONE	(202) 462-1340
KOREA (SOUTH)	90 DAYS, M	P	N	N	15 DAYS	NONE	NONE/NONE	(202) 939-5660
MACAU	N/A	P	N	N	60 DAYS	NONE	NONE/NONE	(202) 332-3007
MADAGASCAR	I MO, M	P,V	Y	Y	N/A	NONE	YF/NONE	(202) 265-5525
MALAYSIA	N/A	P	N	N	3 MOS	NONE	YF/MAL	(202) 328-2700
MALDIVES	N/A	P	Y	Y	CALL	NONE	YF/NONE	IN SRI LANKA
MALTA	N/A	P	N	N	3 MOS, E	NONE	YF/NONE	(202) 462-3611

		NONE	Y	Y	30 DAYS	NONE	CALL	
MARSHALL ISLANDS	N/A							(202) 234-5414
MARTINIQUE	N/A	P	Y	N	3 MOS	NONE	YF/NONE	(202) 944-6000
MAURITANIA	3 MOS	P,V	Y	N	N/A	NONE	YF/MAL	(202) 232-5701
MAURITIUS	N/A	P	Y	Y	3 MOS	NONE	YF/MAL	(202) 244-1492
MEXICO	N/A	NONE	N	Y	3 MOS	NONE	YF/MAL	(202) 736-1000
MICRONESIA	N/A	NONE	N	N	1 YEAR	NONE		(202) 223-4383
MONACO	N/A	P	N	N	3 MOS	NONE	NONE,NONE	(202) 944-6000
MOROCCO	N/A	P	N	N	3 MOS, E	NONE	NONE,NONE	(202) 462-7979
MOZAMBIQUE	30 DAYS	P,V	N	N	N/A	NONE	YF/MAL	(202) 293-7146
MYANMAR (BURMA)	14 DAYS	P,V	Y	N	N/A	R	YF/MAL	(202) 332-9044
NAMIBIA	N/A	P	Y	Y	90 D	NONE	YF/MAL	(202) 986-0540
NAURU	CHANGES	P,V	Y	N	CHANGES	NONE	YF/NONE	IN GUAM
NETHERLAND ANTILLES	N/A	P,V	N	N	3 MOS	NONE	YF/NONE	(202) 244-6300
NEW CALEDONIA	N/A	P	NO	NO	1 MO	NONE	YF/NONE	(202) 944-6000
NEW ZEALAND	N/A	P	Y	Y	3 MOS	NONE	NONE/NONE	(202) 328-4800
NICARAGUA	N/A	P	Y	Y		NONE	YF/MAL	(202) 939-6631
NIGERIA	6-24 MOS	P,V	Y	Y	N/A	LOI	YF/MAL	(202) 822-1522
OMAN	3 WKS	P,V	CALL	CALL	N/A	I, LIBYA	YF/MAL	(202) 387-1980
PALAU	CHANGES	NONE	Y	N	30 DAYS	NONE	NONE/NONE	(202) 624-7793
PANAMA	CHANGES	P	Y	N	30 DAYS	NONE	YF/MAL	(202) 483-1407
PAPUA NEW GUINEA	CHANGES	P	Y	N	30 DAYS	NONE	YF/MAL	(202) 745-3680
PERU	CHANGES	P	DEPENDS	N	90 DAYS	NONE	YF/MAL	(202) 833-9860
PHILIPPINES	59 DAYS	P	Y	N	21 DAYS	NONE	YF/MAL	(202) 483-1533

COUNTRY	TIME GRANTED FOR VISA	PASSPORT AND VISA REQUIRED?	ONWARD TICKET REQUIRED?	PROOF OF FUNDS REQ'D?	HOW LONG W/O VISA?	CODE	VACCINATIONS REQUIRED/ RECOMMENDED	CONSULATE PHONE NUMBER
PORTUGAL, AZORES, MADEIRA	CHANGES	P	N	N	60 DAYS	NONE	YF/NONE	(202) 332-3007
ST. KITTS AND NEVIS	N/A	NONE	Y	N	6 MOS	NONE	YF/NONE	(202) 833-3550
ST. LUCIA	N/A	NONE	Y	N	6 MOS	NONE	YF/NONE	(202) 463-7378
ST. MARTIN	N/A	P	Y	N	3 MOS	NONE		(202) 944-6000
ST. MAARTEN	N/A	P	DEPENDS	DEPENDS	90 DAYS	NONE	YF/NONE	(202) 244-6300
ST VINCENT AND THE GRENADINES	N/A	NONE	Y	N	6 MOS	NONE	YF/NONE	(202) 462-7806
SENEGAL	N/A	P	Y	N	90 DAYS	NONE	YF/MAL	(202) 234-0640
SEYCHELLES	N/A	P	Y	Y	1 YEAR	NONE	NONE/NONE	(212) 687-9766
SIERRA LEONE	3 MOS	P,V	Y	Y	N/A	NONE	YF/MAL	(202) 939-9261
SINGAPORE	N/A	P	Y	N	3 MOS	NONE	YF/NONE	(202) 667-7655
SOLOMON ISLANDS	N/A	P	Y	Y	2 MOS	NONE	YF/MAL	(202) 462-1340
SOUTH AFRIICA	1 YEAR	P,V	Y	CALL	N/A	NONE	YF/MAL	(202) 966-1650
SPAIN	N/A	P	N	N	6 MOS	NONE	NONE/NONE	(202) 265-0190
SRI LANKA	1 MO	P	Y	Y	1 MO	NONE	YF/MAL	(202) 483-4025
SUDAN	3 MOS	P,V	Y	CALL	7 DAYS	NONE	YF/MAL	(202) 338-8665
SURINAME	2 MOS,M	P,V	CALL	CALL	N/A	NONE	YF/MAL	(202) 244-7488
SYRIA	6 MOS	P,V	CALL	CALL	N/A	NONE	YF/MAL	(202) 232-6313
TAHITI	N/A	P	NO	NO	1 MO	NONE	YF/NONE	(202) 944-6000

TAIWAN	2 MOS	P,V	CALL	CALL	N/A	NONE	YF/NONE	(202) 895-1800
TANZANIA	30 DAYS	P,V	CALL	CALL	N/A	NONE	YF/MAL	(202) 939-6125
THAILAND	60 DAYS	P	Y	N	15 DAYS	NONE	YF/MAL	(202) 234-5052
TOGO	N/A	P	N	N	3 MOS	NONE	YF/MAL	(202) 234-4212
TONGA	N/A	P	Y		30 DAYS	NONE	YF/NONE	(416) 781-0365
TRINIDAD AND TOBAGO	N/A	P	N	N	2 MOS	NONE	YF/NONE	(202) 467-6490
TUNISIA	N/A	P	Y	N	4 MOS	NONE	YF/NONE	(202) 862-1850
TURKEY	N/A	P	N	N	3 MOS	NONE	NONE/MAL	(202) 659-0742
TURKS AND CAICOS	N/A	NONE	Y	Y	3 MOS	NONE	CALL	(202) 462-1340
UNITED KINGDOM	N/A	NONE	Y	Y	3 MOS	NONE	NONE/NONE	(202) 896-0205
URUGUAY	N/A	P	N	N	3 MOS	NONE	NONE/NONE	(202) 331-1313
VANUATU	N/A	P	Y	N	30 DAYS	NONE	NONE/MAL	(202) 462-1340
VIRGIN ISLANDS, BRITISH	N/A	NONE	Y	Y	3 MOS	NONE	NONE/NONE	(202) 462-1340
WESTERN SAMOA	CALL	P	Y	N	30 DAYS	NONE	CALL	(202) 833-1742

CHAPTER 2
HITCHING A RIDE

LEARNING THE NECESSITIES

Your first step is to learn what you need to know to prove yourself qualified when the captain checks you out. Chances are he will take you out for a day sail for this reason, if he has time. He might even offer to have you on board for the first leg of the journey, with no promises to let you sail any farther. In this case you can bet he will be watching you and examining your seamanship abilities and your attitude. It is important to know enough to make yourself useful and to show you are a fast learner. Your first crossing is the most important because it is the most difficult to get, and with the experience of an open ocean crossing under your belt, you will have a much better chance of getting on for subsequent voyages. Because of the importance of the first voyage, I strongly recommend that you endeavor to learn some seamanship from library books before you go out looking for a yacht and then make an attempt at boarding a boat or two on the weekends to transform your knowledge to skill. After that, read over your resources again and try to extract more information from them. Don't let your lack of basic understanding get in your way.

One of the best methods that I touch upon throughout this book is that of visiting the boat yards in your area. Spend time looking around and talking to yachtsmen who are preparing for lengthy crossings, then find a yacht owner you like and help him with his repairs. Spend a week or two working for meals and a place to sleep so that he can see you in action, and he will likely take you along. I know several people who have used this approach to get on extended journeys.

TAKE A SAILING CLASS

If you live near a harbor or have a friend who does, make use of the privileges provided by the harbor community and local yacht clubs. If you have time, take a sailing class. Most harbors on the U.S. coasts have a wide range of classes, designed to give you an opportunity to charter their small yachts and become proficient at sailing. In these classes you might meet somebody who has a friend or dad with a boat who is willing to let you sail with him. Talk with the instructor and tell him of your quest. He can probably help you by lining you up with local yachties who frequently look for crew, or in some cases he will have a yacht of his own. There are professional organizations that have sailing courses that range from beginning sailing to advanced offshore navigation, and they are described in depth in my section on education in the next chapter. This method is not recommend for the reader of this book because of the time and money involved. I feel that you can use the money for keeping yourself alive while searching for a yacht in a tropical locale, and you can use the time for sailing in an open water crossing with the skipper as your guide 24 hours a day. Once you have learned the sailing and the navigation necessary, you can always challenge the courses you avoided, to obtain the certificate you desire.

JOIN A SAILING CLUB

Most harbors have sailing clubs(or yacht clubs), and for a small fee provide members with a chance to sail on the boats owned by other members. You don't have to own a boat to join, so you will be able to step into the sailing community and meet those who can help you get the experience you need. Sailing clubs and sailing classes are windows of great opportunity that should be used to your advantage. Call the individual harbors and marinas that are listed in the appropriate chapters (such as *Ports in the Atlantic*) and ask about sailing clubs.

GET OUT FOR DAY SAILS

Whether you plan to spend any time in the coastal areas of the US before your trip or not, you should know that it is easy to find a yacht to sail on for the day just by walking the docks. Unfortunately, many docks have gates that keep out non-residents, so in some cases you will have to find your own way to come into contact with these people. Put a notice of your own up on the board at the club (sometimes there are boards at the gate, or close by) with your local phone number and the days you are available. There are hosts of yacht owners who don't get out as much as they like just because they have a hard time finding crew. There are more who miss days of sailing because of last-minute dropouts and will phone you anxiously the night before or the day of the sail. Leave your number everywhere. In many cases you will find that the yacht clubs and sailing clubs will keep your number on hand just for these emergencies. Ask the local yacht clubs for calendars of upcoming regattas or weekly races and plan to be at the harbor for these events. In my sections of the ports that line the US coasts, I have listed some of the yacht clubs that host such races and described their policies.

OTHER OPPORTUNITIES

In the classifieds of national sailing magazines, there are many advertisements showing opportunities for crewing positions, monthly newsletters and placement organizations. Although the positions are rarely paid, the experience is free and it could be a great way to get your first crossing under your belt. Experience is usually not a requirement, but it helps. In addition, many local sailing magazines have classified ads for crews of a more structured nature. Check them out. Consider placing ads in such periodicals yourself and submitting your name in the electronic matching databases such as the *Crew Directory*. It costs some money and may not help you if you have no experience, but the exposure is hard to beat.

VISITING THE HARBORS

From the time you first get to the harbor you intend to leave from until the day you leave on a yacht, you should have your notice up at the board advertising your availability for a long crossing. Even if you intend to spend a couple of weeks going out on day sails, getting your message out early will help. The sailor planning for a long voyage will spend months, and in some cases years, preparing, and if he can spend a few weeks getting to know you, he will feel more comfortable about your coming along. The more people who see your message the better, as eventually the word will get to the interested sailor provided somebody he knows sees it. On the east coast, where there are countless harbors and facilities, the transient sailor becomes the rule rather than the exception, and word doesn't spread as rapidly. There, you must post your ad in more places to cover the community. Spend some time on the phone asking the proprietors of the yacht clubs, boat yards and marinas if they know of any opportunities, and ask if they would post your message if you mailed it to them. It's worth a try.

SELLING YOURSELF

Have you ever been driving down the freeway and seen a dirty, scraggly looking guy with his thumb out and thought, 'He's not dressed as though he wants a ride. I wonder if he knew he wouldn't be driving when he left home'. You might say the same thing if you saw the hitchhikers around the world trying to get on boats. These guys have the same fate out at the docks that they have on the road: they never go anywhere. I have hitchhiked many times on the road and at the docks, and with a clean appearance I have never waited long. If you put yourself in the shoes of the captain, you would come to realize that if you look as if you cannot manage your own personal hygiene, you probably cannot manage the appearance of his boat. If you look like a freeloader, you had better hope that he needs crew real bad. If you want to grow your hair long and look like a salty dog, wait until you sign on and you have proven your worth.

Talking to the captain about getting on for a crossing is in many ways like a job interview, and it is important that you dress and groom yourself appropriately before you talk to the captain or owner. Walking the docks will require nothing more than a pair of trunks and flip flops, but keep a decent pair of cotton pants and a button-down shirt on hand for when somebody tells you he would like to talk to you over dinner or a beer. Use the rest of your interview tactics, and realize you will be scrutinized more about your personal habits, as you will be looking for a 24-hour-per-day job where personalities and personal traits can ruin a voyage. Be honest and sincere.

DECISIONS

TO PAY OR NOT TO PAY

Sometimes you will be asked to pay a bit of cash into a food fund, which can be a good or a bad idea. In my experiences, the fee has been just a few US dollars daily, enough to keep everybody fed without making anybody rich. Realize that it is very inexpensive to sail and if you were to drop the anchor every night, your expenditures would be limited to food, fuel and necessary repairs. For those sailors cruising around on shoestring budgets, these expenses can kill their trips, and you should expect to pay a regular ante. If you are asked to pitch in for a fund such as this, your reaction should be to view it objectively and weigh the factors. If, for example, you are faced with shelling out forty bucks for a two-week crossing from Hawaii to Tahiti and you have no experience, you might view it as a great deal. On the other hand, if a captain wants you to put a great sum of money up front, view the request with suspicion and keep searching.

Another pattern that has been emerging in recent years is that of the 'cheap charter,' or the opportunity to sail as a crew member on a private yacht, helping to finance somebody else's circumnavigation in exchange for a one- to two-week sailing vacation in an exotic locale. These trips are set up by domestic travel agents and aren't cheap by hitchhiking standards, being comparable to the prices of regular yacht charters. For example, one such yacht I recently ran across is the *Jennifer,* a 50-foot Beneteau which was making its way across the Pacific over two years. The owner was offering berths on this voyage for $575 per week, all-inclusive (call Dominic Macan for similar yacht trips at (415)332-4681). A yacht charter generally costs two to three thousand dollars per week for a 50-foot sailboat in the Caribbean or the South Pacific, but it is difficult to find room for only one person on such a charter. For those with a very tight schedule and plenty of money this type of trip is far more practical, but this book is not intended for that audience. There are many nearly free opportunities.

ASSESSING THE CAPTAIN AND CREW

At times, the owner of a yacht will advertise in the harbors for crew members to avoid spending a season in paradise alone, and is willing to share his yacht with compatible and spirited people. In this case, one must take a long, hard look at his underlying intentions and make a decision. Usually one will find his objectives are straightforward, but be careful. This is especially so for a young lady looking to sign up with an all-male crew. Be sure to have a protector you can trust or have a good feeling for the crew, as there are no laws at sea and you can get into trouble. Look for a journey along a coast in short hops at first to get to know the others.

Be wary of wholesale crew abandonment or a malcontented crew. The captain can make life pure hell if he has a reason to, and many times his or her nasty side surfaces at sea. Take a member of the crew aside and ask a few simple questions. Find out how long he and other members have been with the boat. If they haven't had a crew change for some time, you should be inclined to accept. Ask why the previous guy left the boat, and what his tasks were. Take a look at the condition of the boat. Is it in good shape? Does the crew seem to care how it looks? Remember that pride is an important indicator on the attitude of the crew. Look at the seaworthiness of the boat, and ask yourself if you will be putting your life in jeopardy by leaving the coast for an extended voyage. Assess the experience level of the crew. With your two days out at sea for a couple of day sails, are you the most experienced person aboard? It is usually easy to get a proper reflection of the attitudes of the crew up front, but take in as much as you can. On coastal sails and island hopping you have plenty of opportunities to jump ship, but on a long crossing you're a captive.

Lastly, look at the destination of the yacht and its plans in your overall scheme, and decide if the crossing will put you where you want to be. If the captain wants you around only until a passage is complete, be sure to look ahead in the appropriate section of this book for the sailing opportunities from there.

THE SKIPPER'S RESPONSIBILITIES

One of the responsibilities a captain has when a crew member departs from his native turf for a sail abroad is to furnish him with a return airplane ticket. It is an accepted practice in the yachting community brought about by the immigration laws of the individual countries. Upon entry to most countries, the captain must sign a document that makes him responsible for getting his crew home in the case of them abandoning the yacht. This is a big responsibility for a yacht owner traveling on a shoestring, and the price of your repatriation can wound his adventure, especially when the host country has the defaulting right to confiscate his home. You can see that his decision can go far beyond speculative personality conflicts and the level of your knowledge, and that he must gain a certain degree of trust in you. If, for example, you sign on in Los Angeles and travel with him to New Caledonia, then you decide to part company, he might be responsible for flying you to your native turf even if it is half a world away. As a result, a wise skipper might ask a crew member to post a personal bond with him, putting it in the boat's strongbox or in a foreign bank account in the skipper's and your name to be drawn upon in the case of such an emergency. That way, you and he can decide up front who will finance your repatriation in the event of you departing the yacht early in the voyage. If, however, you and the skipper get on well while still in the states and he is not worried much about the money it will take to ship you home, the issue might never come up. In any case, just keep in mind that if the skipper takes you from your native home, he should be responsible for getting you home. If he only takes you from one foreign country to another, you should be responsible for getting out of your country of destination. A skipper who has had a hassle of this sort will make it his business to keep on top of these matters for the rest of his seagoing life, and those skippers who haven't dealt with it before have certainly heard about it from others. Be responsible for yourself and don't try to pull a fast one on a skipper by wrangling a free airline ticket out of him. You could ruin your vacation, ruin his voyage or find yourself treading water somewhere between Easter Island and the Galapagos. If you are in the position of possibly embarking upon an extended voyage, be sure to bring up these matters before he does. If you lay down your intentions up front and show him that you take the responsibility into your own hands, he will feel great about having you on board, and he will gain a measure of trust in you. This is the stickiest of all of the skipper's concerns with taking on crew members, so remove any of his doubt. Also, if you find yourself competing with other hitchhikers for a spot on a yacht, be prepared to make concessions regarding your repatriation. If you are in the States looking to sail off to the Panama Canal, offer to place the price of a plane ticket in the safe to be used in any port from which you might depart the yacht. Even though it might never be used, it may give the skipper the peace of mind he needs to select you over the others.

HITCHHIKING ON COMMERCIAL SHIPPING LINES

I mentioned briefly in my section entitled *What to take* an experience I had finding a berth on a freighter crossing the ocean. I have known people who have done this successfully many times, I have one friend who was allowed to take his motorcycle along with him, gratis. Most of these circumstances have been with individuals who were experienced engineers, seamen or electricians, and they spent a few days searching for a ship. I also spent some time in San Francisco harbor and in Darwin, Australia looking for passage briefly, to no avail. I just was not aggressive enough. Do not view it as impossible. There are many ships that will take you on board readily provided you spend the time to find one, but you may search for weeks. This subject is beyond the scope of this book.

CHAPTER 3
TRAINING AND PROFESSIONAL OPPORTUNITIES

LEARNING TO SAIL

In the previous chapter, I described the ease in which one can learn to sail in the unstructured environment of the deck of a person's personal yacht when hitching a ride. In this section I will describe the other, more formal alternative of learning in the classrooms and on the yachts managed by the many professional sailing schools in the United States and surroundings. This is, of course, the least adventurous way in which to introduce yourself to the world of offshore sailing, but in many ways it can be the most rewarding. If time and money are on your side, then this may be the method for you. The advantage here is the earning of a certificate, which may or may not be globally accepted for bareboat chartering, but in any case will convince the captain of any yacht you may approach that you are able, educated and had the patience to complete a structured course in sailing and/or navigation. In addition, it must be noted that most yacht owners do not have the capability or the interest to teach a person how to sail correctly. Thus, a sailing school remains the only way to be sure you will receive a complete education.

The different organizations around the country are described here and then the individual sailing schools are listed with phone numbers. Contact the organizations for the complete lists of their members. I have included a list of the more popular tall ship and offshore yachting schools, an expensive alternative but one with a guarantee of wet and wild sailing.

AMERICAN SAILING ASSOCIATION

There are many schools situated in the harbors of the continental United States that offer fantastic opportunities for the aspiring sailor.

The one organization that clearly sets the standard for sailing instruction in the US. and in the Caribbean is the American Sailing Association out of Marina Del Rey, California. There are currently about 125 sailing schools in the US that are members of that association, and teach the classes that were written by them. They offer a series of basic sailing and navigation courses leading to the bareboat charter certificate which can be used in most places around the world where bareboat charters are available. The person who holds this certificate has the most respected and internationally known document to prove their ability to sail.

The schools that use the ASA certification process differ in their prices and the content of their classes, which has been the main point of contention of those schools that have remained independent. The bottom line is that to gain the certificate offered by the ASA, everybody has to pass the hands-on test and the written examination administered by the ASA for each level of instruction. They seem to be an efficient self-governing body for the professional sailing community, and it appears that those organizations that choose to fight them will be left in the dust for years to come.

There are three basic classes that lead to the daysailing bareboat certification, five classes that lead to the bareboat certificate of boats to 50 feet. When comparing schools make sure you are not comparing apples and oranges, but compare the time and money required to obtain one of these certificates. Ask which ASA certificate you will receive upon successful completion of the course. Here is a rough breakdown of the certificates offered, but keep in mind that the space here prohibits me from giving too many details. For a more complete breakdown, call the ASA at the number below.

The **ASA Bareboat Chartering Certification** (able to act as skipper on a yacht to 50 feet for coastal sailing during the day) costs about $1000 and takes about two weeks to attain.

The **ASA Advanced Coastal Cruising Certification** (able to act as skipper on a yacht to 50 feet day and night in any weather), takes an additional $300 and another three days of instruction.

The **ASA Offshore Sailing Certification** (the same as the certification above but for offshore passages), an additional 400 dollars and another three days is required. This is the ultimate certificate, the most advanced given.

Since the ASA is a self-governing body and cannot get involved with the true licensing standards which must be followed in the maritime industry, all professional skippers of yachts involved in running of commercial vessels (such as those engaged in chartering) must be licensed by the US Coast Guard. These licenses are described briefly at the end of this chapter.

ASA facilities are found in almost all major harbors in the US, with a few in the Caribbean. Two that stand out on the West Coast are the Olympic Circle Sailing School in Berkeley, Ca and Sailing Solutions of San Diego, Ca. An alternative to sitting in a classroom to get the instruction towards your certificates is offered by the Ocean Incentives School of Sailing out of St. Thomas, USVI. They offer charters in the Virgin Islands that teach you sailing as you go, although the price is appropriately high. To get a brochure that lists the ASA facilities and their addresses, call them at (310) 822-7171.

OTHER SAILING ASSOCIATIONS

Although the ASA is the benchmark for sailing instruction in the US, there are other associations that have attempted to do the same thing with less success. One such organization is the **National Sailing Industry Association,** which represents chartering firms and sailing schools around the country, but is not wholeheartedly dedicated to sailboat instruction. They can be reached at (312) 836-4747, and will provide you with a list of their affiliates in your state.

Cal Boating is the instructional arm of the US Coast Guard, and will provide you with information on classes in your area that are offered by the US Coast Guard Auxiliary. They are quality courses ranging from basic boating and marine engine repair to advanced coastal navigation and are free of charge except for a nominal fee for the textbooks and the use of the classroom. To reach this organization, call (800) 869-SAIL.

Local and county organizations offer similar courses that are not as structured or as recognized but are softer on the budget. Call the harbor in your area and ask about the federally assisted summer programs sponsored by your local city or county.

INDEPENDENT SAILING SCHOOLS

Here is a list of the private schools offering quality instruction that are not associated with the ASA at the time of this printing. Keep in mind that this is not a complete list for all classes offered in the private sector, but it covers those that are well known and recognized. Note that some of these schools have since joined the ASA, and it is likely that more will in the future.

US WEST COAST AND HAWAII
Mahina Tiare Sailing Expeditions, Friday Harbor, Wa. (800) 875-0852
Cal Adventures, Berkeley, Ca. (510) 642-4000
Club Nautique, Alameda, Ca. (800) 343-SAIL
Pyzel School of Navigation, Santa Barbara, Ca. (805) 640-0900
Bluewater Sailing, Marina Del Rey, Ca. (213) 823-5545
Ragtime Sailing Ltd., San Pedro, Ca. (213) 514-9347
Orange Coast College Sailing Center, Newport Beach, Ca. (714) 645-9412
Calypso Marine, Newport Beach, Ca. (714) 645-7100
Aventura Sailing Association, Dana Point, Ca. (714) 493-9493
Honolulu Sailing Co. Honolulu, Hi. (808) 235-8264

US GULF COAST
Texas Sailing Academy, Austin, Tx. (512) 261-6193
MacPherson Sailing Enterprises, Pensacola, Fl. (904) 438-6514
Gulf Wind Yachting, Naples, Fl. (813) 775-7435
Offshore Sailing School, Fort Myers, Fl. (800) 221-4326

US EAST COAST
Norrad Sailing School, Camden, Me. (800) 421-2492
Island Time Sailing School, Marion, Ma. (508) 748-1148
J-World Sailing School, Newport RI. (401) 849-5492
Newport International Sailing School, Barrington, RI. (401) 246-1595
RCR Yachts, Henderson Harbor, NY. (315) 938-5494
Gold Coast Sailing School, Jersey City, NJ. (800) 532-5552
Annapolis Sailing School, Annapolis, Md. (800) 638-9192.
Sail Harbor Academy, Savannah Ga. (912) 897-2135
Florida Yacht Charters, Miami Beach, Fl. (800) 537-0050
Chapman School of Seamanship, Stuart, Fl. (706) 887-7966

OFFSHORE PROGRAMS
A growing number of programs are available for novice sailors to learn advanced skills while sailing offshore to exotic locales. This type of class started as outward-bound style trips for American youth to get exposed to adventure away from the inner city, but has evolved to accept everybody. The vessels range from conventional offshore cruising yachts to restored, fully functional square riggers, with the

programs having one thing in common: a high price tag. They usually do not include any type of certificate, but do guarantee adventure and a degree of offshore sailing instruction which can give you the experience you need to set out on your own for later trips around the world. Expect to pay between $900 and $1600 for a one-week trip, not including airfare, although the trips vary greatly in length, quality and price. For a more complete and in-depth list, contact the American Sail Training Association at (401) 846-1775. Their brochure contains a listing of more than 100 programs worldwide, but costs $15. Here is an incomplete list that might have the program you are looking for.

On the west coast there is the *Alaska Eagle*, run by Orange Coast College at (714) 645-9412; the *Californian,* run by the Nautical Heritage Society of Dana Point at (714) 661-1001; the *Pacific Swift,* operated by the Sail and Life Training Society out of British Columbia at (604) 383-6811; and other programs set up by the University of California, Berkeley at (415) 642-6586.

On the gulf coast there are opportunities at Action Sail in Sarasota, Fl at (813) 924-6789 and at the Galveston Historical Foundation, which offers experiences aboard the *Elissa,* a 200-foot sailing vessel. Contact them at (409) 765-7834.

The East Coast offers the widest range of these voyages with most of the vessels being of the more traditional type. The first is the *Ernestina,* a 112-foot schooner run by the Massachusetts Schooner Ernestina Commission of New Bedford, Ma., (508) 992-4900. The *Spirit of Massachusetts* runs in the Caribbean and is managed by the New England Historic Seaport during winter months at (617) 242-1414. In the spring and fall the ship is run out of the University of Long Island, which can be reached at (516) 283-4000. The schooner *Westward* and brigantine *Corwith Cramer* are run from the Sea Education Association of Woods Hole at (508) 540-3954. You can earn college credit on either one of these vessels. Trips aboard the *Brilliant* are organized by the Mystic Seaport Museum at (203) 572-0711. The *Clearwater* takes on month-long apprentice positions to help with short day sails out of New York Harbor, and can be contacted at (914) 454-7673. The *Pride of Baltimore II,* a 157-foot topsail schooner, runs two-week trips out of Baltimore, call (301) 625-5460.

Other organizations that run similar trips in different parts of the world include the Cousteau Society at (804) 627-1144; Earthwatch at

(617) 926-8200; Outward Bound at (800) 341-1744; and the Sea
Education Association at (617) 540-3954/3955.

THE PROFESSION

If you find yourself enjoying life out at sea on a sailboat and you
feel it may hold your interest for years to come, you might want to
consider going the professional route, and approach the US Coast
Guard for a captain or mate's license. The licenses are set up in the
categories outlined below, but for more complete rules contact one of
the Coast Guard offices, or call them at (800) 869-SAIL. Here is a
brief discussion on what it takes to obtain a license from the Coast
Guard and what you can expect it to do for you.

TYPES OF LICENSES

The first and most popular license is something called the
Operator of Uninspected Passenger Vessels, commonly known as
the 'OUPA' or 'six-pack' license. To charter a vessel or make money in
any way while taking passengers on a private or commercial vessel or
to marry people at sea, you must, at least, have this license. The
insurance companies that insure yachts against the loss of a vessel at
sea often require that the skipper has this license, even if the yacht is
not used for chartering. In most cases they will reduce the premiums
that the owners are required to pay. As a result, most owners of sizable
yachts will require their captains to be in the possession of this ticket,
or the more desirable master's license. 360 days aboard a vessel similar
to the one described on the license is required for this license, which
must be presented at the time of application. The categories are
divided into boat size and area of operation, and the required sea time
must be of the appropriate type. The tonnage limits for the licenses are
set by the examiner, and are categorized as either 25-, 50-, or 100-ton
uninspected vessels. The license will also be categorized as Inland
(restricted to harbors) or near coastal (to 100 miles offshore). The near
coastal requires 90 days of the 360 days of sea time to be along the
coast. This license is good for taking a maximum of six persons, soon
to be changed to twelve.

The **Master of Steam or Motor Vessels** is the big license,
requiring 360 days for the inland license and 720 days for the near
coastal. The near coastal is good for 200 miles offshore, and both
licenses are valid for boats up to 100 tons. This license is good for

inspected vessels, which means the vessels the licensee can operate can take more than six (or shortly twelve) persons.

The **Mate, Steam or Motor Vessels** license has been set up for the mate who wants to assist the captain, allowing him to rest or sleep on longer crossings. The Master's license allows the skipper to pilot the boat for only 12 hours at a time, so if the boat is involved on a longer transit, a mate or another master is required to be on board. The seatime requirements are half of those required for the Master's ticket.

The **Launch Operator** license is for those who run small launches or ferries, and is usually obtained as a term of employment. One would never get this license to prove his worth on a sailboat.

CLASSES AND EXAMS

The examination is not exceedingly difficult, provided you have spent the time to learn the rules, but its length can be nerve-wracking. The test can last from one to two days, with no time limit for each section. It is recommended that you take one of the correspondence courses advertised in boating magazines or a class in one of the schools that cater to the prospective examinee. These classes are about 40 hours and take two weeks, and some will even guarantee that you pass the exam. Call the Coast Guard office in your area for a recommended study center, to apply for a license and to schedule your exam in one of the seventeen examination centers. Your sea time must be documented and notarized with the skipper's signature.

CHARTERS

There are a great deal more bareboat charter companies around than there are crewed charter firms. However, more and more people have been deciding that it is more practical to have a hands-off vacation and let a professional crew give them the comforts they have earned. This trend is providing more opportunities for employment on crewed yacht charters, and if you feel it is the life for you, contact them for employment prospects. In my research I found that most of these charter firms hire most of their crew people from the professional placement services I described above. In any case, it cannot hurt to send out resumes well in advance, provided you have a great deal of experience or some kind of license or certificate from the Coast Guard or the American Sailing Association. For a list of crewed charter firms operating worldwide, see Appendix 1.

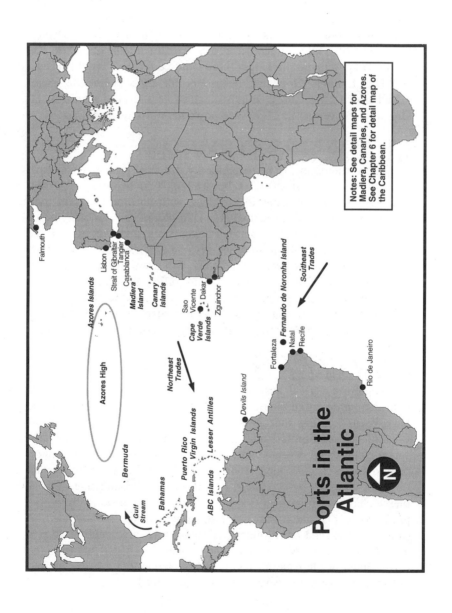

Ports in the Atlantic

Notes: See detail maps for Madiera, Canaries, and Azores. See Chapter 6 for detail map of the Caribbean.

Falmouth

Lisbon
Strait of Gibraltar
Tangier
Casablanca
Madiera Island
Canary Islands
Azores Islands

Azores High

Sao Vicente
Dakar
Ziguinchor
Cape Verde Islands

Northeast Trades

Fernando de Noronha Island
Natal
Recife
Fortaleza
Rio de Janeiro
Southeast Trades

Devils Island

Puerto Rico
Virgin Islands
Lesser Antilles

Bermuda

Bahamas

Gulf Stream

ABC Islands

N

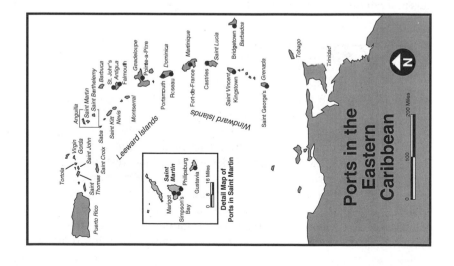

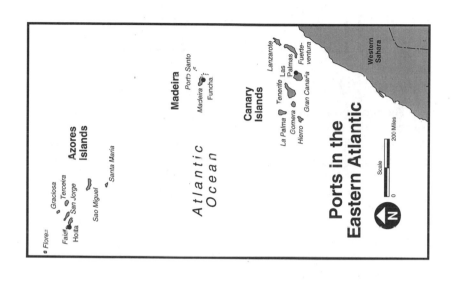

CHAPTER 4

ROUTES IN THE ATLANTIC

THE POND

The most crisscrossed ocean in the world is by far the Atlantic with boats on a constant move between Europe and the Caribbean with the change of the seasons. The 5000 or so yachts that cross through the Straits of Gibraltar annually warrants a big discussion so that the right ports can be visited at the right times of year. This chapter breaks the Atlantic Ocean and the Caribbean Sea into pieces, showing the times and directions of frequented voyages by region. Details of the individual countries and the ports and facilities within are described in the next two chapters.

The Atlantic is a very big ocean with passages of all lengths, and the Caribbean is usually visited in a series of short hops from island to island. It is also the most logical learning ground for the ambitious sailor and a favored stopover spot for circumnavigating yachts. So whatever your aim, this close-to-home paradise can launch you into an adventure of any length you choose.

WESTBOUND

The northeast trades, which blow throughout the year from east to west in the tropical waters north of the equator carry sailors along at a comfortable clip all year long. But being one of the nastiest breeding grounds for hurricanes in the world, most boats wait until late October to choose such a crossing. The route for most transoceanic sailors is firmly in the lap of the northeast trades when sailing west, although many choose to travel with the southern hemisphere counterpart, appropriately named the southeast trades. This southern route is relatively unpopular because of the lack of decent ports of departure and ports of destination and its separation from the rest of the Atlantic by that strip of windless misery commonly known as the doldrums.

The only sailors that use the southeast trades on a large scale are those moving north from the cape of Africa. One interesting note about the south Atlantic Ocean: hurricanes do not develop there, so the southeast trades are safe all year.

The northeast trades, on the other hand, offer a tantalizing downwind sail to the Caribbean Sea with nothing to impede the voyage. This wide conduit of warm air over tepid seas is bordered by the doldrums in the south and the moderate and uncertain winds of the Azores high in the north. As a result, sailors will use the trades to carry them gleefully to the paradise they spend those journeys dreaming about. The voyages are started in the southern Islands and the African seaports of the northern tropics such as Madeira; the Canary Islands; the Cape Verde Islands and Dakar, Senegal and are finished in one of many islands in the Caribbean or on the US Coast. Even voyages started from northern Europe, Scandinavia and UK usually run south to the transatlantic step-off points mentioned above, usually between May and August. The port of Falmouth on the southwest corner of Cornwall is the last place for sailors to stop before continuing across the English Channel, and so it is the logical place for you to go at this time of year to find a berth heading for warm water. The step-off points from Europe are Gibraltar and Lisbon, Portugal usually heading south from May to October. In the Canary islands, the most likely place for boats to land is Las Palmas; the most likely spot to leave from is Arrecife for the trip westward. The Portuguese island of Madeira is the departure point of choice for boats intending to head for the northern Caribbean such as the Virgin Islands, the leeward islands or the Bahamas, but most yachts continue on to the Canary Islands before making their crossings. Sailors depart Senegal for the Canaries before the December crossing to the US, but they also depart Dakar in April to make it up to Europe and the Mediterranean. Ports south of Dakar have unreliable winds.

Las Palmas on Gran Canary island sees more that 1000 yachts per year pass through on their way to the Caribbean, only about 75 of which are of US registry. Most of the 300 or so yachts there in late November are part of the Atlantic Rally for Cruisers (ARC) which leaves on the last Saturday in November for Barbados. Some boats are charters being shuttled between the Mediterranean and the Caribbean between seasons. About 90% of the yachts that call into the Canaries are there for a transatlantic crossing.

The Atlantic crossing is almost exclusively made from the Canaries with most boats leaving late November or December, but the rush continues until April. After that, although the northeast trades remain favorable, the hurricane season threatens the passages. November and December are favored over later departures so as to arrive around Christmas time to have the entire season to sail the Caribbean. One factor to consider is that the northeast trades (as with all trades and westerlies) shift with the sun throughout the season, i.e. north in the summer and south in the winter. Yachts that leave from the Canaries intent on making passage to the northern ports in the dead of winter (December) can find themselves sitting in the horse latitudes at the end of their crossing while the wind is south for the winter. Since this is such an ugly prospect, most yachtsmen plan to shoot for the southern Caribbean islands in these early months, or wait to sail from the Canaries for the US coast or Bermuda once the winds have moved back to the north. This seasonal wind shift also offers excellent prospects of finding passage from Dakar in December to these southern destinations in the Caribbean sea.

The four destinations of Christopher Columbus when he sailed on his four voyages from the Canaries were, in order: San Salvador, Bahamas; Dominica; Trinidad (with a stop in the Cape Verde Is.); and Martinique. The destinations of today's transatlantic sailors have changed somewhat, but the winds still blow them into the same vicinity. Boats now tend to land in Barbados, Grenada, Antigua and Martinique about three weeks after departure. Those boats from Europe that are planning a return trip to the Mediterranean will aim for one of the islands in the south and cruise north to avoid having to backtrack before their crossing to Bermuda. Those yachts continuing through the Panama Canal will aim for the northern islands of the Leewards, then sail south and make their crossing to Panama hugging the Venezuelan coast. The southern Caribbean is also the place to sit out the hurricane season, as hurricanes don't go down there.

Barbados has become the favored landfall in recent years, mostly because it is upwind of everything else. About 75% of the 300 or so yachts that call in Barbados each season are sailing from the other side of the Atlantic, of which most landings are made in December, before Christmas.

BRAZIL

Brazil covers nearly half of the South American continent, has about one-third of its shoreline and has a river navigable 2300 miles upstream, yet is not as important to yachtsmen as one might think. Brazil has some pristine cruising grounds, has fairly lax entrance requirements and an annual party to end all parties; however, the country is plagued with the light, variable and highly undependable winds of the doldrums. The principal attraction for cruising sailors is with this party, Carnival, which begins on the Friday before Ash Wednesday and lasts for weeks. Rio de Janeiro is the place to be when this occurs, although the party is in strong force all over Brazil and most of the rest of South America to a lesser extent.

In the southern part of the country, the only area of attraction for cruising sailors is in the City of Rio de Janeiro and the bays and islands to the west. The entire coast of southern Brazil, however, is plagued with poorly charted reefs, northeast winds and currents that run along the coast to the southwest, so the sailors you will find there have a very difficult sail ahead of them no matter where their next destination is. Some sailors leave for South Africa from November to March, and some set sail for the north from March to June with their ultimate destinations lying far beyond the Lesser Antilles. If aiming for Europe, they leave anytime between April and September, planning to use a great deal of fuel and a great deal of diligence to avoid the tropical cyclones that plague parts of their route throughout the northern hemisphere summer. Whatever their intent is, they are in for an ordeal that few sailors choose to put themselves through. As a result, the international cruising sailors you will find in Rio are very serious about their sailing and very competent.

In the northern part of the country, the primary intent is to get in and get out. The coast is plagued with reefs and rocks like the rest of Brazil, but the opacity of the water brought about by the Amazon run-off brings more uncertainty to the picture as the shallow reefs cannot be seen from above. Since the temptation of water sports is directly related to the clarity of the water, few sailors will find much attraction to the things he or she came to the tropics looking for, so the islands to the north beckon with ferocity. The coast north of Recife is easily sailed and more easily sailed away from as the winds and currents lead yachts northwest, towards the Caribbean Islands and the superior shores of Venezuela.

IN THE CARIBBEAN:

Given no further information, it would seem prudent for a sailor to choose his route through the Caribbean from windward to leeward (south to north). However, the direction of the prevailing winds is almost perpendicular to the lay of the Islands, enabling a southbound direction to be accommodated almost as readily. The flow of cruising yachts still tends to be to the north for the reasons discussed above, but the number of boats in the Lesser Antilles (the windwards and leewards) during the winter season is very high, and both directions see more than enough traffic for the needs of a hitchhiker. If you want to leave these Islands for the Venezuelan coast or the ABC Islands, the flow of yachts leaving from St. Lucia, Martinique and Grenada are concentrated in the months of December and January. From there they journey back to the Lesser Antilles in April and May or, more commonly, on to transit the Panama Canal late January or February to reach the Marquesas with good weather afoot.

Many sailors plan the crossing to the Panama Canal to match arrival in the South Pacific at the end of that hurricane season without realizing that the northeast trades, blowing across the huge fetch of the Atlantic and Caribbean, cause big swells and very rough following seas during these months. For this reason, the experts recommend crossing to Panama before or after the heart of the Caribbean season, although there are always plenty of yachts sailing in February and March and braving the seas. If you plan to leave the southern Caribbean for Panama, it is more comfortable in late April or May when the conditions are more pleasant. If you find yourself there that late, be sure to stay on good terms with the captain, as it will be a bad time to find a yacht sailing to the south Pacific.

If you find yourself in Panama, Venezuela or the ABC islands and you want to go elsewhere in the Caribbean, you will probably not find a yacht that will attempt a north or northeast crossing during the height of the northeast trade season. Boats will sail in all directions in November and early December, and then again at the end of this season in April, May or June, before the likely occurrence of hurricanes sets in. More and more boats are leaving the Caribbean side of the Panama Canal for points in the northwest Caribbean to sail the Bay Islands of Honduras, Guatemala and the Yucatan Peninsula of Mexico, then continuing a clockwise circuit of the Caribbean. The best time for this trip is from late October to early December to avoid the seas generated by the northeast trade winds and the dangerous northers that blow out of the States from November to April. From April to June when the trades tend to set more from the southeast, yachts will find their most comfortable sailing, but with the impending hurricane season they will be looking for the safety of the northern ports and will not be interested in seeking paradise.

Panama is by far the best spot in all of Central America to latch up with long distance sailors, as approximately 200 yachts cross from the Pacific to the Atlantic and approximately 350 pass from the Atlantic to the Pacific every year. The reason this is such a great spot is that the canal is difficult to transit and many yachts need assistance. To transit the canal on a yacht, you must have four 100-foot lines and handlers for each one, not including the captain. As the average size of a yacht's crew is three persons, there is always the need for an extra person. The going rate for a local line handler is fifty dollars per day, so your volunteering can save the captain some money. This affords you the opportunity to meet the captains of these boats, work with the crew for most of the day, and perhaps catch a ride for the South Pacific or the islands of the Caribbean. Pleasure boats now begin their transits on Mondays and Wednesdays; larger yachts (over 65 feet) can complete the transits in one day, for smaller yachts it takes two.

Boats sailing from the ABC Islands and Venezuela for the Lesser Antilles also make the journey before and after the height of the trades. For this reason, it would be best to seek out a berth pointing north from Aruba, Bonaire or Margarita around November to sail to St. Vincent, Grenada or the Grenadines and enjoy the entire season from there with the wind at your back. If you plan to head to the Virgin Islands or other points in the northern Caribbean or to the US, note that boats will not attempt this crossing until the late trades have shifted more to the south, in April or May.

After a seasonal sail in the Caribbean, most yacht owners choose to bring their yachts home with them or head off to the Mediterranean for the sailing season there. This is usually done around the months of April and May, but stragglers continue leaving throughout the next couple of months despite the hurricane threat. English Harbor, Antigua is the most popular spot in the entire Caribbean for shoving off to cross the Atlantic back towards Europe. In 1987, for example, 436 yachts checked out of English Harbor, most on their way to Bermuda. This launching culminates at the end of April or the beginning of May after Antigua Sailing Week and lasts until mid-

June, then northbound traffic ceases. If leaving for the southern states, try St. Thomas Harbor in USVI or San Juan, Puerto Rico.

For those leaving for the northern US ports and the Mediterranean, the midway stopping point of choice is Bermuda. A visit to this beautiful and friendly island in May or June will put you in the path of yachts tracking in both directions, as it is a favored resting zone for those sailors crossing the Atlantic from the ports on the US continent and those returning there from the Caribbean. Bermuda is one of the busiest hubs for transoceanic sailors on earth. In addition, this island is the first place for those long-distance voyagers to jettison troublesome deck hands, a place where yachts traditionally juggle crews. You will likely have a better chance of scrambling onto a yacht as a green sailor than somebody who was thrown off another.

All told, Bermuda sees approximately 1000 yachts per year, almost half heading towards the States in May and June, a quarter heading for the Azores in April to June, and another quarter heading to the Caribbean in October and November. This is a great place to go for a trip across to the Azores in May or south in October.

FROM THE US

The most logical place for a Yankee to leave for points unknown is from his own turf, so here are some recommendations for leaving the US from east coast ports. From Newport, RI; Norfolk; Cape Cod; Boston; and New York, the likely first destination for offshore sailors is Bermuda with onward trips across the Atlantic to the Azores and Europe or south to the Caribbean. From Beaufort, NC and ports to the south, boats usually go directly to the Virgin Islands without stopping in Bermuda, as the winds are more favorable in that direction and the weather more pleasant. This sail is made directly to St. Thomas in November. Yachts leaving Beaufort for the Virgin Islands leave religiously on November first. All of the above mentioned ports on the U.S. East Coast have boats that depart for Bermuda in May and June, for those with ultimate destinations of the Caribbean, primarily from northern ports, will leave for Bermuda in November. Boats leaving Florida ports can go directly to the Bahamas from November to April but will have to rely largely upon their engines. From the Miami area, yachts leave for the Caribbean during the entire Caribbean sailing season and also for Bermuda during May and June. One of the most popular events that bring cruisers together and offer the opportunity for potential crew members to join boats for an offshore trip to the Caribbean is the Caribbean 1500 cruising rally. They start out at three or more different cities around the end of October and set sail for Bermuda and then the Virgin Islands. Contact the race organizers at (401) 848-0302.

From West Palm Beach to Miami there are few places for yachts to depart, as the continuous Intracoastal Waterway has only a few inlets. The northern inlets of Sebastian and Lake Worth are used when the Grand Bahamas Island is the destination, while Hillsboro, Fort Lauderdale and Government Cut (Miami) are used when yachtsmen are sailing for the islands of Bimini and farther south. Along this stretch of coast there are other inlets, but they are not entirely safe in most cases and are used infrequently by sailors unfamiliar with the waters.

Virtually every yacht crossing to Europe will stop in the Azores, and this spot, as with Bermuda, is a great re-shuffling port where a great number of boats dump crews and pick up others for the remainder of their voyage. Your advantage here is that you have a good chance of picking up passage eastbound while only competing with others who have been dumped off other boats. In many cases, the disgruntled crew member will press his right for a free re-patriating plane ticket, leaving the Azores with one person too few. Since the majority of remaining crewmen on yachts in the Azores have blue water experience from the first part of the voyage, the yacht captains there will not usually mind having an inexperienced member aboard. If you do chose such an outpost for your initial crossing, you will have a good introduction to the Mediterranean sailing season, giving you blue water experience and a chance to stay on the same yacht for the booze-cruising hob-nobbing in the Mediterranean. The months that yachts pass through the Azores are May to September, with some boats sailing to Bermuda, the Canaries and Madeira in May to July and others sailing to the North Sea in June and July. It is reported that about 750 yachts pass through the port of Horta, Faial, Azores annually. Buying an airplane ticket to the Azores is a gamble, but the cards are stacked well in your favor.

SOUTH AFRICA

South Africa is one of the many countries important to both circumnavigators of the world and circumnavigators of Africa, being the last place to touch land before the lengthy transequatorial sail to the Caribbean, South America or Europe. Although it is possible to find yachts sailing the other direction in the months of October to January from Europe and from the U.S. East Coast in November, by far the greatest movement is to the north. The city of departure is Cape Town, but with different destinations, the times change a few months either way. The first boats leave Cape Town for the Caribbean starting in November and continue through March, but sail only from January through April to the Azores and Bermuda via stops in St. Helena and/or Ascension Island. The preferred routes are aimed at Brazilian ports and the Lesser Antilles to meet the cruising season there. It is estimated that an average of 200 yachts stop in St. Helena on their passages to Europe and the Caribbean. Another interesting note is that the best place to cross the equator is right around 30° west, so a stop at the island of Fernando de Noronha off the coast of Brazil is in the line of most yachts heading for the Caribbean.

Durban, South Africa and Cape Town are opportune places to find yachts arriving and leaving, respectively. It does not warrant a special trip down there, but if you find yourself in South Africa after an adventure southbound through the interior of that continent, the prospects of finding passage to Brazil or the Caribbean are excellent if your continental trip ends sometime between November and March. I have two friends who did that just recently and they both found passage, on different yachts, one for Brazil and one for Grenada.

CHAPTER 5
PORTS IN THE ATLANTIC
PORTS ON THE AFRICAN CONTINENT
MOROCCO

If you are to visit the coast of Morocco looking for a ride west across the Atlantic directly, you are clearly in the wrong place. If, however, you are looking to sail south along this rarely sailed coast or are trying to find a ride out to Madeira, this is the best place to look. Keep in mind that the facilities are very primitive and the harbors devoid of yachts for the most part.

The first port you will encounter on your journey south is the small harbor of Tangier. There are no services or facilities for yachts, just a small harbor full of fishing boats. Occasionally a foreign yacht will pull in. In Casablanca, visit the yacht club on the south end of the town dock. There are several workshops and a few small boat yards scattered around the port area, but any yacht large enough to warrant a visit will be anchored off or moored in front of the club. El Jadida is the next harbor south along the coast, about 50 miles from Casablanca. There is a small yacht club, only accessible by dinghy, and you will be hard pressed to find a yacht using its facilities. About 170 miles south from there you will encounter the small harbor of Agadir which has another small yacht club and you may find a yacht or two anchored offshore.

SENEGAL

The places to visit in Senegal are Dakar and Ziguinchor. But despite the reputation of being a transatlantic step-off pad, Dakar has very little to offer the cruising sailor except good provisioning. If you were to visit the city of Dakar in the wintertime, you will find yachts sailing off to the Cape Verde Islands or directly to the South American coast or the Caribbean. At other times of the year the trades are still too far north. In Dakar, have a look in the newly constructed wharf that may allow yachts to tie up from time to time. In Ziguinchor, look for yachts at the main wharf. This is the farthest south transient yachts will regularly venture as the variable winds characteristic of the doldrums keep the next 500 miles to the south still.

THE ISLANDS

MADEIRA

The only reason for the popularity of these two islands in the world of yachting is their position between the mouth of the Mediterranean and the Canary Islands. They do not warrant a visit in their own right as there is very little to do there. Yachts are found passing through the entire year, primarily in the months of October and November, and even those yachts that choose their crossing of the Atlantic without a stop in the Canaries will usually put in for a rest and a refuel because of this group's proximity to their route. Other yachts that pull in are those European sailors shuttling back and forth from the Canaries for the winter and the American yachts making the summer loop of the Atlantic, wishing to avoid the Mediterranean. As this pair of islands is not within the strip of the northeast trades, it does not see many visitors on seasonal trips as do the Canaries. But the seasonal strengthening and shifting of the trades and the impending transatlantic departures bring many yachts to this refuge. In the early winter season it is not unusual to see thirty yachts tied up along the Funchal quay.

In Funchal, the main port of entry and departure, the hub of activity is at the Clube Naval du Funchal, offering services and haulouts to 35 tons. The actual club is somewhat out of the port area, but they have an office at the Funchal quay. There is also a marina in the harbor.

The Porto Santo harbor has limited facilities for yachts, but it is the only other port of entry and the only other harbor in the country.

THE CANARIES

This group of islands is very important in the international sailing scene, as virtually all sailors stop here on their trips across the Atlantic. In addition, the Canaries are gaining in popularity by their own merit of superior sailing, excellent weather, a welcoming population and varying sights and beauties unique to the western tourist. They have no bad seasons and no serious storms except for the occasional Sirocco blowing sand out of the Sahara Desert to obscure vision and make people cough. As a vacation spot the Canaries have their attractions, including some of the best wind surfing in the world. In the months of November through about February, this group is worthy of a flight from Europe or even from the States, as a hitchhiker stands a fantastic chance of finding a ride across the pond and then likely a season of free sailing through the islands of the Caribbean. In November it is not unusual to find thirty or forty yachts anchored in Santa Cruz de la Palma ready to voyage, possibly with vacant bunks. Gran Canaria and Tenerife are even better than that. If one was to look for a yacht sailing west from the mouth of the Mediterranean, that person could scour every harbor in southern Spain and Gibraltar and not find all the yachts making the seasonal crossing. If a trip to the Canaries was made instead, virtually every yacht would be seen. There have been more and more European yachts in recent years wintering in the Canaries, and shuttling back and forth between seasons. In addition, the Atlantic Rally for Cruisers (ARC) runs hundreds of cruising yachts across the Atlantic together on the last Saturday in November.

On the island of Gran Canaria, primarily in Las Palmas, you will find the greatest number of yachts preparing for the transoceanic passage. Arguineguin, Puerto Mogan, Puerto Rico and Pasito Blanco are all decent ports with good facilities including travelifts (traveling boat hoists). This is clearly the best island to visit in the chain. Be advised that although the Real Club de Gran Canaria is sort of a centerpiece of the local yachting community, it is unfriendly to all foreign yachts.

Lanzarote is the second most visited island in the chain for foreign yachts, specifically the harbor of Arrecife. Arrecife is one of the places yachts stop first on their tour of the islands and one of the popular departure points for the journey. Visit the Casino Club Nautico de Arrecife, but be on your best behavior. Also visit Puerto Calera and Playa Blanca.

Tenerife is another good spot, Santa Cruz on the northern peninsula being the place to go. Although there are limited supplies, it is a port of entry and a recommended departure point. There is a boatyard with haul-out capabilities at Los Cristianos and marinas at Puerto Colon, Los Gigantes, Radazul and Puerto de Guimar.

On La Palma, visit Santa Cruz de la Palma for its repair facilities and the yacht club there.

The friendliest yacht club in the whole group of islands currently is the Club Nautico on La Gomera, but do your best to preserve this warm welcome by being on your best decorum.

The last island worth mentioning is Fuerteventura, which has a 30-ton travelift and a full service marina at El Castillo. Also visit Morro Jable, Corralejo and Puerto Rosario.

CAPE VERDE ISLANDS

This small group of 14 islands almost 400 miles off the coast of Senegal is becoming one of the premier stopping places for transoceanic sailors who leave from the African coast. In the months yachts cross the Atlantic for the Caribbean, primarily November until March, the winds are south for the winter and most sailors need to sail south from the Canaries to find the trades. This brings them fairly close to this group of islands, and many take the time to explore. However, the islands are largely uninteresting and not worthy of a trip on their own. If you do find your way to this lonely group of islands by way of another yacht or by ignoring reason and flying there on your own, here is where and when you can expect to find yachts sailing west.

The main port of call is Mindelo (Porto Grande) on Saõ Vicente island, and that is where foreign yachts spend most of their time. The Clube Nautico is the center of attraction, and most yachts use it to clear in, clear out and arrange repairs at the two small boatyards close by. The other notable harbor is Praia, on São Tiago. Most yachts that stop here do so only to take on fuel and fresh veggies.

Yachts start leaving for Brazil in late October, but the main exodus begins around November and early December when the crowd from the Med passes through on their way to the Lesser Antilles. This tapers off steadily until April, then some yachts pass through from West Africa on their way to the Azores. Those yachts transiting from Europe to South Africa cross the region of the Cape Verde Islands in November and December, however, their number is small.

PORTS OF SOUTH AMERICA

BRAZIL

In Rio de Janeiro there are many marinas scattered around the bay, the best one being Marina Gloria, east of the center of town. The Rio Yacht Club is reportedly very unfriendly to visitors on foreign yachts. Marina Gloria has repair facilities of its own, but the best establishment in which to seek yachts getting work done is at the shipyard in Angra Dos Reis, seventy-five miles west of Rio in the pristine cruising grounds of the Ilha Grande Bay. There you will find many yachts of foreign origin, good bars and everything else you could hope for. On the eastern lip of the entrance to Rio de Janeiro Bay at the town of Niterói there is a good, welcoming yacht club with repair facilities and supplies. At the Yate Club de Santos, close to São Paulo, you will find more good repair facilities, although most of the members of the yacht club are the owners of power boats.

About 300 miles southwest of Recife there is a huge bay and the city of Salvadore, the southernmost landing spot for those yachts ultimately heading for the Caribbean. There are no marinas or yacht clubs in the area, but the repair facilities are good and many yachts use them for the problems they develop on their trips across the Atlantic from the coast of Africa. On the eastern cape of Brazil is a very good boatyard at Praia de Jacaré. This small port town is reputed to be a good spot to leave a yacht for a trip to the interior.

The island of Fernando de Noronha is one of the most visited places for foreign yachts in all of Brazil, as it is a convenient resting place on the trip up from South Africa. In addition, there are usually no Immigration officials on the island, so a visa is rarely needed. The facilities there are primitive, and it certainly does not warrant a special trip from Brazil.

Although no cruising guides presently mention Fortaleza, which lies on the northern coast of Brazil, virtually all yachts bound for the Caribbean from South Africa stop there. The yacht club is very receptive to foreign yachts and provisions are plentiful, the beer is cheap, and there are reportedly very beautiful, loose women all over town. Now I'm not going to validate this last factor as a satisfactory reason for a group of transatlantic sailors to visit this place, but with the nature of men being what it is you can expect this port to gain popularity as more and more of them learn of its lack of virtue. It is not unusual for the bay in front of the yacht club to have twenty or thirty transatlantic yachts in it at any one time during the season, and being the first harbor for most of these yachts to touch mainland ground in several weeks, there is a natural affinity for them to exchange crew and a natural urge for some of those crew members to hit the ground running. I will put this harbor as one of the best in all of the Atlantic for catching a ride to points far away.

The only other recommended places to visit are the yacht clubs at Natal, on the northeast corner of Brazil, and Belém in the alluvials of the Amazon. Natal is a recommended departure point for the Caribbean islands.

FRENCH GUIANA, SURINAME AND GUYANA

These three countries have no interesting cruising areas but are mostly alluvial flatlands and the entrance formalities are very restrictive. The only places cruising yachts ever visit are the Iles du Salut offshore of French Guiana, which includes Devil's Island, the island made famous by *Papillon.*

PORTS ON THE NORTH ATLANTIC ISLANDS

BERMUDA

The two harbor areas in Bermuda are St. George's and Hamilton Harbor, both receiving yachts year-round in large numbers. Besides these yacht-laden harbors, there are islands and reefs giving visitors fabulous places to cruise and anchor for the night. The diving is superb all over the country, and the beaches are the best in all of the Atlantic. As described in more detail in the chapter *Routes in the Atlantic,* the primary times for a visit are April to June when yachts arrive from all over the Caribbean for the trips home and for yachts crossing to Europe from the states, and then again around November for those sailing from the US to the Caribbean. There are many races and cruising rallies from the U.S. East Coast to Bermuda and back in the months of April, May and June such as the semi-annual race from Marion, Mass. which commences around the 25th of June on odd-numbered years.

First, it is prudent to mention *The Yachting Guide,* put out by the Bermuda Department of Tourism. It will give you the facts you need and the information will be more current than mine.

St. George's is one harbor that sees all of the traffic that passes through the country, due to the government's requirement for them to clear in there. If a yacht does not plan to get any major work done or stay for more than a week or so, there is no urge to round the island and brave the intricate network of reefs and partially exposed rocks to get to Hamilton Harbor. In St. George's, all visiting yachtsmen coming ashore must dinghy in or tie up to the fueling and watering dock at the town quay. The huge bay is dotted with yachts in the busy months and the St. George's Boatyard at the west end of the harbor has facilities for hauling out yachts needing major or minor repairs. The St. George's Dinghy and Sports club welcomes yachtsmen from all over once a nominal fee is paid.

Until recently Hamilton Harbor was like St. George's with its lack of marinas and facilities, but now the Marina Real del Oeste stands where the Royal Naval Dockyard used to, on Ireland Island. It is now crammed with international yachts for most of the year, as is the boatyard next door. In Hamilton proper, yachts dock at the two yacht clubs: the Royal Hamilton Amateur Dinghy Club and the world famous Royal Bermuda Yacht Club. Yachts using the latter must be members of respectable yacht clubs back home, and if you want to enter the club you need to dress accordingly. For those yachts anchoring in the bay, the recommended tie-ups for their dinghies are at the center of the waterfront by the flagpole, at one of the clubs mentioned above and at the Gas dock beside the Princess Hotel. The two yacht maintenance areas are at Offshore Yachting and Maintenance and Mills Creek Marine. Visit the Pearman Watlington Marine Center in town and ask if they know of anybody looking for crew. Ely's Harbor in Mangrove Bay is worth a look, as is the small boatyard at St. David's on the northeast end of the main island.

THE AZORES

This tight group of picturesque islands is located well off the coast of Portugal, about three quarters the way across the Atlantic from The United States. The Azores has one of the biggest annual congregations of yachtsmen in all the world, seeing almost one thousand yachts pass through during the season. It is one of those places that is known as a great re-shuffling area for yachts to flush their crews in exchange for others, and the presence of yachts is so strongly felt that the entire area around Horta harbor caters almost exclusively to them. Although the other islands see a fair amount of yachts during the sailing seasons, Faial is where most of the yachts aim for and only a very small percentage of those clearing into the Azores ever see the waters that splash the other islands. One of the attractions that Horta has that is exclusive to this harbor is a wall on which virtually all transatlantic sailors paint a picture depicting their yacht. You can see these paintings as you walk along the waterfront, and view the history of modern seafaring like no other place on earth.

The newly constructed marina in Horta on the island of Faial is the overwhelming favorite for sailors passing through. There are no adequate boatyards, and yachts can be hauled out of the water only in case of emergencies. There are, however, a few workshops in town and a work yard where you might be able to meet up with yacht captains and crews, but the best place to go to come into contact with these people is at the Café Sport right next to the marina. Talk with Peter Azevedo, the proprietor of this world famous bar about how to get in touch with yachts looking for crew. Or just stick around and spend a few bucks, loosen up and don't be shy. The alternative is Club Naval right next door, which is as welcoming and as friendly as its neighbor, but not so well known. If you have a small bit of social sense or a fairly friendly face, you will not have to go any farther than Horta. Remember, there is an almost complete turnover of yachts every week or so in this group of islands, so if you drink too much and do something stupid in full public view, you will only have to hide out for a short time before all is forgotten.

Ponta Delgada on São Miguel is the second spot to visit if things don't work out in Horta, and a newly constructed marina makes a visit here a must. This marina, called Marinaçores, opened in 1993 and reportedly rivals the marina at Horta in size and services. There are also repair facilities in Praia da Victoria and at Angra do Heroismo on Terceira, the latter having a good yacht club as well.

PORTS IN THE US

Because of the large number of yachting centers along this coast and the others in the US, I have listed the facilities in tabular form. It is difficult to process this amount of entries by stating the relative attractions of the thousands of worthy yacht clubs, marinas and yacht yards without giving a tangible measurement, so I have simply stated the attractions of each. My tour starts on the coast of Maine and ends at the tip of mainland Florida. Those highly recommended are indicated with a diamond.

MAINE

EASTPORT AREA

Eastport City Dock (207)853-4614. Room for 7 transient yachts, deep, repairs.
Moose Island Marine 853-6058. room for 6 transient yachts, haul-out repairs.
Sorrento town dock 422-6889. Room for 4 transient yachts, not much else.
Bar Harbor Municipal Pier 288-5571. Room for 5 transient yachts.

MOUNT DESERT ISLAND

♦Northeast Harbor Marina (207) 276-5737. Room for 60 transient yachts, large yachts.
Mount Desert Yacht Yard 276-5114. Room for 10 transients , large yachts.
Clairemont Hotel 244 5036. Room for 10 transient yachts, but shallow.
The Hinkley Company 244-5531. Boatyard that handles sailboats. 75 ton lift capacity.

PENOBSCOT BAY AND RIVER AREA

Bangor Landing Park (207) 947-5251. Room for 10 transient yachts.
Wayfarer Marine Corp., Camden 236-4378. Room for 12 transient yachts, boatyard with a 120- ton lift.
♦Castine town dock 326-8579. Room for 160 transient yachts.
♦Billings Marine Service 367-2328. Room for 35 transient yachts, a 400 ton travelift and a large yard.

ROCKLAND

Knight Marine Service (207) 594-9700. Room for 12 transient yachts, a 50-ton travelift.
Journey's End Marina 594-4444. Room for 12 transient yachts, a 50-ton travelift.

BOOTHBAY HARBOR

Coveside Marina, Damariscotta River (207) 644-8282. Room for 12 transient yachts.
♦Boothbay Harbor Yacht club 633-5750. Room for 60 transient yachts.

Carousel Marina 633-2922. Room for 12 transient yachts, a small travelift.
Brown's Wharf Marina 633-5440. Room for 10 transient yachts, a small travelift.
Robinhood Marine Center 371-2525. Room for 10 transient yachts, a 30-ton travelift.

YARMOUTH / FREEPORT AREA

Casco Bay Rigging, So. Freeport (207) 865-3183. Room for 10 transient yachts, travelift.
South Freeport Marine 865-3181. Room for 10 transient yachts, travelift.
Handy Boat Service, Yarmouth 781-5110. Room for 25 transient yachts, a 35-ton travelift.

PORTLAND AND SOUTH PORTLAND

Centerboard Yacht Club (207) 799-7084. Room for 20 transient yachts.
Spring Pointe Marina 767-3213. Room for 25 transient yachts, a 35-ton travelift.
Channel Crossing Marina 767-4729. Room for 10 transient yachts.

KENNEBUNKPORT

Chick's Marina (207) 967-2782. Room for 40 transient yachts.
Kennebunkport Marina 967-3411. 16 transient yachts and a small travelift.
Rumery's Boat yard, Biddeford. 282-0408. Room for 6 transient yachts, a 25-ton travelift.

NEW HAMPSHIRE

Wentworth By the Sea Marina (603) 433-5050. Room for 35 transient yachts and lots of anchorage.
Prescott Park Dock 431-8748. 30 transient docks.
Harbor Place Marina 569-2443. 10 transient docks.
Great Bay Marine, Newington 436-5299. 20 transient docks, a 30 ton travelift.

MASSACHUSETTS

NEWBERRYPORT

Merri-Mar Yacht Basin (508) 465-3022. room for 10 transient yachts.
City Boat Works and Marina 465-1855. 10 transient docks.
Windward Yacht Yard 462-6500. A 70-ton travelift and large yard.

GLOUCHESTER AREA

Studio Restaurant (508) 283-4123. Room for 15 transient yachts.
Brown's Yacht Yard 281-3200. Room for 8 transient yachts, a 35-ton travelift.
Cape Ann Marina Resort 283-2112. Room for 25 transient yachts, a 70-ton travelift.

SALEM

Danversport Yacht Club (508) 774-8620. 50 ton travelift.
Fred J. Dion Yacht Yard 744-0844. 6 transient docks, a 100 ton travelift, large yard.
Barnegat Transportation Co. 745-6070. Room for 10 transient yachts.
Pickering Wharf Marina 744-2727. Room for 12 transient yachts.
Hawthorne Cove Marina 745-3061. 10 transient docks, 20 ton travelift.

MARBLEHEAD

Marblehead Trading Co. (617)639-0029. A 100-ton travelift, lots of yard space.
West Shore Marine 639-1290. 12 transient docks.
Marblehead Transportation Co. 631-0259 Room for 10 transient yachts.

BOSTON HARBOR AND SURROUNDINGS

Seaport Landing Marina, Lynn Harbor (617)592-5821. Room for 30 transient yachts, 25-ton travelift.
Crystal Cove Marina 846-4494. 15 transient docks, 30-ton lift capacity.
Admiral Hill Marina 889-4002. 25 transient docks, 50-ton travelift.
Marina at Rowes Wharf 439-3131. 38 transient docks, very exclusive in downtown.
Wally's Yacht Service 561-8408. 50-ton travelift, lots of yard space.
♦Shipyard Quarters Marina 242-2020. Many transient slips, room for 400 boats total.
Constitution Marina 241-9640. 50 slips for transient yachts.
Waveland Marina 925-2828. 15 transient docks, 35-ton travelift.
♦Marina Bay Marina 847-1800. 50 transient docks.
Bay Pointe Marina 471-1777. 15 transient docks, a 50-ton travelift.
Tern Harbor Marina 337-1964. 10 transient slips, 35-ton travelift.
Mill River Marine Railways, Cohasset Harbor 383-1207. 2 transient docks, 50-ton travelift and lots of yard space.

CAPE COD BAY

Harbor Marina, Green Harbor (508) 837-1181. Room for 20 transient yachts, a 35-ton travelift.
Long Point Marina, Doxbury 934-5302. 35-ton travelift.

♦Plymouth Marine 746-4500. Room for 60 transient yachts, a 60-ton travelift.
Provencetown Marina 487-0571. 35 transient berths.
Provencetown Yacht and Marine 487-2938. 30 transient docks.
Flyers Boat Shop 487-0518. 10 transient berths, 100-ton travelift with a large yard.
Northside Marina 385-3936. 15 transient berths, a small travelift.

MARTHA'S VINEYARD AND NANTUCKET ISLAND
♦Nantucket Boat basin (800)NAN-BOAT. Room for 140 transient yachts.
Menemsha Texaco Service (508) 645-2641. 20 transient berths.
Menemsha Town Dock 645-2846. Room for 20 transient yachts.
Coastwise Wharf Co. 693-3854. 20 transient berths, 30-ton travelift.
The Pilothouse Marina 693-0720. 40 transient slips.
♦Oak Bluffs Marina Harbor 693-4355. Room for 92 transient yachts.
Martha's Vineyard Shipyard 693-0400. A 25-ton travelift, lots of room for repairs.
Edgartown Marine 627-4388. A 35-ton travelift.

SOUTH COAST OF CAPE COD
Harwich Boat Works, (508) 432-1322. 50-ton travelift.
Mill Pond Boat Yard, Chatham 945-1785. 50-ton travelift.
♦Hyannis Marina 775-5662. Room for 40 transient yachts, 35-ton travelift, large yard area.
Lewis Bay Marina 775-6633. 30 transient docks.
Hyannis Yacht Club 778-6100. 10 transient docks.
Crosby Yacht yard, Osterville 428-6958. 10 transient berths, a 40-ton travelift.
Oyster Harbor Marine, Osterville 428-2017. 18 transient berths, a 50-ton travelift.
♦Green Pond Marine 548-2635. 15 transient docks, a 60-ton travelift.
Edwards Boat Yard 548-2216. 4 transient berths, a 50-ton travelift.
♦MacDougall's Marine Service, Falmouth Harbor 548-3146. 25 transient berths, three 100-ton marine railways. Very large, highly recommended.
East Marine 540-3611. A 35-ton travelift.
Falmouth Marine 548-4600. 15 transient berths, a 70-ton crane.

BUZZARD'S BAY
Quissett Harbor Boatyard (508)548-0506. 20 transient berths, small travelift.
Fiddler's Cove Marina 564-6326. 10 transient berths, 35-ton travelift.
♦Kingman Marine 563-7136. 235 slips open to transient yachts, 60-ton travelift.
Onset Bay Marina 295-0338. 12 transient slips.
Brownell Boatyard, Mattapoisett 758-3671. 16 transient slips, 60-ton travelift.
Mattapoisett Boatyard 758-3812. 35-ton travelift.

◆D.N.Kelley & Sons, Fairhaven 999-6266. 10 transient docks, three marine railways and a 150-ton travelift. Very large boatyard.

◆Fairhaven shipyard 996-8591. 12 transient berths, 300-ton marine crane and lots of yard space

F.L Tripp & Sons, Westport 636-4058. 3 transient berths and a 25-ton travelift.

RHODE ISLAND

NEWPORT AREA, NARRAGANSETT BAY

Standish Boatyard, Sakonnet River (401) 624-4075. Room for 12 transient yachts; travelift and marine railway.

◆Pirate Cove Marina, Sakonnet River 683-3030. 100 transient slips, a 40-ton travelift.

Dutch Harbor Boatyard, Jamestown 423-0630. 25-ton travelift.

Jamestown Boatyard 423-0600. 50-ton travelift and lots of yard space.

Conanicut Marine Service 423-1556. Room for 10 transient yachts, small travelift.

◆East Passage Yachting Center, Newport 683-4000. 50 transient berths, 70-ton marine crane.

◆Little Harbor Marine, north of Newport 683-5700. 50 transient berths and three travelifts to 160 tons.

Newport Yacht club 846-9410. 20 transient berths, very exclusive.

Long Wharf Landing 849-2210. 20 transient berths.

Newport Harbor Marina 847-9000. 60 transient docks.

Bannister's Wharf, Newport 846-4500. 30 transient docks.

Oldport Marine, Newport 847-9109. 30 transient docks.

Newport Yachting Center 847-9047. 30 transient docks.

Cristie's of Newport 847-5400. 30 transient docks, for large yachts.

Newport Marina 849-2293. 45 transient docks.

PROVIDENCE AND GREENWICH AREA, NARRAGANSETT BAY

Cove Haven Marina, Providence (401) 246-1600. 4 transient slips, 150 ton marine crane.

Pawtuxet Cove Marina 941-2000. 6 transient berths, 25-ton travelift.

Carlson's Marina 738-4278. 4 transient slips, 25-ton travelift.

Greenwich Bay Marina Club 884-1810. 10 transient slips, a 35-ton travelift.

Brewer Yacht Yard 884-0544. 35-ton travelift.

◆Norton's Marina and Shipyard 884-8828. 50 transient docks and a 35-ton travelift.

East Greenwich Yacht Club 884-7700. 10 transient berths.

Harborside Lobstermania 884-6363. 14 transient docks.

Wickford Shipyard 884-1725. 10 transient berths and a 60-ton marine crane.

BLOCK ISLAND
Chaplain's Marina and resort (401) 466-2641. 100 transient berths.
Block Island Boat Basin 466-2631. 65 transient berths.
Payne's Dock 466-5572. 50 transient berths.
Smuggler's Cove 466-2828. 14 transient berths.
Old Harbor Dock 466-2526. 40 transient berths.

EAST RHODE ISLAND
Point Judith Marina (401) 789-7189. 30 transient slips and a 30-ton travelift.
Long Cove Marina, Wakefield 783-4902. 45 transient slips.
Ram Point Marina, Wakefield 783-4535.10 transient berths, a 30-ton travelift.

PAWCATUCK RIVER
Westerly Yacht Club (401) 596-7556. 25 transient berths.
Avondale Boat Yard (401) 348-8187. 12 transient slips, 35-ton travelift.
Dodson Boat Yard, Stonington, Ct. (203) 535-1507. 40 transient slips, 35-ton travelift.
Northwest Marina, Pawtucket River, Ct. (203) 599-2442. 30 transient slips, 35-ton travelift.

CONNECTICUT

MYSTIC RIVER
Mason's Island Marina (203) 536-2608. 6 transient slips, 35-ton travelift.
♦ Seaport Marine 536-9681. 60-ton travelift, 100-ton marine railway.
Brewer Yacht Yard 536-2293. 10 transient slips, 35-ton travelift.
Mystic Shipyard 536-9436. 30 transient slips, 35-ton travelift.
Fort Rachel Marine Service 536-6647. 30-ton travelift.
♦ Mystic Seaport Museum 572-0711. 40 transient slips.
Spicer's Marina 536-4978. 12 transient berths, small travelift.

NEW LONDON AREA
Burr's Yacht Haven, New London (203) 443-8457. 25 transient berths. 20-ton travelift.
Crocker's Boatyard 443-6304. 25 transient slips, 2 travelifts to 75 tons. Huge marina, big yard.
Baureuther Boat Yard, Niantic 739-6264. 10 transient docks, 35-ton travelift.

CONNECTICUT RIVER

Yankee Boat Yard and Marina, Portland (203) 342-4735. 12 transient berths, travelift.
Portland Boat Works 342-1085. 10 transient slips, travelift.
Connecticut River Marina 526-9076. 10 transient berths, 25-ton travelift.
Deep River Marina 526-5560. 10 transient berths, small travelift.
♦ Essex Island Marina 767-1267. 75 transient berths, 30-ton travelift.
♦ Brewers Dauntless Shipyard 767-2483. 103 transient berths, 35-ton travelift.
Essex Boat Works 767-8276. Two sling hoists to 50 tons
Essex Yacht Club 767-8121. 22 transient berths.
Brewers Chandlery East 767-8267. 10 transient berths.
Oak Leaf Marina, Old Saybrook 388-9817. 8 transient berths, 25-ton travelift.
River Landing Marina, Old Saybrook 388-1431. 25 transient berths, 75-ton marine crane.
Saybrook Marine Service 388-3614. 10 transient slips, 30 ton travelift.
Saybrook Point Marina 395-2000. 15 transient berths, lots of room.
Harbor One Marina 388-9208. 35 transient slips.

WESTBROOK AREA

Pilots Point Marinas-East, North and South (203)399-7906. Each of these three marinas have 100 transient docks and a 80-ton marine railway and travelifts.
Pier 76 399-7122. 20 transient slips.
Cedar Island Marina, Clinton 669-8681. 50 transient berths and a 30-ton travelift.

NEW HAVEN AREA

Guilford Yacht Club (203) 453-8746. 20 transient berths.
Pier 66 Marina 488-5613. 35-ton travelift.
Goodsell Point Marina 488-5292. 2 transient berths, 50-ton marine hoist.
Dutch Wharf Boat Yard and Marina 488-9000. 35-ton travelift, good size yard.
West Cove Marina, New Haven 933-3000. 10 transient berths, a 35-ton travelift.
Milford Boat Works, Milford 877-1475. 20 transient berths, 35-ton travelift.
Milford Harbor Marina 877-1475. 20 transient berths.
Port Milford Marina 877-7802. 4 transient berths, 35-ton travelift.
♦ Stratford Marina 377-4477. 20 transient berths, 35-ton travelift. A huge marina.

BRIDGEPORT TO GREENWICH

Captain's Seaport, Bridgeport (203) 335-1433. 30 transient docks, 85-ton marine crane.

♦Norwalk Cove Marina 838-2326. 120 transient berths, a 70-ton travelift.

Norwest Marine, Norwalk 853-2822. 6 transient berths, 30-ton travelift.

Rex Marine Center, Norwalk 866-5555. 5 transient berths, 35-ton travelift.

Stamford Landing Marina 965-0065. 20 transient docks.

♦Yacht Haven Marine Center East and West 359-4500. 50 transient docks at each facility, a 60-ton marine crane at the west facility.

Greenwich Harbor Club 869-8690. 10 transient docks, a 30-ton travelift.

NEW YORK

EAST LONG ISLAND (THE FISHTAIL)

Modern Yachts (516) 728-2266. 6 transient berths, 40-ton marine crane.

Jackson's Marina 728-4220. 6 transient berths, 75-ton marine railway.

Larry's Lighthouse Marina, Flanders Bay 722-3400. 25 transient berths, 30-ton marine hoist.

Great Peconic Bay Marina, Flanders Bay 722-3565. 20 transient docks, 25 ton travelift.

Captain's Cove Marina, Montauk Inlet 668-5995. 15 transient docks, 35-ton travelift.

Offshore Sports Marina, Montauk 668-2406. 25 transient docks, 50-ton travelift.

Three Mile Harbor Boatyard 324-1320. 10 transient berths, 40-ton travelift.

Harbor Marina, Three Mile Harbor 324-5666. 10 transient slips, 30-ton marine travelift.

Sag Harbor Yacht Club 725-0567. 15 transient docks.

Sag Harbor Yacht Yard 725-3838. 35-ton travelift.

Jack's Marine, Shelter Island 749-0114. 45 transient docks.

Piccuzzi's Dering Harbor Marina, Shelter Island 749-0045. 35 transient slips

Coecles Harbor Marina & Boatyard, Shelter Island 749-0700. 30 transient slips, 30-ton marine hoist.

The Island Boatyard and Marina, Shelter Island 749-3333. 30 transient slips, 25-ton travelift.

Port of Egypt Marine, Southhold 765-2445. 20 transient slips.

Claudio's Marina, Greenport 477-0355. 30 transient slips.

♦Greenport Yacht and Shipbuilding 477-2277. 20 transient slips, 350-ton marine railway.

♦Stirling Harbor Shipyard & Marina 477-0828. 50 transient slips, 50-ton travelift.

Townsend Manor Marina, Greenport 477-2000. 51 transient slips.

NORTH LONG ISLAND

♦ Mat-A-Mar Marina, Mattituck (516) 298-4739. 40 transient berths, 50-ton travelift, 9 acres of yard

Bayles Docks, Port Jefferson 928-5200. 100 transient berths.

Old Man's Boatyard, Mt. Sinai 473-7330. 30 transient berths, 20-ton travelift.

Brittania Yacht Club, Northport 261-5600. 6 transient slips, 50-ton travelift.

♦ West Shore Marina, Huntington Harbor 427-3444. 50 transient slips, 35-ton travelift, a huge marina.

Willis Marine Center 421-3400. 10 transient slips, 35-ton travelift.

Coney's Marine 421-3366. 10 transient slips, 50-ton marine crane.

Knudson's Marina 673-0700. 10 transient berths, 35-ton travelift

Jacobson Shipyard, Oyster Bay 922-4500. 150-ton travelift, lots of yard space.

Sound View Marina 628-8688. 40 transient slips, travelift.

Glen Cove Marina 679-2213. 20 transient slips, 35-ton travelift.

Glen Cove Yacht Service 676-0777. 10 transient slips, 60-ton marine hoist.

Manhasset Bay Marina 883-8411. 25 transient berths, 80-ton marine hoist.

Capri Marina East & West 833-7800. Each facility has 40 transient berths and a 30-ton travelift.

WEST LONG ISLAND SOUND, NY

Derecktor Shipyard, Larchmont (914)698-5020. 11 transient berths, 120-ton marine hoist

Imperial Yacht Club, Davenport Neck (914) 636-1122. 10 transient docks, 70-ton marine hoist.

Kretzer Boat Works (212) 885-2600. 6 transient docks, 60-ton travelift.

North Minneford Yacht Club (212) 855-3143. 30 transient slips.

Marineland at Minneford (212) 885-2000. 30 transient docks, 35-ton travelift.

Consolidated Yachts, City Island (212) 885-1900. 6 transient slips, 60-ton travelift.

SOUTH SHORE OF LONG ISLAND

Shinnecock Canal Boat Basin (516)567-1700. 48 transient docks.

Jackson's Marina 728-4220. 20 transient slips, 75-ton marine hoist.

Hampton Boat Works 728-1114. 5 transient docks, 40-ton travelift.

Bath and Tennis Yacht Club, Westhampton Beach 288-0380. 25 transient docks, small marina.

Dockside 500 Marina, Patchogue 289-3800. 30 transient slips, 30-ton marine travelift.

Weeks Yacht Yard, Patchogue 475-1675. 40-ton travelift, large yard.

Davis Park, Fire Island 597-6830. Over 200 transient berths.

Watch Hill National Seashore Marina 597-6644. 150 transient berths.

Seaborn Marina, Islip 665-0037. 75-ton travelift.

Wantagh Park Marina 785-7777. 50 transient docks.
Tobay Beach Marina 785-1800. 130 transient slips.
Mako Marina, Freeport 378-7331. 5 transient docks, 60-ton travelift.
Guy Lombardo's Marina, Freeport 378-3417. 30 transient slips.
Bay Park Yacht Harbor, East Rockaway Channel 766-4112. 35-ton travelift.
Crow's Nest Marina, East Rockaway Channel 766-2020. 15 transient docks,
  35-ton travelift.

FROM NYC UPSTREAM TO PEEKSKILL

Viking Marina, Jamaica Bay (718) 444-3506. 35-ton travelift.
Brooklyn Marine Corp., East Mill Basin (718) 531-1616. 15 transient slips,
  50-ton marine hoist.
Liberty Harbor Marina (718) 451-1705. 60-ton marine hoist.
Newport Marina, Jersey City, NJ (201) 626-5550. 70 transient slips.
Port Imperial Marina, Jersey City, NJ (201) 902-8787. 15 transient docks, 35-
  ton travelift.
Julius Peterson Inc., Nyack (914) 358-2100. 6 transient docks, 60-ton travelift.
♦Haverstraw Marina 429-2001. 60 transient piers, 30-ton travelift.
Viking Boat Yard 739-5090. 12 transient docks, 60-ton travelift.

NEW JERSEY

SANDY HOOK AREA

Channel Club, Shrewsberry River (212) 222-7717. 10 transient docks, 70-ton
  marine hoist.
Irwin's Yacht Works, Navesink River 530-9222. 20 transient docks, 25-ton
  travelift.
Lockwood Boat Works, Raritan River 721-1605. 8 transient docks, two
  travelifts to 35 tons
Sandy Hook Bay Marina 872-1450. 10 transient slips, 50-ton marine hoist.
Atlantic Highlands Municipal Harbor 391-1670. 50-ton marine travelift.

EAST COAST, NJ

Belmar Marina, Shark River (201) 681-2266. 130 transient berths.
Brielle Yacht Club, Docks A,B,C,D 528-6250. 20 transient docks at each
  facility.
Brielle Marine basin 528-6200. 8 transient slips, 35 and 70-ton travelifts.
Johnson Brother's Boat Works 892-9000. 100-ton marine crane.
Wehrlen Brothers Marina 899-3505. 40-ton marine crane.
Winter Yacht Basin, Mantoloking 377-6700. 6 transient berths, assorted
  cranes and a marine railway, to 80 tons.
Harrah's Marina 441-5315. 107 transient docks.

Farley State Marina 441-8482. 200 transient Docks.
Albert C. Westcoat & Co. 345-1974. 60-ton marine crane.
Harbour Cove Marina, Somer's Point 927-9600. 10 transient docks, 25-ton travelift.
Canyon Club Marina, Cape May 884-0199. 30 transient docks, three travelifts to 60 tons.
Roseman's Boatyard, Cape May 884-3370. 50-ton travelift.
South Jersey Marina 884-2400. 50 transient berths.

DELEWARE BAY, MARYLAND, PENSYLVANIA, NEW JERSEY

Philadelphia Marine Center (215) 931-1000. 25 transient docks, travelift.
Seyfert & Wright, Neshaminy Creek, Pa (215) 788-2951. 15 transient berths.
Riverside Marina, Dredge Harbor, NJ (609) 461-1077. 10 transient docks, travelift.
Shafer's Canal House, C&D Canal, Maryland. (301) 885-2204. 40 transient docks.
Greenwich Boat Works, Bridgeton, NJ (609) 451-7777. 20 transient docks.

MARYLAND

EAST COAST, CHESAPEAKE BAY

Georgetown Yacht Basin (301) 648-5112. 35 transient slips, 45-ton marine crane.
Sassafras Boat Co. 275-8111. 30 transient slips, 70 -ton marine crane.
Granary Marina 648-5112. 50 transient slips.
Skipjack Cove Yachting Center, Georgetown 275-2122. 25 transient slips, 30-ton travelift.
Green Point Marina 778-1615. 60 transient slips, 15-ton marine travelift.
The Wharf at Handy's Point 778-4363. 16 transient slips, 35-ton marine travelift.
Worton Creek Marina 778-3282. 80 transient slips, 30-ton travelift.
Mears Great Oak Landing 778-5007. 50 transient slips, 50-ton travelift.
Tolchester Marina 778-1400. 5 transient docks, 50-ton marine crane.
Long Cove Marina 778-6777. 10 transient slips, 60-ton marine crane.
Piney NarrowsYacht Haven 642-6601. 25 transient slips, 50-ton marine crane.
Mears Point Marina 827-8888. 30 transient slips, 35-ton travelift.
Pier 1 Marina, Stevensville 643-3162. 30 transient slips, two travelifts to 70 tons.
Kentmorr Harbour 643-4201. 20 transient slips.
St. Michaels Harbour Inn and Marina 745-9001. 60 transient slips.
St. Michaels Town Dock Marina 745-2400. 50 transient slips.
The Tilghman Inn and Lodging 886-2141. 15 transient slips, small travelift.

Severn Marine Services 886-2159. Room for 12 transient yachts, 30-ton travelift.

Harrison's Chesapeake House 886-2123. Room for 15 transient yachts, 20-ton travelift.

♦ Yacht Maintenance Co., Cambridge 228-8878. 10 transient slips, lifts, cranes, marine railway to 200 tons Very large yard, lots of boats.

Oxford Boat Yard 226-5101. 25 transient slips, 60-ton marine hoist.

Mears Yacht Haven 226-5450. Room for 20 transient yachts.

Town Creek Marina 226-5131. 30 transient slips.

Crockett Brothers Boatyard, Oxford 226-5113. Room for 15 transient yachts, 30-ton travelift.

Port of Salisbury Marina 548-3176. Room for 15 transient yachts.

Logan Marine Services, Inc., Crisfield 968-2330. 30 transient yachts slips, travelift.

Somers Cove Marina 968-0925. Room for 50 transient yachts.

Shad Landing Marina 632-2566. 23 transient yachts slips.

Pocomoke City Municipal Docks 957-1333. 60 transient yachts slips.

Kings Creek Marina, Cape Charles, Virginia 331-2058. Room for 15 transient yachts, 10-ton travelift.

NORTHERN WEST COAST OF CHESAPEAKE BAY, ANNAPOLIS AREA

Bay Boats Works, North East, MD (301) 287-8113. 40-ton travelift.

McDaniel's Yacht Basin, Inc., 287-8121. 50-ton travelift.

The Log Pond Marina 939-2161. Room for 75 transient yachts.

Tidewater Marina 939-0950. 10 transient slips, 30-ton travelift.

Bowleys Point Condomarina 335-3553. 15 transient slips, 30-ton marine hoist.

Markley's Marina, Middle River 687-5575. 60-ton marine hoist.

Deckelman's Marina 391-6482. 6 transient yachts docks, 40-ton travelift.

White Rocks Yachting Center, Pasadena 255-3800. Room for 25 transient yachts, 25-ton marine hoist.

♦ Anchorage Marina, Baltimore 522-4007. Room for 20 transient yachts, 30-ton travelift, huge facility.

♦ Henderson's Wharf Marina, Baltimore 342-2060. 100 transient slips.

Tidewater Harbor 625-4992. 60-ton marine hoist.

Inner Harbor Marina, Baltimore 837-5339. Room for 80 transient yachts.

Baltimore City Docks 396-3174. 100 transient yachts docks.

Gibson Island Club 255-7632. Room for 100 transient yachts.

Whitehall Marina Services 974-1342. 10 transient slips, 50-ton marine hoits.

Mears Marina/Severn River Y.C. 268-8282. 50 transient slips, 20-ton marine crane.

♦ Port Annapolis Marina 269-1990. 35-ton travelift.

A&B Yachtsmen, Inc. 263-9073. Room for 30 transient yachts, two 20-ton travelifts.

Chesapeake Harbor Marina 268-1969. 20 transient slips.

White Rocks Marina, Annapolis 268-5300. 60-ton marine hoist.
Petrini Yacht Yard 263-4278. 50-ton travelift.
AnnapolisYacht Basin 263-3544. Room for 30 transient yachts.
Mariner's Wharf, Severn River 757-2424. 60 transient berths.
Hartge Yacht Yard, West River 867-2188. Three 60-ton marine railways, two 20-ton travelifts.
Galesville Yacht Yard 867-7517. 30-ton travelift.

SOUTH TO PATUXENT RIVER

Herrington Harbour North (301)867-4343. Room for 20 transient yachts, 35-ton travelift.
Shipwright Harbor 867-7686. 20 transient slips, 15-ton travelift.
Harbor Island Marina 326-3441. 25 transient slips, 15-ton travelift.
Town Center Marina 855-1504. Room for 20 transient yachts, 50-ton marine hoist.
♦ Zahniser's Sailing Center 326-2166. Room for 20 transient yachts, marine railway and travelift to 60 tons
Shepherd's Yacht Yard 326-3939. 35-ton travelift.
♦ Chris Washburn's Boat Yard 326-6701. 75-ton marine hoists, room for 800 boats in yard.
♦ Spring Cove Marina 326-2161. Room for 20 transient yachts, 35-ton travelift.
Calvert Marina 855-1633. 25 transient slips, 30-ton travelift.
White Sands Marina 586-1182. 40 transient slips, marine railway.

POTOMAC RIVER, MARYLAND

Point Lookout Marina, Smith Creek (301) 872-5145. 15 trasient docks, hoists and railways to 100 tons.
Dennis Point Marina, St. Marys River 994-2288. Room for 10 transient yachts, 25-ton travelift.
Tall Timbers Marina 994-1508. 17 transient slips, 20-ton travelift.
Dock 'o the Bay Marina 475-3129. Room for 20 transient slips.
Aqualand Marina 259-2123. 20 transient slips, 20-ton travelift.
Robertson's Crab House 934-9236. 20 transient slips.
Full Tilt Marina 932-1407. Room for 20 transient yachts.

VIRGINIA

POTOMAC RIVER

White Point Marina, Yeocomico River (804) 472-2977. Room for 10 transient yachts, travelifts and marine railway to 90 tons.

Yeocomico Marina (804) 472-2971. 20 transient slips, 30-ton travelift.

Bay Yacht Center, Colonial Beach (804) 244-7230. Room for 20 transient yachts, 20-ton travelift.

Stanford's Marine Railway (804) 224-7644. Marine railways and travelifts.

E-Z Cruz, Inc,. Neabsco Creek (703) 670-8111. 50-ton travelift.

Fort Washington Marina, downtown (301) 292-7700. 20 transient slips, 30-tonn travelift.

Washington Marina (202) 554-0222. 40-ton travelift.

SOUTH CHESAPEAKE BAY

Jennings Boatyard (804) 453-7181. Room for 10 transient yachts, 100-ton marine crane.

Buzzard's Point Marina 453-3545. 35 transient slips, travelift.

Windmill Point Marine Resort 435-1166. Room for 30 transient yachts.

Miller's Marine Railway 776-9662. 250-ton marine railway.

Dozier's Dockyard 776-6711. 10 transient slips, 50-ton travelift.

The Tides Lodge and Marina 438-6000. Room for 44 transient yachts.

Southside Marine Service 758-2331. 10 transient slips, 40-ton travelift.

Deagle & Sons Marine Railway 776-9741. Cranes and marine railways to 500 tons.

Narrows Marina 725-2151. Room for 50 transient yachts, 40-ton travelift.

Horn Harbor Marina 725-3223. 9 transient slips, 75-ton travelift.

Shelter Harbor Marine, Inc. 642-2800. 25 transient slips, 35-ton travelift.

♦ York River Yacht Haven 642-2156. Room for 30 transient yachts, 35-ton travelift.

York Haven Marina 868-7829. 50-ton marine hoist.

Salt Ponds on the Bay 424-5722. Room for 100 transient yachts.

Superior Marine, Inc. 238-3906. 68-ton marine crane.

Smithfield Station 357-7000. 30 transient slips.

NORFOLK AREA

♦ Willoughby Harbor (804) 583-4150. 100 transient slips.

Portsmouth Boating Center 397-2092. 70-ton marine hoist.

Waterside Marina, Portsmouth 441-2222. Room for 60 transient yachts.

♦ Tidewater Yacht Agency, Portsmouth 393-2525. 100 transient slips, 60-ton marine hoists.

NORTH CAROLINA

NORTH CAROLINA SOUNDS

Tates Marine Railway, Coinjock (919) 453-3281. Room for 26 large transient yachts.

Elizabeth City Ship Yard 335-0171. 20 transient slips, 100-ton marine railway.

Edenton Marina 482-7421. Room for 15 transient yachts, 10-ton travelift.

Belhaven Marina 943-3773. 25 transient docks, two 100-ton marine railways.

Carolina Wind at McCotter's 946-4653. 15 transient slips, 30-ton travelift.

Point Marina, Inc., Whartonville 745-4460. 25 transient slips.

Sheraton Marina, Trent River 638-3585. 50 transient docks.

Ramada Inn Marina, Trent River 636-3637. 50 transient docks.

Whittaker Creek Yacht Harbor, Oriental 249-0666. 20 transient docks.

Minnesota Beach Yacht Basin 249-1424. 5 transient slips, 60-ton travelift.

Manteo Waterfront Town Docks 473-2188. 45 transient slips.

Mill Landing Marine Maintenance, Roanoke Island 473-3908. 40-ton travelift.

Ocracoke Public Dock 928-4531. 28 transient docks with time limit of two weeks, constant activity.

MOREHEAD CITY AREA

Dockside Marina (919)247-4890. 20 transient berths.

Town Creek Marina 728-3819. 20 transient docks, 35-ton travelift.

♦Beauford Docks 728-2503. 81 transient docks and a lot of activity. The Dockhouse, beside the Dockmaster's office is one of the best places on the entire east coast to get on as a crew member. Put up an ad at their board and tell the dockmaster of your intentions.

Taylor Boat Works 726-6374. 50-ton marine railway.

Spooners Creek Harbor 726-2060. 25 transient slips for large yachts, 60-ton travelift.

SOUTHERN COAST OF N. CAROLINA

Dudley's Marina, Swansboro (919) 393-2204. 10 transient slips, 100-ton marine railway.

Carolina Yacht Yard, Wilmington 686-0004. 100-ton marine hoist.

Seapath Transient Docks, Wrightsville Beach 256-3747. 24 transient slips.

Southport Marina, Inc. 457-5261. 25 transient docks, two travelifts to 75 tons.

Bald Head Island Marina, Southport 457-5000. 25 transient docks.

Holden Beach Marina, Supply 842-5447. 5 transient docks, 70-ton travelift.

Shallotte Boatyard 754-6476. 60-ton travelift.

Marsh Harbor Marina, Calabash 579-3500. Room for 25 transient yachts.

SOUTH CAROLINA

NORTH COAST, S. C.

Myrtle Beach Yacht Club, Coquina Harbour (803) 249-5376. 25 transient yachts docks.

Harbour Gate Marina, North Myrtle Beach 249-8888. 20 transient docks.

Hague Marina, Myrtle Beach 293-2141. Room for 15 transient yachts, 35-ton travelift.

Bucksport Plantation Marina 397-5566. 20 transient slips, 50-ton travelift.

Hazzard's Marina, Georgetown 546-6604. 10 transient docks, 30-ton railway.

McClellanville Boat Yard, Inc. 887-3220. Cranes and marine railway to 100 tons.

CHARLESTON AREA

Wild Dunes Yacht Harbor, Isle of Palms (803) 886-5100. 20 transient docks.

Darby Marine, Mt. Pleasant 884-8541. Travelifts to 150 tons.

Patriot's Point Marina 849-4100 or 884-6568. 50 transient slips available.

George M. Lockwood Marina, Ashley River 724-7356. 25 transient slips.

Ashley Marina 722-1996. 40 transient docks.

Buzzards Roost Marina 559-5516. 25 transient slips.

Bohicket Marina Village, Johns Island, S.C. 768-1280. Room for 40 transient yachts, 60-ton travelift.

SOUTH COAST, S. C.

Marsh Harbor Marina (803) 524-4797. 50-ton travelift.

Downtown Marina Beaufort 524-4422. 25 transient slips.

The Marina at Lady's Island 524-3949. Room for 20 transient yachts, marine railway.

Skull Creek Marina, Hilton Head Island 681-4234. 25 transient docks, 30-ton travelift.

Palmetto Bay Marina 785-3910. 25 transient docks.

Shelter Cove Marina 842- 7001. Room for 26 transient yachts.

GEORGIA

Thunderbolt Marina, Savannah (912) 352-4956. Room for 30 transient yachts.

Sail Harbor Marina, Savannah 897-2896. Room for 8 transient yachts. 30-ton travelift.

Golden Isles Marina, St. Simons Island 638-7717. 35 transient docks.

FLORIDA

NORTHERN INTERCOASTAL WATERWAY, JACKSONVILLE AREA

Fernandia Town Marina (904)261-0355. Deep, accepts transient yachts, no drydock.

Amelia Island Yacht Basin 277-4615. Extensive transient dockage, haul-out repairs.

Sisters Creek Marina 251-3306. Many transient berths, drydock.

Trout River Marina 765-9925. Many transient docks, travelift.

Harbormasters Marina, Jacksonville 399-8536. Deep, very large.

♦Ortega River Boatyard, Fred Abel's Boatyard 387-5538. The best haul-out facility in the area, highly recommended.

Ortega Yacht Club 389-1199. First rate facility, accepts transient yachts.

Huckins Yacht Corporation 389-1125. Full repair facilities.

♦Lamb's Yacht Center 384-5577. Many transient docks, extensive crane facilities for haul-out repairs, large yard.

♦Pablo Creek Marina, Pablo Creek 221-4228. Huge facility with travelifts to 150 tons. Extensive transient docks.

♦Beach Marine 249-8200. Another huge complex, with almost 400 docks and haul-out facilities.

ST AUGUSTINE AREA

St. Augustine City Marina (904) 825-1026. Lots of transient docks.

Oasis Marine Services 824-2520. Deep, many transient docks, travelift.

Palm Coast Marina 445-0843. Accepts transient yachts, very exclusive.

DAYTONA BEACH AREA

Halifax Harbor Marina (904) 253-0575. 440 docks total, a huge marina which accepts transient yachts.

♦Daytona Marina and Boat Works 252-6421. Very impressive boatyard, lots of room in the yard and in the transient slips.

Seven Seas Marina, Port Orange 761-3221. Accepts transient yachts, has a travelift and a large yard.

Inlet Harbor Marina 761-6033. Extensive transient slips, drydock facilities.

Lighthouse Boat Yard 767-0683. Extensive transient dockage, a large yard with travelifts.

New Smyrna Beach has four marinas and a boatyard, none of them notable but all worth checking if in the area.

CAPE CANAVERAL AREA

Titusville Municipal Marina (407) 269-7255. Many transient slips in this modern marina, most services except drydock.

Westland Marine 267-1667. More transient slips, a 100-ton travelift.

Kennedy Point Yacht Club 383-0280. Many transient docks.

♦ Harbor Square Marina 453-2464. One of the finest Marina complexes in the area, Harbor Square accepts transient yachts and has a travelift and completes all kinds of repairs.

Inland Marina, South Banana River 453-5912. Travelift for small boats.

Banana River Marine 452-8622. Another marina for lifting out and repairing small yachts.

♦ Port Canaveral Marina 783-5480. Very large marina facility, deep with lots of transient slips, very rugged and well built docks and complete haul-out facilities.

♦ Cape Marina 783-8410. almost a carbon copy of the marina above.

Indian Cove Marina, Cocoa 452-8540. Transient yachts accepted, haul out facilities and a large boatyard

Whitley Marine 632-5445. Transient yachts accepted and a travelift on the premises.

Diamond 99 Marina 254-1490. Lots of transient slips.

Anchorage Yacht Basin, Dragon Point 773-3620. Lots of transient slips and haul-out services to 35-feet.

♦ Indian Harbor Marina 773-2468. Very large, very accomodating to transient yachts, with boat yard and the whole works.

Eau Gallie Yacht basin 254-1766. Another large marina, supplying room for transient yachts and a travelift.

♦ Intracoastal Marina of Melbourne 725-0090. Many transient yachts, another large boatyard and travelift.

Melbourne Harbor Marina 725-9054. A large marina with lots of transient space.

VERO BEACH AREA

Summit Landings Marina 664-3029. Accepts transient yachts and has hull repairs including a travelift, but the most attractive aspect is the huge and very lively bar and restaurant on the waterfront.

Sebastian Inlet has a series of marinas, none stand out but the area is worth a look around.

Indian River Marina 231-2211. Full of facilities, open to transient yachts.

Vero Beach Municipal Marina 231-2819. Another mediocre marina in the thousands along this coast.

Riomar Bay Yacht Club 231-4976. Lots of transient parking.

Riverside Marina, Fort Pierce 464-5720. Accepts transient yachts, Haul-out facilities available.

Cracker Boy Boat Works 465-7031. Another fine yacht yard.

♦ Harbortown Marina 466-7300. Heaps of transient dockage and extensive boat yard facilities including haul-out facilities for yachts up to 185 tons.

Fort Pierce City Marina 464-1245. More transient spaces in this fine marina.

Pelican Yacht Club 464-1734. A great place for yachts to provision for a long sea passage, a great place for you to check.

STUART AREA

Bailey Boat Co. (407) 334-0936. Large travelift and a lot of yard space, but the harbor is very shallow and the size of yachts here are limited to their draft.

♦ Indian River Plantation 225-3700. Part of a huge resort complex, the huge marina is open to a few transient yachts, although you will not find shoestring sailors here.

♦ Manatee Pocket on the mouth of the St. Lucie river inlet has a great deal of marinas with haul-out facilities. They all have transient docks available and at least one travelift. Here are those worth visiting: Sailfish Marina 283-1122. Pocket Watch Marina 283-6270. Mariner's Cay Marina 287-2900. Pirate's Cove Marina 287-2354. David Lowe's Boatyard 287-0923.

SOUTH FROM ST. LUCIE

Note: there are dozens of fine marinas and boatyards on the Okeechobee Waterway up to the lake. But with the availability of equally fine facilities along the Intracoastal waterway, I will not list those away from the coast.

Blowing Rocks Marina (407) 746-3312. Many transient slips available.

Maxon Marina 746-8311. Shallow, but has haul-out facilities for smaller yachts.

Jib Yacht Club Marina 746-4300. Large marina complex, transient dockage available and haul-out services are sometimes available.

Jupiter Marina 747-7877. Transient slips available, can haul out yachts only to 30 feet in length.

♦ Frenchman's Creek Marina 627-6358. A huge and very well run facility, has extensive transient dockage but no below waterline repairs.

The Way's Club 622-8582. Do-it-yourself boatyard, the best kind for meeting transient sailors looking for crew.

E&H Boarworks 622-8550. Another do-it-yourself boatyard, lots of yard space.

♦ Soveral Harbour 622-6910. One of the finest boatyards in the area, has extensive transient docks and a couple of travelifts.

PALM BEACH AREA

Harbor Point Marina (407)622-6890. This marina has lots of slips open for transient yachts.

♦North Palm Beach Marina 626-4919. Absolutely huge with endless transient slips, a good boatyard and extensive repairs available.

♦Old Port Cove Port Marina and Yacht Club 626-1760. Another huge marina complex with every service available except haul-out repairs.

Riviera Beach Municipal Marina 842-7806. Another fine Marine facility that accepts transient yachts.

Old Slip Marina 848-4669. A good full-service haul-out repair facility with transient slips.

Canonsport Marina, Singers Island 848-7569. A real laid-back facility with lots of transient spaces.

Rybovich Boat Works 844-4331. Transient berths and travelifts.

♦Spencer Boat Company 844-3521. Extensive transient slips and several travelifts.

NORTH OF FORT LAUDERDALE

♦Boca Raton Club Marina, Delray Beach (407) 395-3000. A very classy spot, open only to transient yachts of fifty feet and over.

Lighthouse Point Marina, Hillsboro Inlet (305) 942-8118. Open to transient yachts, with travelift and yard space.

Merritt's Boat and Engine Works 941-0118. Haul-out facilities for smaller yachts.

Sands Harbor Marina 942-9100. A fine marina, with limited space for transient yachts.

FORT LAUDERDALE

♦Pier 66 Yacht Harbor (305)525-6666. The first of many giant Fort Lauderdale marinas, lots of transient docks, repairs at dockside.

♦♦Bahia Mar Yachting Center 764-2233. This has to be the largest marina in the world. acres of transient slips and repairs.

♦Marina Inn and Yacht Harbor 525-3484. Another gigantic marina, famous for being able to house a yacht of any size.

♦Portside Yacht Club Marina 527-6782. Very large marina, lots of transient slips.

♦Lauderdale Marina 512-8507. Another large marina with travelifts and yard space, the main attraction the a fuel dock, a popular place for yachties to fuel up as they are heading out to sea, giving you an opportunity to get on for a day sail or better at the last moment.

Cable Marine 462-2822. A great boatyard with extensive haul-out facilities.

NEW RIVER AREA OF FT. LAUDERDALE
♦In the New River area, check the following boat yards: Chinnock Marine 763-2250. Summerfield Boat Works 525-4726. Allows do-it-yourself work. River Bend Marine 523-1832. Specialize in repairs and long term storage of sailboats. Lauderdale Yacht Basin 522-3655. Jackson Marine Center 792-4900. Rolly Marine Service 583-5300. Cable Marine service 587-4000. Hurricane Harbor Yacht Basin 583-0007. Bradford Marine 791-3800. Art Marine 587-3883. New River Marina 584-2500. Roscioli Yacht Center 581-9200. Check the following marinas: Marina Bay 791-7600. Marina '84' 581-3313. Municipal marina (305)761-5423.

SOUTH OF FORT LAUDERDALE
Harbour Towne Marina, on the Dania Canal (305)926-0300. The first of many first rate marinas along this canal. This one, unlike most, also has transient docks and a big marina.

Playboy Marine Center 920-083. An extensive professional yacht yard.

♦Derecktor-Gunnell Boat Yard 920-5756. A great boat yard, lots of large yachts.

Royale Palm Yacht Basin 923-5900. Another good yard.

♦Hollywood Marina 921-3035. A big marina with lots of room for transient yachts.

Waterways Marina 935-1252. A big marina with transient slips.

Maule Lake Marina 945-0808. A good marina that accepts transients.

MIAMI AND MIAMI BEACH AREA
Flamingo Yacht Basin (305) 861-5343. Accepts transient yachts, full service.

Fountainbleau Docks 538-2000. This marina, unlike the ones next to it, accepts transient yachts.

♦The Miami Beach Marina 673-6000. Lots of transient slips, very modern.

♦Sunset Harbor Marina 673-0044. Lots of room for transient yachts.

Keystone Point Marina 940-6236. Transient slips, travelift.

♦Biscane Marriott Hotes and Marina 374-4900. Many transient slips.

Dupont Plaza Marina 358-2541. Lots of transient docks, deep.

♦Miamarina 579-6955. Literally stuffed with transient yachts, one report is that it usually has more transient yachts than residents.

SOUTH OF MIAMI AND THE MIAMI RIVER
♦Rickenbocker Marina, Virginia Key 361-1900. Very large, very friendly, lots of large transient yachts and haul-out facilities.

♦Visit these boatyards in the Miami River: Miami Shipyard (305)854-5227. Allied Marine 643-0332. Poland Yacht Basin 325-0177. Nutta's Boatyard 325-0680. Norseman Shipbuilding 545-6815. Merrill-Stevens 324-5211.

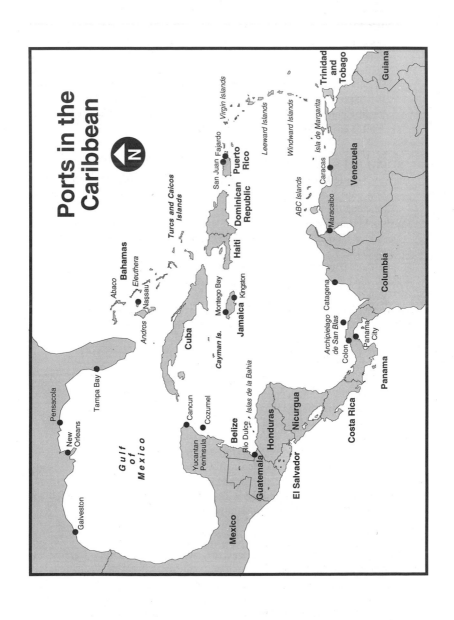

Ports in the Caribbean

N

Pensacola
New Orleans
Galveston
Tampa Bay

Gulf of Mexico

Mexico

Yucantan Peninsula
Cancun
Cozumel

Abaco
Eleuthera
Bahamas
Nassau
Andros

Turcs and Caicos Islands

Cuba

Cayman Is.

Montego Bay
Kingston
Jamaica

Haiti
Dominican Republic

San Juan Fajardo
Virgin Islands
Puerto Rico

Leeward Islands

Windward Islands

Isla de Margarita

Caracas

Venezuela

ABC Islands
Maracaibo

Columbia

Catagena
Archipielago de San Blas
Colon
Panama City

Panama

Costa Rica

Nicurgua

Honduras
Islas de la Bahia

Belize
Rio Dulce
Guatemala

El Salvador

Trinidad and Tobago

Guiana

CHAPTER 6
PORTS IN THE CARIBBEAN AND THE GULF OF MEXICO
PORTS IN MEXICO AND CENTRAL AMERICA

MEXICO

The Mexican state of Quintana Roo encompasses the best of the Caribbean sailing area of Mexico, making up the entire eastern face of the Yucatan Peninsula. As with the waters of Belize and most of the Caribbean islands, the Yucatan Peninsula has been endowed with some of the best sailing anywhere. With the clear water, beautiful beaches and the full strength of the northeast trades blowing for the entire season from November to May, one can hardly wish for anything more in a sailing vacation.

I will describe the ports from the north to the south because that is most likely the direction you will be looking to go in your quest to get away from the States and into warmer water. The easiest route to sail is to the north, as the Yucatan Current moves at a clip of about three knots along the coast in that direction. But in the winter when the wind has more north in it, the flow of yachts is heading to the south. The method of sailing in this direction is by short hops in the day and anchoring at night, with the coast providing sheltered anchorages every thirty or forty miles to make this possible. By sailing the coast in only the daytime, the yachts can stay close to the reef where the current is minimal.

ISLA CONTOY AND ISLA MUJERES

There are two islands in the northern state of Quintana Roo that are worth describing in detail for their unique situations. Isla Contoy is the northernmost island along the Yucatan cruising route and one that yachts visit frequently. The problem is, there are no places to stay on the island as it is a bird sanctuary. Also, Isla Contoy is not a port of entry, so the yachts that are sailing to or from the US cannot land here until they check in or out at Isla Mujeres, and then plan to visit this beautiful island within that window. For this reason, I strongly suggest that if you plan to visit this region for a sail along the coast of Quintana Roo, go to Isla Mujeres. Your next stop might be Contoy anyway.

Isla Mujeres is still a sleepy town compared to Cancun and Cozumel, but an excellent choice for finding a ride south along the coast. The lodging and food are a great deal cheaper and the atmosphere is more laid back, but there is also less boating activity. The best thing about this island is that it is the primary port of entry for yachts sailing from the U.S., and you will have a good chance at the beginning of the season as these yachts start to arrive, as many are ready to dump the crew they barely tolerated on the long passage from the States. At the end of the season, a host of yachts set to make for the Florida Keys or points down the Gulf Stream, and this is the place for you to approach them just before they set sail.

Isla Mujeres has three marinas at this time, and all three are jammed at both ends of the hurricane season, which are the recommended times to make the passage to or from the States. Again, in November the primary flow is from the States, and May is the time of the mad rush back home. Close to town is the Club De Yates with eighteen slips and facilities; south of town by the airport is the Marina Paraiso with 24 slips; another half mile south of that is the Marina Mujeres with 22 slips and a small charter fleet.

CANCUN

Despite being a major tourist center known worldwide for the fishing, diving and fabulous beaches, Cancun is not set up adequately for yachts. There are three marinas in the Cancun area, but two of them are located in the lagoon with low concrete bridges on both ends, disabling yachts from entering. The one marina that is available is the Playa Blanca Marina on the mainland on the southern end of Las Perlas Beach. The other areas I recommend are adjacent to the main anchorages offshore from the Hotels El Presidente, Fiesta Americana and the Casa Maya. In contrast to the other beach front areas of the Caribbean, Cancun caters more to the land-based tourists than it does to the yachties, and the hangouts in town will be barely diluted by them.

COZUMEL

Probably the best place in Caribbean Mexico to come in contact with yachts is Cozumel. The Club Nautico Marina is a huge complex with facilities for yachts up to 100 feet long and services to match. It is located about a mile and a half north of downtown Cozumel. The other harbor is south of town about four miles in a natural lagoon called Bahia Caleta. Many yachts prefer to anchor off the town of San Miguel or to tie up on the north side of the town dock. As with Cancun, the restaurants and bars are focused on the hotel crowd, so it is unlikely that you will find a yachtie hangout. The only exception is the bar at the yacht club itself.

PUERTO AVENTURAS

This is the last real port of call along the coast heading south, and might be the best one on this coast. It is a huge private marina and coastal development with a large yacht club, brand new and squeaky clean. This is the last worthy spot for you to try to hitch a ride on your way south into Ascension Bay and farther south to the finer cruising waters of Belize.

BELIZE

There are some beautiful sailing grounds in Belize, but the only places I recommend that you visit are the official and unofficial ports of entry. The reason for this is that the cays are very difficult to get to without the benefit of a boat, but if you are to get there by other means, it is worthwhile to look around. These islands see much yachting activity in season. The people who bring their yachts here are not as much interested in seeing the people of Belize or the towns and ruins along the coast as they are in visiting the cays and beaches of the world's second largest barrier reef. For this reason, it is advisable to try to get onto a yacht sailing off to the reef from the ports of entry, as all yachts are required to stop there upon entering the country.

There are only three official ports of entry in Belize: Dangriga, Punta Gorda and Belize City. Another port that is used frequently is

San Pedro, on the southern point of Ambergris Cay, near the Mexican border.

SAN PEDRO

This small and friendly town is a very convenient place for yachts to stop on their way down the coast of Mexico or from the northern Caribbean, and yacht captains frequently check into the country there by flying an official down from Belize City for the day to avoid having to sail to that crowded and uncomfortable port. Chances are there will be a Port Captain stationed there soon to respond to this demand.

It only costs about $30 US to fly into San Pedro from Belize City, and it is well worth a visit both for its yachting crowd and its ambiance. There is only one marina in this area, but a very large anchorage and a series of docks along the waterfront. The marina is rather small and primarily for the local dive boats that work out of the area, but pay it a visit at least for a bite at the bar and grill. There are many good bars and restaurants in town, I recommend you visit the Tackle Box Bar, the Barrier Reef Hotel and the Navigator Bar, which are the sailors' hangouts.

BELIZE CITY

No longer the capital of Belize, Belize City is still its largest city and hosts the largest commercial shipping fleet, which is why most yachts prefer to get out of there in a jiffy once they clear customs. The anchorages are open to winds from all directions and the long walks between official offices make clearance activities difficult. At the easternmost point of Belize City is the Fort George Hotel, where most yachts calling into Belize clear customs. This is the only practical place in town to go looking for cruising yachts, but the hotel is a good gathering spot for westerners. A prominent cruising guide for the area recommends that yachts bring their problems to a small establishment on 91 North Front Street called `Beth La Croix's Personalized Service.' Beth LaCroix immerses herself in the comings and goings of the cruising world, which may warrant your paying her a visit to see what is going on with the yachting community. If somebody is looking for a reliable crew member, she will know it and be able to set you up. There are two notable marine suppliers in Belize City, both with hauling out facilities and boat yards. Blackline Marina is capable of hauling out yachts up to 30 tons, and the marine railway run by Arthur

Hoare can haul out vessels much larger. Both are located in Haulover Creek.

There are a number of places near Belize City that yachtsmen use to anchor while doing business in the city or awaiting parts, but I will give no more than a mention to them as they are hard to reach for the boatless. Moho Cay, which has the only bareboat charter fleet in Belize, and Peter's Bluff are very close to the mainland and to Belize city. Banister Bough and Robinson Point are popular areas within ten miles of Belize City, and you will find yachts anchored there in season.

DANGRIGA

The port of entry south of Belize City is only thirty miles south at the town of Dangriga. There is no reason for yachts to visit this place except to clear in or out of the country or to provision in the supermarket. Yachts anchor off the town dock by the radio antenna, or on the south side, east of the commercial pier. Once finishing those duties, the owners of the visiting yachts clear out of town right away. The problem is not crime or poverty, but boredom.

PLACENTIA

Probably the best place to visit in all of Belize is the town of Placentia, located about 50 miles south of Belize City. Placentia is called the most beautiful town in Belize and is a very pleasant place to hang out. It is growing in popularity for yachts as it provides a perfect spot to take a break from exploring the cays. I recommend visiting Sonny's Bar, the Galley restaurant and the Turtle Inn to talk to the crews of the yachts calling there. Placentia is more of a spot to relax and enjoy the surroundings than the other recommended places in Belize. Those who stop here are not interested in carrying out official business, but in simply enjoying the place.

PUNTA GORDA

Punta Gorda is the third and last port of entry along the coast of Belize, but remains relatively unpopular with yachts due to its remoteness. The town itself is quite pleasant and has some good places for yachts to provision. A greater number of yachts are finding the beauty of the islands in this region worthy of exploring, as these cays are arguably the most attractive on the barrier reef. Punta Gorda is the gateway to these islands, and the place most likely for yachts to stop last on their way out to explore them. In addition, the yachts moving up from Guatemala and points south will clear here before visiting the rest of Belize.

THE RIO DULCE OF GUATEMALA

The Rio Dulce area is the only place to visit along Guatemala's short coast, but what a place. It has developed a cruising community on its own, some of the yachts have been there for years and have no intention of leaving. There are many reasons to go there for both the yachtsmen and for you, from the 300-foot high jungle clad cliffs on either side of the river, the manatees swimming in its fresh water, hot springs along the river, a river almost clean enough to drink. The Mayan ruins close by, just now being carved out of the tropical rain forest, are rivaled only by the Egyptian pyramids and the wildlife alone is worth the visit. The cultures are intact and the region has no bad season and no bugs, the fresh water lakes have no rough weather and the colors are fantastic. Have I talked you into going there? Then this is what you'll need to know:

There are a few decent towns to visit along the Rio Dulce including Livingston and Fronteras, but the best place to go is to the lake of El Golfete. There were four marinas there as of the summer of 1992, with its popularity growing all the time. Nigel Calder, author of *The Cruising Guide to the Northwest Caribbean,* calls this possibly the best place to leave your boat in the entire Caribbean. The four marinas should all be visited, as there is always activity there and many cruisers. Visit the Catamaran Hotel and Marina; the Mañana Marina; Susana's Laguna Restaurant and Marina; and Mario's Marina. The marinas are mostly American owned and run, and all services are available. You can get to El Golfete by an uncomfortable four or five hour bus ride from Guatemala City.

HONDURAS

The mainland of Honduras is not a practical place to sail, the banks rise up too fast and the coast is almost completely devoid of protected harbors. This leaves only the Bay Islands, just a few miles offshore, for cruisers to enjoy. The same topography that makes the mainland difficult to navigate makes the Bay Islands breathtaking in indigenous beauty. Roatan, the most important island in this group, is growing in popularity all the time as a tourist center and dive charter boat base. Yachting is also becoming popular here, but the filthy conditions and bribery in the harbors discourage many yachts from visiting. One thing that the Bay Islands has is the proximity of the sailing routes from Panama, and many yachts stop there on their way north after the canal transit.

The Island of Roatan now has regular flights from Houston and Miami and a great deal of good resorts, and, although I would not recommend a flight here to seek out a ride on a boat, the harbors are well worth a visit once here. The main yacht harbor in Roatan is the French Harbor Yacht Club, even though it only has room for seven yachts. French Harbor is worth a visit for its haulout facilities, among the best in the northwest Caribbean, and the yacht club is the recommended spot for leaving the boat for journeys into the mainland. The facilities at Brick Bay are also worth a visit as they have a marine railway and some facilities that used to belong to the Caribbean Sailing Yachts charter fleet.

PANAMA

The entire coastline of Panama is rather dull except for a few very interesting places: the San Blas Islands, the entrance to the Panama Canal and the small port of Porto Bello are the notables. The entrance to the Panama Canal is the only place worth visiting if you are solely determined to find a berth on a yacht. Up the coast from Colon there is no real boating activity at all. The ports are few and the sailing conditions are terrible, all the way to Guatemala. Down the coast from the canal the cruising grounds are made up primarily of the San Blas Islands. These islands are popular to traveling sailors and tourists alike, but the only way to find a yacht cruising these islands is to hang out at one of the jump off points on the mainland.

The entry point in the east is Puerto Obaldia at the Colombian border, but it is obvious to all who visit this mess of a harbor that the only reason to stop is to gain a cruising permit to the San Blas Islands. The few yachts venturing through Panama in this direction will all stop there, but it is not a comfortable place to await passage to the islands. I suggest that you stop only if you are passing through anyway. On the other side of the San Blas Islands lies the odoriferous and crime-ridden port of Colon. Despite its reputation as a town, however, it is a good place to park your yacht and get some work done.

In recent years the yachting community has come to realize this, and consequently it has become a fantastic place to join a yacht awaiting an impending transit of the Canal. The Panama Canal Yacht Club is the place to go to find transit through the canal, as yachtsmen can take care of all the transiting formalities on the grounds. The club also functions as a meeting place for the yachting community. I suggest that you spend time at the yacht club and volunteer to handle lines on any yacht needing your assistance. Even if a crew member is not needed for the Pacific crossing, several yachts go through the canal together, and they will all be able to see you in action. Become part of the community. See the Caribbean section of *Routes in the Atlantic* for more information on the canal crossing. The Port of Cristobal is also a good place to check for yachts looking to transit the canal and for those that have just come through.

For those yachts not transiting the canal, the Club Nautico in the port of Colon welcomes visiting yachts with open arms, and if you find yourself in the area, you should visit it so everybody knows your name.

US GULF COAST

Because of the large number of yachting centers along this coast and the others in the US, I have listed the facilities in tabular form. It is difficult to process this amount of entries by stating the relative attractions of the thousands of worthy yacht clubs, marinas and yacht yards without giving a tangible measurement, so I have simply stated the attractions of each. My tour starts on the southern tip of the Florida mainland and works its way along the gulf towards the west. The most highly recommended are indicated with a diamond.

FLORIDA

SOUTHERN COAST OF WESTERN FLORIDA

Rod and Gun Club, Everglades City (813) 695-2101. Accepts transient yachts.

Marco River Marina 394-2502. 10 transient docks, fine marina. 35-ton travelift.

Factory Bay Marina 642-6717. Lots of transient slips for yachts under 45 feet.

Naples Yacht Club 262-7301. A very respectable marina, carrying lots of room for transient yachts, but only for members of other yacht clubs.

Naples city dock 434-4693. Fully open to transient yachts, 30-ton travelift.

Marco Island Marina 649-7776. Travelifts and yard space.

Turner Marine 261-6188. Excellent boatyard with all kinds of yard space, a 50-ton travelift and room for 8 transient yachts.

In Fort Myers, check the following marinas: Moss Marina 463-6137. Palm Grove Marina 463-7333. Fort Myers Beach Marina 463-9552.

South Seas Plantation Marina, Captiva Island 472-5111. Classy marina, accepts transient yachts.

Miller's Marina, Gasparilla Island 964-2283. 25 transient slips, full service.

TAMPA BAY AND SOUTH

Palm Island Marina (813) 697-4356. Many transient slips, full service marina.

Venice Marine Center 485-3388. Very complete marina, room for 15 transient yachts. 40-ton travelift.

Crow's Nest Marina, Venice 484-7661. 25 Transient slips.

Marina Operations, Sarasota 955-9488. Deep, crowded and lots of traffic moving past. 30 transient slips.

Longboat Key Marina, Sarasota 383-8383. Another fine marina, plenty of transient space.

Bradenton Beach Marina 794-1235. Good marina with 30 transient slips, full haul-out facilities

♦ Snead Island Boat Works 722-2400. Very extensive haul-out facilities.

Bradenton Yacht Club 748-7930. Deep, accepts transient yachts.

♦ Regatta Pointe Marina 729-6021. One of the best marinas in all of western Florida. Accepts transient yachts.

Bradenton City Marina 747-8300. A nice marina, 5 transient docks.

♦ ♦ The Harborage, Salt Creek 821-6347. Very, very large and very extensive services in everything a captain would ever want. A great boatyard and a fantastic lounge full of the yachties staying in the area, the best place to meet them. A unique place to find a yacht.

♦ ♦ St. Petersberg Municipal Marina (800) 782-8350. An absolutely giant marina that saw 1000 transient yachts visit in 1991. One of the biggest marinas you will ever see.

St. Petersberg Yacht Club (813) 895-4779. It pales in contrast, but is a good spot nonetheless. 15 transient docks.

Tampa Yacht Club, Hillsborough 839-1311. A good yacht club, very classy. Accepts transient yachts from other clubs.

Davis Island Yacht Club 251-1158. Good transient dockage, very friendly.

♦ Harbor Island Marina 229-5324. 70 transient slips.

NORTH OF TAMPA BAY

♦Maximo Marina, Boca Ciega Bay (813) 867-1102. 350 total slips, room for 150 yachts in drydock. a 35-ton travelift.

Gulfport Municipal Marina 321-6319. Big marina with transient slips, repair services.

Tierra Verde Marina 866-0255. Big and deep, with room for 110 total yachts, 10 transient slips.

Warren's Marina 360-1784. Accepts transient yachts, do-it-yourself boatyard.

Pass-A-Grill Yacht Club 360-7069. Lots of room for transient yachts.

♦Tierra Verde Yacht Basin 866-1487. A huge marina with all conceivable amenities. 10 transient slips.

Village Marine Center 391-0700. 35 transient slips, very large travelifts.

Madiera Beach Municipal Marina 393-9177. 10 transient slips available.

♦Clearwater Municipal Marina 462-6954. Deep and full of life, 20 transient yachts accepted and a great deal of room.

Marker One Marina 733-9324. Large marina with full services, accepts transient yachts.

In Tarpon Springs, visit the following: Port Tarpon Marina 937-2200. Anclote Sailport Marina 934-7616. Sail Harbor Marina 938-4660. Reis Boat Yard 937-2798.

NORTHERN WEST COAST

Riverside Marina, Yankeetown (904) 925-6157. Accepts lots of transient yachts.

Pride of the Points Marina 349-2511. One of the only deep water marinas in the area, lots of room for transient yachts, mechanical repairs. 40-ton travelift.

Carabelle Marina, Carabelle, Florida 697-3351. 9 transient slips.

The Moorings at Carabelle. 697-2800. 10 transient slips.

Rainbow Marina, Apalachicola, Fl. 653-8139. 25 transient slips, 40-ton travelift.

Frog Level Marina, Apalachicola, Fl. 653-8000. 12 transient slips, 40-ton travelift.

PANAMA CITY

Sailor's Marina, Panama City. 769-5007. Transient yachts.

Panama City Marina 785-0161. Huge and deep. 15 transient slips.

Bay Point Yacht Club and Marina, Panama City in Grand Lagoon 235-6911. 15 transient slips.

Panama City Boatyard, Panama City, Grand Lagoon 234-3386. Biggest in area with transient yachts, 50-foot travelift.

Passport Marina and Boatyard, GL. 234-560. Transient yachts and repairs.

Treasure Island Marina, GL. 234-6533. A few transient yachts.

Sun Harbor Marina, St. Andrew Bay, Panama City. 785-0551. Small, but has 10 transient slips.

CHOCTAWHATCHEE BAY

Baytowne Marina at Sandestin. (904)267-7777. Huge resort but limited marina, 50 transient docks

Bluewater Bay Marina at Rocky Bayou. 897-4150. Transient yachts and all services (except haulouts)

Lighthouse Key Marina, Boggy Bayou. 729-2000. Transient yachts and services, haulout to 26 ft, deep

Destin in Choctawhatchee bay, many marinas, but for small boats and few transient yachts.

Robroy Lodge and Marina, 837-6713. A few transient yachts.

Harbor View Marina 837-6172. 8 transient docks.

FORT WALTON BEACH AREA IN C BAY.

Shalimar Yacht Basin, (904)651-0510 Accepts transient yachts, 35-ton travelift.

Hudson Marina (919)862-3165. 20 transient slips and has haulout facilities, is very deep with facilities for larger yachts.

Fort Walton Yacht Club (904)243-7102. Very modern, very nice. Located on Smack Point in the southern end of C Bay. You might have a hard time getting into this exclusive facility.

FORT WALTON BEACH AREA

Deckhands Marina (904)243-1598. Good yard and a decent marina. Accepts transient yachts. 35-ton travelift.

Marina Motel 244-1129 right next door to above. Liollios Marina next to the restaurant of the same name 243-5011. Good for large transient yachts.

♦ The Boat Marina 244-2628 Has a lot of yachts, a lot of yard facilities and extensive transient dockage.

Fort Walton Yacht Basin. 244-5725. Not as good but decent. Accepts lots of transient yachts.

PENSACOLA AREA

Pensacola Yacht Club, Boca Chica (904)433-8804. Has some transient yachts.

♦ Brown's Marine Service (904)453-3471. The biggest and best in the area. Accepts transient yachts, has extensive haul-out facilities and is well run. 60-ton travelift.

♦ The Pensacola Shipyard (904)455-6966 is an absolutely huge facility that can lift out any craft with its huge crane. Probably the biggest and best repair facility in all of the Florida panhandle.

BIG LAGOON, AT THE END OF FLORIDA

Rod and Real Marina (904)492-0100. Accepts transient yachts, has below waterline repair and a 25-ton travelift.

Southwind Marina 492-0333. Deep outer piers, accepts large transient yachts at 10 transient docks.

ALABAMA

PERDIDO PASS AND COTTON BAYOU

Perdido Pass Marina (205)981-6481. Big, deep, clean and accepts transient yachts.

Zeke's Marina at the end of Cotton Bayou 981-4007. Accepts transient yachts, first rate facility.

♦ Coastal Yacht Service 981-9755. A fantastic boat yard in Terry Cove. CYS has haulout facilities for yachts to 60 tons.

WEST OF MILL POINT IN THE ICW

Bear Point Marina (205)981-3991. Small but deep, accommodates large yachts. 20 transient docks.

♦ Pirates Cove 986-7910. Has haulout facilities to 20 tons, lots of room, 20 transient docks.

FAIRHOPE

♦ Eastern Shore Marine on Fly Creek (800)458-7245. Very big with haul-out facilities, room for 10 transient yachts and a charter fleet.

DOG RIVER ON WESTERN MOBILE BAY

♦ Turner Marine Supply. (205)476-1444. Very big, 20 transient slips, an excellent haul-out facility. Mostly for sailboats. Very deep.

Beachcomber Marine 443-8000. Deep, good yard, lots of room, a bit more casual. 15 transient slips, a 40-ton travelift.

♦Grand Mariner 443-6300. Very deep, 15 transient docks and a 35-ton travelift.

Dog River Marina (205)471-5449. 20 transient slips and a 60-ton travelift. Mostly caters to power craft.

MISSISSIPPI

PASCAGOULA RIVER AND BILOXI AREA

♦Point Cadet Marina (601)436-9312. Built specifically to encourage transient yachting to the Biloxi area. Lots of slips and facilities, brand new. 30 transient berths.

Bay Marine Boatworks 432-2992 and Rebel Boat Works (601)435-2762. Both can haul out huge yachts.

Kremer Marine Boatyard 896-1629. A top notch yard but very isolated, and rarely visited. Warrants a phone call. Can haul out a 100-foot boat.

Broadwater Beach Marina. 388-2211. First class, but most of the slips are covered. Accepts transient yachts but does not have haul-out facilities.

GULFPORT

Gulfport small craft harbor (601)868-5713. Fairly deep and accepts transients.

Gulfport Yacht Club 863-2263. Accepts transient yachts from other clubs.

Misco Marine 864-1492. Good haul-out yard.

BAY ST. LOUIS

Pepper's Discovery Bay Marina (601)452-9441. Accepts transient yachts, has comforts but is shallow. Located at Bayou Portage in the east bay.

Bay Cove Marina 467-9257 on the Jordan River. Fairly deep, accepts transient yachts, has some big sailing yachts.

LOUISIANA

NORTHERN LAKE PONTCHARTRAIN AND NEW ORLEANS

♦Oak Harbor Marina (504)641-1044. Located on the north of the lake. An absolute first rate facility with every amenity except haul-out repairs. Very deep and has very large docks. 30 transient slips.

VAC Marine 643-4543 on the south shore of Bayou Bonfouca. A decent repair facility but a bit out of the way. Also on the north shore of the lake. 35-ton travelift.

♦ The Yacht Works/Prieto Marine, Mandeville 626-7847. Two very complete facilities with haul-out repairs and transient yachts accepted.

♦ Mariner's Village 626-1517. Another first rate marina located just west of Mandeville. No haul out repairs but lots of boats. 10 Transient slips.

Madisonville Boat Yard 845-8788. A good yard, capable of hauling out yachts to 80 tons.

Marina Del Rey 845-4474. A good marina with 25 transient slips.

M.G. Myers Yacht Services 945-2268. Transient yachts, 100-ton crane.

Marina Beau Chene 845-3454. A very good, quiet marina. Deep, but no repairs available.

South Shore Harbor (504)245-3152. By the Lakefront Airport, it is a quiet marina but has good facilities. 15 transient docks available.

WEST END HARBOR

Southern Yacht Club (504)288-4221. One of the oldest in the country, very exclusive. The finest yachts will be here. Very few transient spots.

♦ New Orleans Municipal Yacht Harbor 288-1431. Keeps 20 slips open for transient yachts. Very popular, very crowded.

Orleans Marina 288-2351. Many transients dock here. A very good spot.

♦ Schubert's Marine 282-8136. A full service marina, has everything any yachtie will ever need. Haul-out facilities and lots of room for transient yachts. 20 transient slips, 65-ton marine hoist.

WESTERN LOUISIANA

Gulf Outlet Marina (504)277-8229. A large, deep marina. 20 transient slips.

Pirates Cove (504) 787-3880. 15 transient slips.

Franklin Marina (318) 923-4486. 10 transient slips.

Danny Richard Marina 893-2157. Transient yachts accepted, a 20-ton lift.

TEXAS

GALVESTON AND CLEAR LAKE

♦ Galveston Yacht Basin (409) 762-6989. Transient berths, a 70-ton travelift.

♦ Seabrook Shipyard (713) 474-2586. 30 transient Docks, haul-outs to 65-feet, very complete, self-service boatyard. The only marine railway in the area.

Lafayette Landing 334-2284. 10 transient slips, good services.
Blue Dolphin Yachting Center 474-4450. 80-ton marine crane.
♦ Watergate Yachting Center 334-1511. 50 transient docks, a 35-ton travelift.
South Shore Harbor (504) 245-3152. 20 transient slips.

FREEPORT AND SOUTH

Bridge Harbor Yacht Club, Freeport (409) 233-2101. 20 transient slips, 70-ton travelift.

House of Boats, Inc., Redfish Bay (512) 729-9018. 6 transient docks, 40-ton travelift.

San Patricio Co. Navigation 758-1890. 30 transient slips.

Island Moorings Marina 749-4100. Many transient slips, many services.

Port Arkansas Yacht Basin 749-5429. 20 transient docks available.

North Shore Boat Works, Corpus Cristi 776-2525. Transient slips available, 60-ton marine hoist.

Port Mansfield Marina 944-2325. 30 transient berths.

Willacy Co. 944-2325. 20 transient slips, services.

Southpoint Marine, Port Isabel (512) 943-7926. Transient yachts accepted, a 35-ton travelift

Sea Ranch Marina, South Padre Island 761-1314. 20 transient slips, services.

PORTS ON THE EASTERN CARIBBEAN ISLANDS

The islands in the eastern Caribbean Sea see more foriegn yachts than any other place in the world. Being close to the United States, generally accepting US Dollars, being warm and extremely varied in scenery while having strong north easterly winds the entire year all contribute to its popularity. The eastern Caribbean has an off season but no bad season. The hurricanes come and go, but more than a couple of days in a row of overcast weather is extremely rare. Some of the best diving in the world with water temperatures always in the high 70's, and the good surfing on the windward side of many islands bring 'water people' from all over the world. The majority of islands are mountainous, so those wanting to get a respite from the tropical heat need only journey a few miles. The eastern Caribbean islands host parties all year; the locals and tourists get involved in them all. Some of the largest charter fleets in the world call the Lesser Antilles islands (the Windwards and Leewards) their home ports, and the Bahamas alone claim 15,000 private yachts visit their waters annually.

Hundreds of yachts each season make the migration between the eastern Caribbean and the Mediterranean, which for you is the best news of all. If you are looking for a free trip across the Atlantic or would like to sail the islands of the Lesser Antilles for a while, the transiting yachts can give you your big chance. The charter fleets have a strong army of crew members to assist sailors who come to the eastern Caribbean each winter; the turnover of many of these crewed charters on some of the Caribbean fleets is astounding. I have included many phone numbers in Appendix 1 for you to call about employment on some of these yachts (paid or unpaid) before you leave home. Your chances will not be very good without experience, but it is worth a few phone calls. I have included the Bahamas and Puerto Rico in this section. I have not included Cuba or Haiti.

There are no vaccinations required for entry to the Caribbean Islands in this section, but to find out more recent information, see my section on vaccinations in chapter 1 or call the health department phone number included there. They do recommend typhoid with booster, tetanus and poliomyelitis. No shots are required for re-entry to the US at this time. The islands require a passport in most cases, but no visas. Length of stay restrictions change from time to time, but I have included the 1993 requirements in Chapter 1.

As you move from island to island and hence country to country, it is unlikely you will want to stay in one place for more than three weeks, which is the length of time most countries grant. If you do need more time, ask for it. The one problem you might have when flying into the country is the usual requirement for an onward ticket, which keeps you from making their country your home. However, if you explain to them that you are getting on a yacht (as you have every intention of doing), you will probably be okay.

If you plan to go to the eastern Caribbean to live cheaply, you will encounter problems. If you are unable to find a yacht to make your home and you only patronize the well-known hotels in town, you will see your bank account dwindle faster than you had planned. In most places you can find inexpensive accommodations not described in guide books simply by asking around. You might not be in the cleanest place in town or have access to 54 cable channels or even a TV at all, but then you are not in the Caribbean to watch TV; your room becomes a place only to hang your pack and lie down to rest. A good source of this wisdom is taxi drivers and restaurant employees, especially in the older parts of town. Tell them you don't want to spend more than ten bucks a night, and they will most likely know a place. Sometimes they will offer to let you stay in their pad or will have a friend with an extra room. The extra money is an unexpected windfall for them, and you will get a chance to see the real Caribbean. Most guide books list "inexpensive" rooms as under $150 per night, so treat your host well.

Transportation in the islands is quite expensive if you prefer air conditioned taxis, but the local buses get you where you want to go in almost all cases. Ask the locals about bus schedules and routes as they change constantly.

Most businesses in the Caribbean aim at the upper end tourists-- wealthy people on a one-week stay not caring much about stretching their dollar. You will inevitably find the underground hangouts among budget travelers and through them key places to stay and eat, but I have been unable to locate a formal guidebook targeting that crowd. My aim here is to get you on a boat, so I will not attempt to line you up with places to stay and eat on the islands, nor will I give an approximation of how much you can expect to spend daily. That is up to your ability to seek out the bargains and to network with other budget travelers. Keep our ears open and smile. Talk to everybody with a backpack.

It seems that the best places to seek out passage on a yacht in the Caribbean are on these islands: St. Lucia; Antigua; Martinique; Bequia, Grenadines; Barbados and Elizabeth Harbor, Bahamas. The best times are in November and December and, to a lesser extent, from then through April and May. There are yachts around all year, but Antigua at the end of April is probably your best opportunity. I will describe each island or group of islands individually starting from leeward to windward, starting in the Caymans, up to the Bahamas, then around the Antilles from leeward to windward in a clockwise circle, finishing at Trinidad and Tobago.

THE CAYMANS

The best reason to go to the Caymans is to dive, as it is arguably the best in the world. But if you were to find yourself there looking for a yacht, check out the Harbour House Marina at the south side of the north isthmus on Grand Cayman. It has a boatyard and is capable of pulling out a 60- foot yacht. Governor's Harbour on the west side of the same sound has anchorages and a marina for yachts, and Georgetown should be checked as well. The Caymans are out of reach of most Caribbean crossings, but you can find yachts crossing from Panama to the Caribbean, landing there the second half of November and from May to the end of July. There are many much better spots, so I don't suggest paying the Caymans too much attention.

JAMAICA

On the Kingston side, the Royal Jamaican Yacht Club has a lot of room and welcomes foreign yachts. Also, Morgan's Harbour Club at Port Royal has a marina. On the northeast corner at Port Antonio lies a beautiful harbor with good facilities, and has become a popular stop for cruisers. Visit this harbor if you have a chance, as there are a great number of things to see and do in and around town besides looking for a yacht. Check the Admiralty Club and the Huntress Marina. Montego Bay, on the northwest corner of the island, has the Montego Bay Yacht Club three and one half miles from town. There is also a small yacht basin in town with a half dozen yachts tied up to the quay and anchored off in the off-season, and a great deal more in the winter. Ocho Rios, the location of my cover photo, has two cruise ship docks and a watersports pier for the local charter yachts and fishing boats. In the basin to the west within the harbor is where the foreigners tie up.

The best times to run into sailors passing through are the months of April/May and November, heading east or west. This, incidentally, corresponds to the rainy seasons. The Southern Ocean Racing Circuit hosts a race from Miami to Montego Bay every March, so you might have an excuse to stay in Jamaica a few months. Like the Caymans, though, Jamaica is out of the path of the trades and is not entirely popular for cruising sailors.

THE BAHAMAS

The Bahamas are bustling with activity all year long, but there are times when they warrant a visit more than others. Boats leave the Bahamas bound for Bermuda in May and June and for the Virgin Islands from April to May and November to Mid December. They sail west to the Panama Canal from April to May and again in November and December, so choose your direction and be there at those times. Yachts arriving in the Bahamas from transatlantic crossings provide you with an opportunity to replace a disgruntled crew member, and you can expect a great amount of yachts moving that way from late

November to mid May. For more specific times and popular cruising routes, see chapter 4.

There are many islands of the Bahamas I recommend visiting, as there are about sixty marinas throughout the islands, many with boatyards and good, lively bars full of yachties. I will list the notables here.

Abaco and its islands are on the northern end of the Bahaman Island chain and are bustling with yachting activity. Visit Marsh Harbor for its three marinas and the Sailors Bar which is across the harbor from the Conch Inn. The Marsh Harbor Town Dock is a great place to find boat owners shopping before a crossing, and the Conch Inn Marina is always crowded. Go to the beautiful Hope Town Harbor and visit its two main marinas: the Light House Marina, which has a dry dock, and the Hope Town Marina which has many berths. Man-O-War Cay also has a dry dock, as well as a 60 berth marina and a noisy boatyard. Treasure Cay hosts the biggest marina in the Abacos; Green Turtle Cay probably has the most marinas plus a boatyard with a dry dock. At the end of June is the Abaco Regatta. The center of activity during this event is in Marsh Harbor, but Treasure and Green Turtle Cays also get involved. The Green Turtle Yacht Club has a regatta in July as well. San Salvador is a popular point in the Bahamas to leave for points north, since it is the most upwind in the island group. It is also a popular landing spot for yachts coming from Europe for those following the Columbus route.

Grand Bahama has many large marinas and a wide array of boating activities, but a great deal of it is aimed at fishermen. Some notable spots for sailing yachts are the Ocean Reef Yacht Club and the Bahama Bay Marina. The marinas in Lucaya which collectively total about 250 berths should be visited, most notably the boatyard at the Running Mon and the Jack Tar Village Marina on the west end with its 100 slips.

The Bimini islands are small but important to sailors and drug runners alike, but you may have problems getting past the complacency of the locals. Bimini's four marinas total about 150 slips for yachts and fishing boats, but the dominant dock is at Captain Brown's, which is the hangout for sailors in the area. You might want to stop by his lively bar to leave a notice of your availability. Also try the End of the World Bar in Alice Town.

The Berry islands is a popular cruising spot, but services are minimal and the two marinas there are not worth the trouble of getting to.

Despite the great length of waterfront on Andros, it is very underdeveloped for the cruising crowd but hosts a regatta in August. Nevertheless, there are better spots.

Nassau, on New Providence Island, is the hub of sailing in the Bahamas. As it is most likely the place you will fly into, it is an excellent starting point for your search. Go directly to the Yacht Haven Marina to check the docks and bulletin board for opportunities, then try the slips and boatyards of the Bayshore Marina, Brown's Boat Basin, and East Bay and Hurricane Hole Marinas on Paradise Island over the bridge. The Nassau Harbor Club is also a sizable marina worth checking.

On Eleuthera, east of Nassau, there are six marinas totaling about 75 berths that may or may not be worth your while. The only boatyard is at the Spanish Wells Marina on the northern tip of the island. Check the bulletin board at the Spanish Wells Yacht Haven while you are there. Hatchet Bay has a 20-slip marina and is home to Eleuthera charters. Get their US number from Appendix 1.

The Exumas are the only other islands that warrant a serious visit for a berth, and this group of islands is full of life. They make up 365 cays, but Great Exuma has most of the boats. George Town on Great Exuma hosts the Family Islands Regatta in April, turning the place into one big all-night, all-day party. Even though the Regatta is technically for the locals, many touring fun seekers get involved and make this a great place to be. Elizabeth Harbour (near George Town) is filled all year with yachts from all over the world and could be the best place in the Bahamas to seek a long distance voyage. Around Christmas time 200 boats cram its anchorages and slips and their crews cram its bars and restaurants along the main street. On New Year's Day there is a regatta out of the yacht club at Staniel Cay in Exuma, which provides a great opportunity to meet some sailors and help them sail their boats. As mentioned earlier, San Salvador is a great landing spot by yachts coming from all directions, especially Europe, as it leaves sailors upwind of the rest of the Bahamas. It is also a popular landfall from the USA and from the windward passage (west of Haiti).

The only other notable cruising grounds are Cat Island, which hosts a regatta in August and is home to the Hawk's Nest Yacht Club, and Long Island, south of Great Exuma, which has three marinas and a boatyard.

TURKS AND CAICOS

The Turks and Caicos Islands are a small group frequently lumped together with the Bahamas for sailing purposes, but are, in fact, politically independent. There is a very limited number of facilities on these islands, but you will find Cockburn Harbour on the south Caicos Island and the marinas on northern Providenciales (such as Leeward Marina and Turtle Cove) to be your best bets. Caicos Marina, Third Turtle Inn and Provo Aquatic Center as well as the two mentioned above all have dry-dock facilities but few berths. It is recommended to visit the Bahamas instead.

HISPANIOLA

The Dominican Republic is not particularly a sailing mecca, but if you find yourself there, head for the capital of Santo Domingo in the south or the Club Nautico in Boca Chica. The Club Nautico is a regular yacht club with reciprocating privileges to other clubs, and if any foreigners were looking for a bit of respite from exploring this land, they would probably end up here. At Puerto Plata in the north there is a commercial harbor and a small boat quay. Fifteen miles to the west there is a new harbor developing, called Luperón that is likely to be the Dominican Republic yachting center in the near future. In La Romana in the south, there is a developing yachting center complete with a 30-ton travelift and the Romana Marina for visiting yachts. The only other places you will likely find foreign yachts are Puerto Manzanillo and Santa Barbara de Samana. If somebody is looking for a crew member, you will probably be the only person around to sign on. If in Haiti, go to the capital and look for the Koka Paol Yachting and Drinking Association.

PUERTO RICO

The main yachting center of Puerto Rico is not in the main cities as one would expect, but in the remote and varied coastline on the eastern end of the island. In the stretch of coastline between Fajardo and Cabo San Juan the largest and most modern marinas on the island have been built, and your chances of finding passage to other parts of the Caribbean are fantastic. Pay a visit to the harbor at Las Croabas, the El Conquistador Marina about four miles north of Punta Fajardo, the Villa Marina and the Marina Puerto Chico at Playa Sardinera (just north of Fajardo). The Isla Marina off the coast of Fajardo on its own island has the best boatyard in Puerto Rico and plenty of room, but there is seldom anything open for transiting yachts.

In San Juan, the Club Nautico welcomes visiting yachts as do some small private marinas in the area. Boats leave Puerto Rico from late April to June to transit to Bermuda, and in April and May sail to Panama. The city of Ponce on the south coast has some room for visiting yachts; the obvious place here is the Ponce Yacht and Fishing Club. There, they will find transient slips, a 40-ton travelift and a fantastic place to leave the boat while traveling inland.

THE VIRGIN ISLANDS

The Virgin Islands mark the eastern end of the great Caribbean sailing. These islands host the largest and finest charter fleets in the world, and make up the most frequently sailed waters on earth.

US VIRGIN ISLANDS

The US Virgin Islands has its yachting hub on St. Thomas Island. The St. Thomas Harbor on the south side of the island is probably the best provisioning site in the entire Caribbean, so in effect, the marinas of Charlotte Amalie and surroundings are possibly your number one best bet in the world for finding a berth on a yacht.

The Yacht Haven Marina on the east end of the harbor has many open docks and anchorages for cruisers with everything available close by. Across the harbor is Avery's Boat House and Marina, which has a boat lift and yachts under repair. Also on the east side of the harbor in Crown Bay is the Leeward Sailing Center and Marina for bigger yachts. A good bar overlooks the docks and the brand new Crown Bay Marina with almost 100 slips for boats up to 170 feet long. This new marina will soon take over from the Yacht Haven as the happening hot spot in the Virgin Islands, where the greatest number of transient yachts will visit, if not entirely filled with charter boats. Flamingo Bay on Water Island has a marina with limited supplies and is only for hotel guests, so it may not warrant a visit. Farther to the east in Jersey Bay is Antilles Boat Yard with a travelift where transient yachts and the local Caribbean Yacht Charters share the services. At the inside end of Red Hook Bay on the east end of St. Thomas is a full service marina called the American Yacht Harbour, but boats avoid it because of its exposure to the wind. More boats usually anchor in Muller Bay to the east, but come ashore at the marina. In St. Thomas I recommend leaving a notice at the American Yacht Harbour, at the marina in Jersey Bay, at the Yacht Haven, at Avery's and at the Crown Bay Marina.

St. John's yachting visitors conduct most of their business and do their shopping in Cruz Bay. There is an anchorage on both the north and south ends of this bay by the ferry dock. It is of particular interest that virtually all yachts tie their dinghies up to the dinghy dock and come ashore in one place. It is a great spot to engage yachtsmen in conversation to get the scoop on the local yachting community. Caneel Bay is a beautiful place with scads of boats at anchor, but they are hard to approach as there are no real services except restaurants and the Plantation Bar. The rest of the island is made up of beautiful beaches with yachts at anchor. The best way to get in touch with them is to rent a scooter at Cruz Bay Scooters and cruise around, stopping at the beaches you find. It is certainly not a bad way to spend the day.

St. Croix has most of its activity in Christiansted with most yachts anchored between Protestant Cay and the beach. Bigger boats, fifty feet or longer, stay a bit to the east either tied off or anchored at the St. Croix Marina. The marina has everything a yachtsman needs and the boatyard and dry storage area is a great place to talk to people working on their yachts. The Green Cay Marina, located two miles east of Christiansted, has all services available and a great deal of room for transient yachts. Three miles down the road is the St. Croix Yacht Club with anchorages and a dinghy dock to allow sailors to come ashore for a drink at the bar. This is an excellent place to hang out if you can talk them into letting you in, but at last word the bar was closing at 5 P.M.

BRITISH VIRGIN ISLANDS

In BVI. the logical place to begin your quest is in Road Harbour, Tortola, with the number of good marinas and services rivaled only by St. Thomas in the USVI. The Road Harbor waterfront is lined with marinas, bars and restaurants crammed with yachtsmen and locals alike. In the harbor at Road Town, visit the following marinas: the Fort Burt Marina, the BVI Yacht Club, both having public bulletin boards; Wickman's Cay Yacht Harbor; and the Village Cay Marina, having 104 slips for yachts up to 140 feet long. Check the Inner Harbour Marina, a bit less expensive than the rest, and the Mariner Inn Marina, which has 90 slips for visiting yachts and 100 yachts in their own charter fleet. The boat yards are found farther to the east on Wickman's Cay II at the facilities of the Tortola Yachting Services and Caribbean Sailing Yacht Charters. Both of these have boat hoists and large yards open for transient sailors. Some of the bars and restaurants in town are worth visiting: Fort Burt is a favorite for casual sailors; Maria's Beach Resort is very popular with cruising sailors and overlooks the harbor; The Downstairs Bar is located at the Village Cay Marina, but is not known for its service. This entire waterfront is in the stretch of two miles.

Off to the west of Road Town is Nanny Cay, a huge marina with 180 slips and a boatyard. Soper's Hole further to the west is a good point of entry and exit to and from the BVI. There is a dinghy dock on the north side of the bay for clearing customs with a great yachtie bar called Pusser's Pub, and a marina on the south side. Out to the east end of Tortola is Maya Cove which hosts visiting yachts as well. Jost Van Dyke Island east of Tortola has a great harbor called Great Harbor with a jetty, dinghy dock and three great, laid-back bar/restaurants called Foxy's, Rudy's and Happy Laury's. East of Tortola is Beef Island with another great anchorage called Trellis Bay where there is a dinghy dock and a fantastic bar/restaurant full of sailors, called the Last Resort. The only other real marina around Tortola is Marina Cay, a full service marina on its own island, east of Tortola. Peter Island, south of Tortola, has a good dock, anchorage and a bar on the beach called the Beach Bar. Clever people, those British.

Virgin Gorda, the other major BVI Island, has Spanishtown with its Virgin Gorda Yacht Harbor with 110 slips and Tortola Yacht Services for dry docking. Have a drink in their pub to say hello and try to hitch a ride to the north end of the island to the Bitter End Yacht Club, accessible only by boat, full of sailors having a hell of a good time.

Visit the Virgin Islands April to June and November to December, depending on where you want to go. Yachts are arriving from the Bahamas, Panama and Venezuela during both of those periods and from Europe, Bermuda and the East Coast of the U.S. in November to mid December. Yachts leave to the Azores, Bermuda and the East Coast of the U.S. in April to early June, to the Bahamas in November to May, and sail west to the Caymans, Jamaica and the Panama Canal April to May and November to Early December.

THE LEEWARDS

ANGUILLA

This island is fairly insignificant in the Caribbean sailing world, with no marinas and few places to leave a yacht for any length of time. But for those seeking out the real Caribbean, it has everything you would want. The beaches are as good as anywhere, as is the diving, and the people are just as friendly. For you, however, it may be a task finding a yacht to sail on as you will find a complete lack of approachable bases. The main yacht anchorage and the only yacht point of entry is at Road Bay on the north side of the island. There are many good restaurants on the beach of the bay that would be worth a visit in the season, but repairs are nonexistent and there are no docks. Check the Riviera, the Ship's Galley and Johno's in Road Bay and Roy's Place in Crocus Bay. Searching for other spots would be senseless as the entire island has good beaches and secure anchorages. As with all other islands in the Caribbean, the leeward side (the eastern side, which doesn't give Anguilla a lot of room because of its east-west lie) is the most protected and is where the comfortable anchorages are found.

ST. MARTIN / SINT MAARTEN

In contrast to the island of Anguilla, Saint Martin (as I will call the entire island) has busy marinas all around. If you are in the leewards looking for a yacht to sail on, this is one of your best spots, even by Caribbean standards. The areas to visit on the northern (French) side are Simpson's Bay, Marigot, Anse Marcel and Oyster Pond. In the southern (Dutch) side, Philipsburg and Simpson's Bay are the spots to go to. There are numerous other anchorages that would be worthy of a mention if it weren't for the extensive services available, but I will leave most out as the marinas are so plentiful. The island is only seven miles long, so you might as well visit them all, but the Dutch port of Simpson Bay you should visit first (mentioned last).

At Marigot there is an entrance to Simpson Bay Lagoon where a great deal of live-aboards stay at anchor. The port itself is not all that spectacular, but there is a haul-out service at SGP in Sandy Ground and good restaurants and bars. The waterfront outside of the lagoon is made up of a lot of sandy beach and a couple of piers, but the crowded docks are inside in the northeast corner of the lagoon. There is no marina per se, but access to the town is facilitated by the three docks provided. Many yachts are at anchor at all times inside and outside the lagoon. Your best bet for coming into contact with the sailing crowd is to visit one of the many good bars and restaurants in town. These include: the Mini Club, the Flamingo, the Bar De La Mer and La Lafayette. As Marigot is the capital of the French half of the island, it is a place of business as well, and the town is the main attraction. The sailing life is better represented in the other ports on the island.

Ance Marcel is the next important center you will encounter as you move east, and it sits on the northern tip of the island. In contrast to Marigot, it was developed solely with the sailor in mind, and all of the resident establishments are there to cater to that crowd. Check the board at the Port Lonvilliers Marina, and if you are interested in engaging the company of charter customers, there are several charter bases here. There are no boatyards in the area, but a few decent restaurants and bars including the Beach Bar at the harbor entrance. The development is quite compact, so within a half an hour or so you will be fully aware of what services the port has.

Oyster Pond is a natural harbor on the east end of the island which is bisected by the border. The French half is where the development is, representing one of the best yachting centers on the island. There you will find the 100-berth Captain Oliver's Marina and the Oyster Pond Yacht Club. Captain Oliver's is a base for the Moorings charter fleet and has perhaps the best yachtie hangout on the French half of the island, right there at the dock. The only other place to go is to Frog's, which is also a lively bar. The yacht club is really only a hotel and restaurant.

Around to the south is one of the best harbors on the island, based in the capital of the Dutch half: Phillipsburg. Every service conceivable is available to the traveling yachtsmen, except dock space. The two marinas on the waterfront, Bobby's and Great Bay, are usually full to capacity in season, but will try their best to accommodate the transient sailor. Regardless, Bobby's Marina is the focal point of the town and has a well used dinghy dock, and those yachts anchored off will use the docks there or at the Great Bay Marina to pass through to find the services they need in town. Bobby's also has a boat yard where the crews are allowed to work on their own boats, and Budget Marine has a great yachting supply business whose owner keeps abreast of the yachting crowd. The best bars in the area are the Greenhouse and Chesterfield's, which are loaded with yachties most of the time.

The last marina area on the island brings us back to the vicinity of the first, in the southern side of Simpson Bay Lagoon in the port of Simpson Bay. So far I have talked about some of the best harbors on the island, but I have saved the best for last. The landlocked nature of the inner marina area is accommodating to those sailors looking for a place to leave their yachts for a while or for a complete boatyard or a marina with room. It is also the closest to the airport, so it is likely the first you will encounter. The most prolific marina in the area is the Port de Plaisance on the eastern side of the lagoon which draws large and luxurious yachts from all over the Caribbean, but also accommodates the smaller ones. There are 73 slips in this harbor and many are open to transients. The Simpson Bay Yacht Club is also a full service facility with 100 slips and a host of decent bars nearby, including the Stop and Shop, the Felix and the Manhattan Bar. Two other small marinas worth checking for transients are Island Waterworld and the Lagoon Marina, the former having cheaper berths and a small marine hoist. Lagoon Marina is very shallow, so only the smaller sailing yachts can be accommodated. Two other bars to visit are the Yacht Club right next to Port de Plaisance and the Turtle Pier.

SAINT BARTS

The official name of this island is St. Barthelemy, but its nickname is used more. St. Barts is a place you will not likely encounter if you are on a tight budget, as it is difficult to get to and costs a lot to stay, and that is why sailors like it. The tourists are kept out by its remoteness, and it has become many sailors' favorite. There are no marinas or boat yards and few services available, but the small harbor of Gustavia is stuffed with visiting yachts as they pick any room available to tie up stern-to the sea wall or to drop the hook in the bay. The restaurants and bars are the main attraction in this port, as the remote and beautiful anchorages are the main attraction of the island. Loulou's Marine is apparently the hub of the yachting world in the port for the few yachts that are really interested in getting anything done, and they also arrange the St. Barts regatta during Carnival. For everybody else, the social life is their aim, and they seem to prefer Eddie's Ghetto and Le Select. Check the local magazine to see what bars seem to be hopping at the time. As with other remote sailor havens throughout the Caribbean, St. Barts can be the spot to sign onto a yacht as few potential crew members are at hand.

SABA, STATIA, ST. KITTS AND NEVIS

Of these four islands, all of them are well worth visiting for the scenery and remote quietness of the land and the beaches, but the lack of development means that you should not visit unless you already have a ride. The possible exception is Basseterre on St. Kitts. Even though it is the biggest coastal town in this group of islands, the extent of travel required to get there is prohibitive enough. Brooks Boat Company is the only group even resembling a yachting service with its limited mechanical service, and the St. Kitts-Nevis Boating Club is the group that organizes the small yearly races. The only recommended bar is the Turtle Bay on the south point of the island.

MONTSERRAT

Like its neighbors to the northwest, Montserrat lacks the services for those except the most self-sufficient and adventurous. The life on the island is lively enough, but the yachting facilities are missing. If you are there looking for a yacht you are probably in the wrong place. Nevertheless, stop by the Yacht Club, the Las' Call, the Oasis and the Plantation Bar for a drink or a bite to eat. If you are in some other part of the Caribbean pondering visiting this island or the four mentioned above, it might be better to stay put and save these gems until you find a yacht sailing that way.

BARBUDA

Barbuda is not a port of entry; yachts must check in at the other half of the country, in Antigua. They can and often do leave from Barbuda to the islands further to the leeward which is, of course, the natural direction of travel. Barbuda, again like the five islands described earlier, is a great place to visit if you have a boat to sail there on, but not a place to look for a yacht sailing onward. The islands and reefs are renowned to have the best diving in the Leewards, and the beaches are some of the most beautiful and remote. For searching out a yacht to sail on, stay in Antigua. If you are here, though, visit the K-Club near the southern Spanish Point and the only boat harbor on the island, called Boat Harbor (those British).

ANTIGUA

I have mentioned Antigua in my Caribbean introduction for its merit as one of the finest islands to visit for many reasons, and have no trouble in saying it is the best island in the Windwards and Leewards to catch a yacht sailing off. For one thing, Antigua Sailing Week, organized by the Antigua Yacht Club, is the biggest event in the Caribbean, and the number one launching pad for those yachts preparing to sail across the Atlantic. The event happens every year beginning on the last Sunday in April. In addition, for those of you looking to see the Caribbean like a rich yacht owner, Antigua is the springboard for jumping off to those beautiful and remote islands described in the passages above. Being directly to windward of such fine cruising grounds you would naturally look for those sailing there, and an island loaded with services for yachts such as Antigua should give you all the reasons you need to visit.

The obvious harbors laden with these services are those of English Harbor and Falmouth, but the facilities don't stop here. I will take you from English Harbor around the island in a clockwise tour, mentioning only those warranting a visit.

Antigua Slipway has the best boatyard in southern Antigua and, although the grounds are fairly small, every square foot is used for holding up sailboats. They allow the crews to work on their own yachts, which is good news for you, and in addition they have complete services and a complete ship's store, which is good news for those transients looking to get some work done. Nelson's Dockyard on the east side of the channel by the customs house is the second most important place of business for you to get to, with its stern-to moorings and full repair facility. You might also want to check the grounds of Nicholson's Yacht Charters on the point north of Nelson's; although they are in the business of selling and chartering yachts, they are known in town to be very accommodating to the transients and have services that are lacking in the rest of Antigua. Falmouth Harbor has a completely different entrance for yachts, but from a pedestrian's point of view can be considered the same area, so I will continue my discussion to include Falmouth. The marine businesses to consider visiting in Falmouth are the Catamaran Club on the northern end of the harbor and the Antigua Yacht Club on the east side. They each have about 30 slips and both are open to transient yachts. Visit the bars and restaurants of Famous Mauro's, Abcadabra, G&T's Pizza (at the yacht club) on Thursday night and the Deck on the weekends.

There are numerous anchorages along the southern and western coasts of Antigua that are frequented by yachts, but they are completely devoid of facilities and services with the exception of the occasional exclusive restaurant and hotel. Deep Bay due west of St. Johns is one such place, but it is among the most frequented because of the Ramada close by and the wreck in the bay which is an attraction to divers. There are no other facilities.

One of the finest harbors outside of English and Falmouth harbors is St. John's Bay. It is a perfectly protected anchorage with a sizable town (the capital of Antigua), a few good restaurants and a marina at Redcliffe Quay on the way. There are reports that the marina is finished at this time, so your concentration should be on that facility. Visit the Lemon Tree Restaurant on a weekend night as this is where the night life is (although a bit too civilized).

On the northern gulf of the island in the vicinity of Parham Harbor lies a fantastic marina facility, recommended without reservation. Crabbs Marina is located on the spit of land east of the bay. A full service boatyard, they let the owners and crew of the yachts work on their own yachts and have plenty of room for yachts to sit for a while. It also has plenty of room out front for yachts to anchor. Visit the boatyard and engage the crews of the yachts into conversation. It might be the best place to go as Antigua Race Week approaches and yachts are being spruced up for the long passages to follow. As I mentioned before, boat yards are great spots to develop long-term working relationships with the crews of long distance voyaging yachts, and this could well be the best place in the entire Caribbean to develop such a relationship. Another facility in the area is Parham Marina in the crotch of the bay, and is really not worth a trip on its own, but on your way to or from Crabbs it is worth a stop. You will find lots of yachts at anchor in front of the marina, but the marina itself is a small repair facility for equipment and cannot dock nor haul out yachts.

The last harbor to mention, Mamora Bay, is just a stone throw from English Harbor to the east and is quite exclusive. The Saint James Club is where all the activity is, and those luxury yachts that can afford it will relax in the splendor of this luxurious resort, but will not likely want to be bothered by hitchhikers. Still, it is always worth a try.

GUADELOUPE

The most important area for yachtsmen on the two islands known collectively as Guadeloupe is Pointe A Pitre in the southern bay between the two islands. There is one mammoth facility there, one of the largest marinas in the entire Caribbean known as Marina Bas-Du-Fort. This facility has room for 900 yachts and has every available service for yachties, and should be your mainstay in Guadeloupe. They have a boat yard on the grounds and a travelift to get the boats there, many good restaurants and bars and a plethora of symbiotic services clinging to mother marina. Seemingly contained in the marina grounds is Porte de la Marina, home to the local Moorings charter fleet and Massif Marine, home to another small charter fleet. North of the marina in the next bay lies Lemair Marine and Forbin Marine. They both have fabulous marine shipyards, Lemaire being the best in all of Guadeloupe. Lemaire can haul out any yacht up to 700 tons and Forbin up to 300 tons. They both allow the crews to do their own work but also make their services available. On the opposite side of the port across the water is the Jarry Industrial area which has the commercial business and a boat yard that will handle any size yacht. There are so many good restaurants in the dock area of the marina it is not necessary to visit the town to meet the crews. In addition, the bars and restaurants are in such a compact area you will see where the action is and where the crews hang out in just a few minutes of walking, and it is not necessary for me to list them. This is one of the best areas in all of the Caribbean to find a ride on a yacht. Spend some time here.

On the southern shore near the eastern tip of the island in the town of Saint François is the Marina Grand Sable. It has about 120 berths for transient yachts but not much in the way of services. It is difficult to recommend after explaining the area of Point A Pitre, but it stands solidly on its own merit.

The islands between Guadeloupe and Dominica are fairly devoid of yachting activity with a barely notable exception. In Marigot, on the island of Terre D'en Haut stands the Roche a Move Slipway and small boatyard. No sense in visiting there unless you are there already.

DOMINICA

Dominica is called the Nature Island. With its lush greenery it surpasses the rest of the Caribbean in beauty. However, most people visit the Caribbean for the beaches, and there are not many here. The rain this island gets gives the surrounding reefs a bit of dirt from the rivers and keeps the diving from being all that good. As a result, it is not a destination yachties chose first when planning a trip to the Caribbean, and is only appreciated when they stumble across it, after they have grown tired of some of the thousands of perfect beaches elsewhere in the Caribbean. The yachting bases are fairly well defined and are situated in the big towns of Portsmouth and Roseau. In Prince Rupert Bay there are a number of worthy places to check, the town of Portsmouth being the least desirable. Pay a visit to the Purple Turtle and the Sunshine Village. The Portsmouth Beach Hotel has some moorings available and offers yachties a good restaurant and tours inland. Go to the desk and ask around for yachts looking for crew. About ten miles south is the Castaways Hotel which welcomes yachts in its fine anchorage and helps them out any way they could, so you might find one or two there in season.

Roseau has two places where yachts can feel fairly safe; those anchorages in front of the Sisserou Hotel and the seawall at the Anchorage Hotel. Many yachts tie up to trees along the waterfront and use the dinghy docks at one of these hotels.

THE WINDWARDS

MARTINIQUE

The most northerly of the Windwards is the squeaky clean Martinique, with its busiest port area at Fort de France, which is the largest city in the Windwards. The main area for entry and departure from Martinique is at the YSM dock there in FDF with the customs office right next door. An area where yachts can tie up stern-to is there at the main harbor, but most anchor close by. FDF is only a spot to check in, check out, repair and provision, so the places I suggest checking are based upon places of business, not of pleasure. The main provisioner is Firmin who can be contacted at 76-05-97 during business hours or stop by Firmin's friendly affiliate, Rama Multi Exchanges, at 34 Rue Victor Hugo between 9 AM and 1 PM. Another good contact is right at YSM; go inside, ask for Gatta and see what is going on. Check also the Crew Bar west of the Caribbean Art Center.

On the west side of the harbor are a couple of boatyards: the Ship Shop Slip with room for many yachts, and Grants (farther along the water). In Cohe de Lamentin, there is Marina de Cohe which caters to boaters who want to work on their own boats in a quiet place. It has a dinghy dock and will have many repair services soon. Anse Mitan, on the south end of the bay has a good marina with many services and is home to a charter fleet of its own. Anse Mitan is also reputed to have fantastic night life and fabulous restaurants and is probably the most important yachting area in Martinique. The Hotel Bakoua has a dock and marina called Avimer Marine which is used for transient docking and fueling. Check the hotel desk for information on boats staying there. The Bamboo Bar is a casual place where yachtsmen stop by for a cheap lunch. If around at night, go into the Hotel Bakoua's night club. Numerous other anchorages are in between FDF and Anse Mitan (and further around the corner with their casual hangouts on the beach), but none really stand out. On the southern end of Martinique lies St. Anne with its own dock but little more. The Club Nautique du Marin, 2 miles north of the town of St. Anne, has room for transient yachts at its docks and more room for anchoring off the yacht club, but services are minimal. The only other notable place on the island is St. Pierre, where there are many yachts at anchor most of the time. Go to the dock and see who's at anchor.

ST. LUCIA

St. Lucia, being closer to the Grenadines and more scenic than Martinique, is a bit more lively and fun for sailors and therefore more populous and set up better for yachting. Rodney Bay is the hub of it all, with a beautiful and modern marina and a customs dock. The marina with its 232 slips is the best place to begin your quest. They have a good bulletin board and can hold messages for you if you post a note yourself. The Rodney Bay Marina Boatyard with its dry dock and 50-ton marine hoist are on the north side of the marina. The A-Frame Docks, another docking area for transients, is on the south side of the same marina. Check Steven's Yachts and the docks at Trade Winds, both charter companies, while in town. The St. Lucia Yacht Club is also worth a visit. If you want to run around the pubs with visiting sailors, it is best to go on a Friday to join the town free-for-all, but all nights are lively in the countless bars and restaurants. The best are the A Frame Bar and Pat's Pub, which are now the big yacht hangouts.

Castries Harbour is another good place to check, but it has nowhere near the quality of sailing life associated with Rodney Bay. A boat yard and 35-ton travelift are located at Castries Yacht Centre in

Vigie Cove. Try also St. Lucia Yacht Services in the same cove. The Wicki-Up Bistro next door is the number one best place to eat, drink and talk to yachties. Marigot Harbor, home to The Mooring's charter fleet, is another excellent stop with most of the action centered around the Hurricane Hole Hotel on the southern side of the harbor end. There is also a dinghy dock on the north side of the harbor at Dolittles with another good bar and restaurant. A free shuttle runs back and forth between here and Hurricane Hole -- use it. Other mentionables are the Hummingbird Hotel & Bar in Soufriere Bay on the southwest side of the island and the Cloud's Nest Hotel on the southern point in Vieux-Fort.

ST. VINCENT

It is wise to approach St. Vincent with the idea of getting on a southbound yacht to the Grenadines, as this is the handiest place to launch from. The Grenadines have some of the best sailing in the world and would be a rewarding training ground for later trips abroad. Caribbean Sailing Yachts of Blue Lagoon has some foreign boats, mostly charters, and would be the best place to start your search. The Caribbean Sailing Yachts docks are usually crowded with their own charters but welcome transients if they have room. They have a good bar as does The Wheel next door. Check with the Caribbean Sailing Yachts hotel and walk the docks. Then wander over to the west side of the lagoon and check Buhler's Boat Yard and go further west to the Young Island Dock (on the mainland) where the crews of the boats at anchor usually come ashore. Have a drink and pizza at The Dolphin, where most transient yachts' crews stop for a bite and a drink.

Kingstown is the port of entry into St. Vincent but is very unpopular with sailors. They do have an anchorage, but it is crawling with boat-stealing kids and heaps of garbage. It is worthy of a check, though, if you are in the area. Although St. Vincent is very scenic, yachtsmen have the Grenadines in mind and are eager to get going.

THE GRENADINES

The best place to shove off for a sail through the Grenadines is from the island of St. Vincent to Bequia, aboard one of the SS Admiral ferries from Kingstown. It takes under two hours and costs about four dollars. Bequia is an island paradise for yachties. They and the locals are likely the only people you'll meet. Admiralty Bay has a number of yacht service companies and many bars and restaurants that warrant a check. Bequia Slip in the northern part of the bay has repair services at its docks. Frangipani Yacht Services, which is the main contact in Bequia, has various yachting services. In addition, there are other small workshops scattered around town. The best bar to sit and socialize in Admiralty Bay is the Frangipani. Besides being the recommended bar, restaurant and hotel, it is a great contact for boats in the region because they arrange charters on many of these private yachts.

For points south of Bequia, I really don't recommend traveling to unless you have a boat at your disposal, as they are quite primitive, and the best places cannot be approached by land. It is best to find a boat to help crew out of Bequia, St. Vincent or St. Lucia.

GRENADA

Grenada, south of the Grenadines, is another choice spot for trips to the Grenadines as well as being a favorite landfall for transatlantic sails. Grenada Yacht Services (GYS) has a lift for boats up to 110 feet and ample room for boats to dock for the short and long term. Rates are so reasonable that many yachties leave their boats there for trips elsewhere. St. George's is a very good place to stock up for longer trips, so finding yachts preparing to leave for Europe is not out of the question. Two bars that you should visit are the Nutmeg and Delicious Landing. Also check S.I.M. Boatyard in Prickly Bay, another great spot to post an ad for yourself.

BARBADOS

Barbados has little available for yachts. Located 100 miles directly into the wind from any other port in the Caribbean, it is very rarely sailed to by anybody doing the Caribbean circuit. There are no harbors, natural or manmade, anywhere on the island. The only place to tie up is at an ugly and unfriendly concrete pier. The anchorages are unprotected from swell and uncomfortable throughout the year, and there are no facilities on the island that cater to yachts. Despite all this, Barbados is one of the best places to find yachts looking for crew in the entire Caribbean due to its geological position, being the most logical place for transatlantic sailors to stop on their way into the Caribbean from the Canaries or Europe. Thus, Carlisle Bay is full of yachts from November through February with little activity the rest of the year. To be the first new westerner to come aboard after a long crossing, many a captain will likely take you on board and dump an irritating deck hand at first sight.

The entire yachting world of Barbados is on the eastern, or leeward, end of the island (for the shelter from the swell) within a two mile radius of Bridgetown. The waterfront in Bridgetown and the dock at the Holiday Inn are good places to start, but the Barbados Cruising Club and the Barbados Yacht Club, both located in Carlisle Bay, are probably the best places to find yachts all year. In season, the noise of the partying yachtsmen alone will bring you to their hangouts and provide you with a fantastic opportunity to buy a beer and raise a toast to their accomplishment of running with the wind for three thousand miles. I can't think of anybody more deserving.

TRINIDAD AND TOBAGO

At the time of this writing, there is little reason to visit either of these islands. Trinidad was once a place where yachting was encouraged and the facilities were being expanded and breakwaters were to be built. In recent years, however, the government has apparently changed its mind and strongly discourages both tourism and yachting. One thing I have learned in my years of travel is that when the government doesn't want you there, it is probably not a very fun place to be. Tobago, in contrast, is quite friendly, but with a generous portion of the world's cruising grounds closer to the US, very few yachts ever find a reason to go there.

PORTS ON THE NORTH COAST OF SOUTH AMERICA

VENEZUELA

To look at a map of Venezuela and try to guess where the best yacht harbors might be, you will most likely guess all the wrong places and wind up leaving the country discouraged. The protected harbors and large cities are reserved for commercial activity or have been left untouched by developers, while the flat stretches of coast that look like nothing on the maps are where the yacht clubs and marinas have been dredged and constructed. My description of Venezuela and subsequently of Columbia will move from east to west, following the wind. These are the only places I will recommend visiting, although there are numerous protected anchorages and small harbors along the coast that you might run across. My job here is to save you the time of searching on your own for the popular places for transient yachts to visit on their exploration of the Spanish Main.

On Isla de Margarita off the coast of Cumana, visit the Puerta Concorde Marina at Porlamar and the Marina El Faro near the Porlamar town dock. The port of entry into Venezuela is in Pampatar on the east end of the island, the first landing spot in Venezuelan waters for yachts coming in from the Caribbean. It is a good place to start if you are there anyway, but it is probably not worth your while to make a special trip to the island.

An excellent place to start your search is in the port of entry in Cumana called Puerto Sucre. Here you will find an unbelievably large marina with accommodations for approximately 200 yachts called the Marina Cumanagoto and a shipyard named Varadero Caribe. I suggest you visit both. For those yachts making their way along this coast from the Windwards to the Panama Canal and spending some time doing it, this is the most likely place to enter the country.

Just west of Puerto La Cruz is the Bahia de Pozuelos, home of another large marina called the Amerigo Vespucchio. There you will find many transients and a small boatyard capable of hauling out yachts.

The best spot to visit along the entire coast of Venezuela is a harbor called Carenero, which has a number of yacht clubs and facilities. The ones worth visiting are the Varadero Cavafa Marina, the Talleres Betancourt Boatyard and the Carenero Yacht Club. Farther west is the manmade harbor of Puerto Azul on Punta Naiguata. The Club Puerto Azul, which has recently been described as the most elegant yacht club in the entire Caribbean, is worth a visit. It may be tough for you to get in without making up an extravagant lie, but it's worth a try. Wear your best blue blazer. Another five miles to the west is Punta Carabellada. There is another classy complex here called the Club Nautico virtually stuffed with yachts, and the Marina Del Mar (which is public). This entire stretch of coast just described is conveniently located close to Caracas and all within a span of fifty miles, so my recommendation is to stay in this area until you find a yacht.

From the Caracas area to the west, there are only four other spots worth mentioning. Although all the yachts moving west will cover this area, there is an unlimited number of places to anchor along the way and no obvious marinas to visit. To check them all would be pointless.

The four places I have described here are the only ones I recommend visiting due to the vastness of this coastline. Puerto Cabello is worth a mention only because of the boatyard at the naval base. The size of the derrick is an attraction to the larger yachts that couldn't be pulled out of the water in the yacht centers around Caracas.

Boca de Sanchez, just north of Tucacas, has a few marinas for smaller boats, but will accept transient yachts and is certainly worth a visit. Try the Marina El Ancla, the Marina Indunave, Las Luisas Marina, and Marina Morrocoy. Morrocoy has a boatyard as well.

Puerto de Guaranao, on the west coast of the Peninsula de Paraguana is a port of entry (albeit for vessels moving in the wrong direction) and hosts the Cordon Yacht Club.

The Port of Maracaibo on the coastline hugging Colombia is also a fantastic place to find a yacht preparing for a long passage. Check the Club Nautico de Maracaibo and the transient docks there as well as the Los Andes Yacht Club. Both welcome transiting yachts.

THE ABC ISLANDS

Commonly known as the Dutch Leewards, the islands of Aruba, Bonaire and Curacao are fabulous places for yachtsmen to stop for a respite of the long crossing to the Panama Canal from the Windwards, and an equally rewarding destination for tourists flying in for a couple of weeks of wind surfing and scuba diving. For you it can be a great spot to begin your journey to the South Pacific; in season there are countless yachts passing through here going in that direction. These islands are friendly, modern and full of history. They have an international airport and a language all their own (Papiamento). Unfortunately, there is a prominent lack of marina facilities here, and this keeps transient yachts from congregating there on a regular basis.

Curacao, the largest of the Netherlands Antilles, also has the best developed yachting centers; principally Willemstad, Spanish Water and Piscadera Bay. Williamstad is primarily a commercial harbor, the second largest Dutch harbor in the world, but is attractive to yachts as well. There are no dedicated marinas as of this writing, but the dock at the Queen Emma Bridge and the Small Craft Yard at Batipanja are the suitable places for you to pay a visit. The yard is primarily used for small commercial vessels, but the yachting community uses it as a repair center as well. In Spanish Water, you will find the greatest concentration of yachts on this group of islands. It is also the best place for leaving the yacht while traveling around the islands. Check Club Asiento, Sairfundy's Marina and the Curacao Yacht Club.

Bonaire has only one harbor, but it does have a small marina and government dock. It is not worthy of a visit on its own.

On the island of Aruba, the only harbor where you are likely to find yachts is Oranjestad. There you will find a brand new marina within its own breakwater. Also check the Aruba Nautical Club for transient yachts.

COLOMBIA

Along the entire coast of Columbia there are beautiful anchorages and pristine cruising grounds. If it weren't for the piracy and drug-running contrabanditos, the place would be one of the foremost cruising areas in the Caribbean. As it is, most cruising sailors know the truth about the danger always present in Columbia, and most avoid even getting close to it. The only place I recommend visiting is the harbor at Cartagena, and maybe Barranquilla.

Barranquilla is a protected harbor about forty miles north of Cartagena and is visited by transiting yachtsmen for its repair facilities and cranes. If you find your way up there, be sure to visit the Club Nautico, the Club de Pesca, and, of course, the commercial wharf.

In Cartagena, you will find by far the best yachting facilities in all of Colombia, which is fortunately close to the premier tourist center in the country. The Club de Pesca is where most of the visiting yachts stay; the rest anchor off, waiting for room in the club's marina. The club also has a haul-out facility for the smaller yachts, but the Compania Vikingos de Colombia across the harbor has a great deal more yard space, six travelifts able to haul vessels to 140 tons and is very hospitable to yachtsmen. For your purposes there is little reason to go anywhere else.

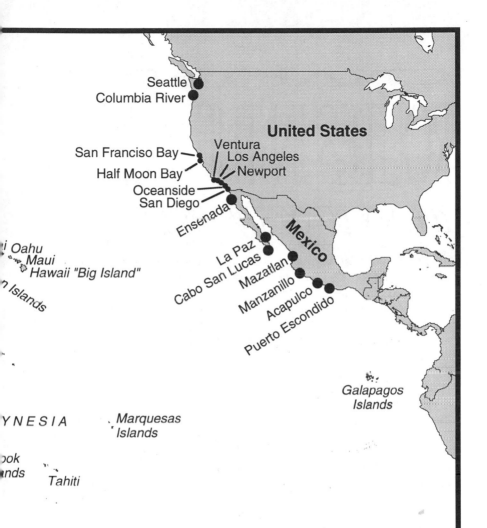

Seattle
Columbia River

United States

San Franciso Bay
Ventura
Los Angeles
Half Moon Bay
Newport
Oceanside
San Diego
Ensenada

Oahu
Maui
Hawaii "Big Island"
Islands

La Paz
Cabo San Lucas
Mazatlan
Manzanillo
Acapulco
Puerto Escondido

Mexico

Galapagos
Islands

Y N E S I A
Marquesas
Islands

ook
nds
Tahiti

Ports in the
Pacific

N

CHAPTER 7

ROUTES IN THE PACIFIC

THE WORLD OF THE PACIFIC

It is now estimated that 1000 cruising yachts are in the islands of the South Pacific at any one time throughout the season with many boats spending more than one season there, giving the Pacific an average seasonal flow of around 300 yachts. On average, 200 of those come from the Panama Canal and the rest from the mainland of the US or Hawaii. Comparing these numbers to the 1000 coming west from the Canaries or the estimated 5000 passing through the Straits of Gibraltar each year, the Pacific is relatively uncrowded, and one can hope it stays that way. The Pacific I will characterize as between the Panama Canal and the Torres Strait, north and west as far as the South China Sea and including all mainlands and islands in between. The main artery runs south from the Canal to the Marquesas, Tahiti, Fiji and off to the Torres Strait with boats entering and leaving this route all the time. Some yachts circle back to the US, some sit out the hurricane season in New Zealand or Australia and others visit more of the islands off the beaten track. The direction is almost entirely westbound as the return trip is both uncomfortable and uncommon.

The season in the South Pacific begins after the last hurricane, usually at the end of March, and continues until the next one, in mid November. This offers six months of sailing in paradise, a length of time one can consider hardly sufficient to see all there is to see and truly enjoy all the South Pacific has to offer. In October and November there is a mad rush of boats getting out of the hurricane belt, which runs in an east to west strip south of Fiji along the South Pacific islands. If you plan to go to New Zealand in April, you will have an excellent chance of getting on a boat on its return trip to the Pacific islands after the hurricane threat has passed, to spend the entire season in the western Pacific.

The directions sailed from the area of Fiji are well defined once the hurricane season is afoot, the biggest destination being New

Zealand in September and New Caledonia and Australia in October. The track of the South Pacific storms runs due west across the islands and then south into Australia. Sometimes hurricanes blow right through the Torres Strait before moving south, so boats in the region are desperate to find secure ports as they don't exist in the islands of Fiji. The only secure harbor used by yachts north of the track to sit out the hurricane season is Rabaul, on the island of New Britain in the group belonging to Papua New Guinea. Many yachts stay in other places scattered around and take their chances.

There is really no reason to be in the South Sea Islands during the southern hemisphere summer months with the cyclone season present. It's more prudent to find someplace else to go until March or April, or plan your trip to be in another part of the world entirely. But as April approaches, cruising yachts leave from New Zealand and Australia for Vanuatu, New Caledonia, Fiji, Papua New Guinea, Samoa, Tonga and the Solomon Islands. As usual, boats will push through these islands throughout the season at no particular rate, as the beginning of the season finds boats entering the trade wind route at countless different points, and everybody moves at a different clip. Since the cyclones that follow these routes in the summer months (December-March) push right through the Torres Straits at times, it is best to be beyond New Guinea by November. From there, your decision on which way to go will naturally be dictated by the yacht you are on. Few boats at this time bother with the Indonesian islands or even the Philippines. Indonesia has some of the best cruising grounds in the world with clear water, steady winds and beautiful paradise islands without people, but the stories of Bogis pirates and the difficulties in obtaining cruising permits are greatly exaggerated among the cruising community and most yachts just stay away. I spent six months slowly weaving my way through these islands and have been back many times, as recently as October 1992 for a surfing expedition on a sailing charter yacht out of Bali, and I am still amazed by the lack of yachts enjoying this paradise.

The Philippines remain lightly touched by the cruising world as well, with few yachts visiting the Vasayas, some of the most beautiful islands I have ever seen. But with the intricate network of ferries running within those islands daily and the extremely low cost of living, it is advisable to fly in, take in the islands on your own and hope to find passage onward to the South China Sea and beyond, or sail to Guam and through the islands of Micronesia.

FROM THE US WEST COAST TO HAWAII

The US Customs Department claims that approximately 1000 yachts registered to ports on the west coast of the US visit Hawaii every year, providing an excellent opportunity for a green sailor to get a crossing under his or her belt. The problem is that there are no ports along the way and if a new member of the crew does not get on well with the rest of the crew or the captain, it makes for a miserable trip. The season for making the crossing is very wide, between May and September, but even outside these months a crossing can be done successfully. If done in November, for example, winds are good, the possibility of a summer hurricane crossing your track is nonexistent, and extra time can be spent in Hawaii before heading to the South Seas. Unfortunately, few sailors put much extra time into their plans, but learn to work it into their schedules once they get into the rhythm of the islands.

If you are on the mainland of the US trying to get out to the islands, it is best to keep in mind that the Pacific Northwest is extremely difficult to sail from, and all yachts from there sail south along the coast to at least San Francisco before encountering favorable winds for the crossing. From there south to San Diego, you will find yachts everywhere preparing for this crossing. One of the most popular events in recent years that has been attracting sailors for the crossing to Hawaii has been the Transpac race. As the event moves from pure racing to more of a cruising rally, it brings more and more cruising yachts with it each year. The Transpac usually starts on the first of July every year to correspond with the best time for the crossing. Get in touch with the Transpac Yacht Club at (310) 983-8790 for crewing opportunities.

FROM HAWAII

There are many great reasons to start your trip in the Hawaiian islands. One of the best is the fact that as a US state there are no visa requirements for American citizens. You can get away with purchasing a one-way plane ticket and not have to hassle with immigration officials on arrival. Once there, you can take your time looking around for a boat and not worry about overstaying your visa. Many yachtsmen sail across the Pacific to Hawaii on their shakedown cruises and don't foresee the changes they encounter in both themselves and their crew members. The sail is long, dull and mostly cold with no islands to break up the monotony, and many yachtsmen reach the islands and decide not to go any farther. Of course, the crewmen who leave those yachts leave vacancies that must be filled by others. The big factor, though, is the number of yachts that are sold in the islands and are purchased by those crafty sailors looking for deals and warm waters. They pick up these yachts cheaper than on the mainland, have their shakedown cruises already completed and start their first journeys in warm water. These new owners need crew, of course, so the benefits for you are obvious. One problem with this is that you have no place to sail for the skipper to check you out, except from one island to the next. To leave the Hawaiian chain you must endure thousands of miles together over the span of a few weeks at least, and if there are problems at the start you will find yourself in a great bind. For this reason, you should take a good, hard look at each other before departing. In addition, a freshly purchased yacht with a newly picked crew has a low experience level, giving the yacht more potential for problems. Be careful.

The other option is to catch a yacht moving from the Hawaiian islands bound for the ports of the US West Coast. The sailing times are in the summer months, as those yachts moving back to the States are concerned with the winds to take them there and the warm weather at their destinations. The yachts that sail for the States intending to do it without the benefit of an engine sail north to take advantage of the northern coastal winds and then turn south once close to the coast. The best winds for the journey occur in the dead of winter as the high pressure center is at its lowest in latitude, but the occurrence of winter storms makes the wind factor seem insignificant. The best weather occurs in the summer months and makes for a more pleasant cruise, even if one must sail farther north to find favorable winds.

From Hawaii to French Polynesia, boats concentrate their departures in the months of May and June to take in the entire South Pacific season, with yachts continuing to depart at a tapering rate throughout the summer months. In April and May each year, several yachts move directly west across the Pacific from Hawaii towards the Far East to Japan, Hong Kong and China. Nonetheless, their numbers are small. Keep in mind that moving to the West Pacific towards Japan, Micronesia and the Carolines requires careful planning as the western Pacific typhoons originate in the Carolines and move towards

Japan in the months of July through October. This gives the northwest Pacific a very tight cruising window.

Wherever you are headed, your best bet is to visit the major ports of the Hawaiian Island chain, which are also the ports of entry. Try to arrive in early April for a voyage south and in June for a trip back to the states. In both cases you will have several months in which to seek out passage.

SOUTH FROM CALIFORNIA

Boats sailing south from California along the coast offer the best deal for a novice sailor, as there are plenty of opportunities for him or her to get off and possibly sign onto another yacht. Boats leave after the summer hurricane season, crossing the southern US border in November and December to spend the dry and sunny winter season in Mexico and Central America. Another advantage is that the winds blow from the north in these months and taper off gradually until around May, when the hurricane potential marks the end of the sailing season. Yachts choosing to return to the US from Mexico or Central America do so at the very end of the season when the winds are not so severe, usually in April and May. In no cases do they return after May.

Many yachts each year sail south directly to Panama or with a few stops along the way. They usually leave around the first part of November to arrive in the Caribbean at the start of the season there.

Many cruising yachts also sail from California directly to the Marquesas a bit later to arrive no earlier than the end of March. In order to avoid the hurricane season that strikes both hemispheres in their summers, yachtsmen have found it best to sail anywhere from the beginning of March to the end of May to meet the arrival of the pleasant season in the South Seas. Most sailors making that journey plan a stop or two on the Mexican coast, primarily at Cabo San Lucas, before the long ocean crossing.

WEST FROM PANAMA

Panama remains a superb place to catch a boat to the South Seas, with virtually all yachts moving from the Atlantic to the Pacific being funneled through the small stream of the Panama Canal. Most yachts sail straight from Panama to the Marquises Islands between the months of February and June, the bulk of them in the earlier part of that stretch, to reach the south seas after the hurricane season at the end of March. The big alternative is to stop in the Galapagos, which is almost exactly en route, but the government there keeps yacht visits to a minimum by granting only about five cruising permits per month and charging excessively. If you find a yacht that is heading that way, then most likely the captain has applied for a cruising permit and submitted a crew list with it. If you hitch a ride after the permit was applied for you will not be officially on that permit, of course, and your presence can cause problems for the captain and for yourself. You do have a good chance of getting permission to stay as a tourist without a visa, but that depends upon the mood of the port captain at the time. If the boat has no official cruising permit, it can still stop for a 3-day rest before pushing on. From Panama, the only other route is up to Hawaii, which is done by approximately 40 boats per year. Sailing north from Panama along the coast is uncomfortable, slow and uncommon.

FRENCH POLYNESIA

The French Polynesian Islands are much more open to cruising than the Galapagos, but if crew changes take place, things can get sticky. If arriving to the country by air, you may have to post a bond for the amount of an exit plane ticket and show you have enough money to support your stay. After your three month stay (which can be easily extended to six), or when you clear out of port, your bond money will be refunded. One other note on French Polynesia in general: the prices are very high and many yachts push on early for this reason. Keep this in mind when you prepare for your stay.

These islands have no real yacht centers except Papeete, Tahiti, which is the place to go to find a berth moving west with the mainstream flow. When yachts provision for a long trip, they usually aim for Papeete, but if going in the opposite direction, it is more practical to load up on food and set sail from the Marquises, principally Nuka Hiva. Passages are made towards Hawaii from French Polynesia at a rate of about 50 yachts per year between April and November, the later months being more common as the sailing season nears its end. Although this number seems small, consider that only about 25 boats sail to Hawaii from Samoa, and less than ten each from the Marshalls and the Cook Islands and two or three from Tonga each year.

WESTWARD FROM TAHITI

The 300 or so yachts sailing west annually from French Polynesia onward to the Cook Islands, Tonga and Samoa move along at different paces, depending upon what they find and how they feel, so the times to visit these places for the hitchhiker are not nearly as critical as they are in other parts of the world. However, the Tahitian celebration of Fété, or Tamure, which is a huge party all over the Tahitian islands but biggest in Papeete, starts around the 20th of July and gives cruisers one scheduled event in an otherwise unscheduled life. Dozens of yachts congregate there each year to join the celebration, lining up for half a mile with sterns tied to the beach. The celebration will last a month or until people get tired of it. After the first few days of this, the yachts start to push westward at a steady flow.

FIJI

The main hub of cruising activity in the South Pacific seems to be Fiji, more specifically Suva on the Eastern end of the main island of Viti Levu. Again, you may be asked to put up a bond for your departure, but if your appearance is good and you are resourceful, you can probably get around this. Suva has about 300 boats moving through from east to west during the season, plus boats leaving for New Zealand and Australia and rejoining the route before and after the hurricane season. Many boats use Tonga for their departure point instead, so a visit to either country in October or November will give you a good chance of finding a ride down to New Zealand for the summer.

NEW ZEALAND

Several hundred yachts arrive in New Zealand during the month of November chiefly from Fiji and Tonga but also from Australia and the islands of Vanuatu and New Caledonia to the west. It's worth noting that a large proportion of these yachts will be hauled out and in repair and their owners and captains can be talked to over this pleasant summer season before they shove off in April and May. In May of 1986, I posted a card advertising my availability on the bulletin board at West Haven Marina in Auckland and got numerous responses and half a dozen offers. At that time of year there are races going off to Australia and also to the islands, hungry for crew members, and the opportunities are fabulous. The main destinations are Fiji and Tonga, but most westbound boats leave earlier, in the summer months of January through April. The cyclone season does not touch New Zealand or the southern (New South Wales) part of the Australian East

Coast without the warm water available to feed dying hurricanes, so the cruisers concentrate on transiting the southern Tasman Sea during those months. If you plan to visit Australia in the summer, a good destination would be Sydney after Christmas to catch a ride to Whangarei or Auckland in time to find passage from New Zealand back into the trade wind route for the season.

SOUTHEAST ASIA FROM PAPUA NEW GUINEA

The Far East has a very long typhoon season, which limits its sailing possibilities to just a few months. You can get to the Far East from the West Coast of the US or from Hawaii by leaving in April or May and miss the typhoon season for some cold water sailing in Japan. Because of the extremely small number of yachts that cruise the Far East, I will not cover this area but will instead introduce the only real way of getting to Indonesia and then the Philippines, that being via Papua New Guinea.

As the alternative to the Torres Strait, circumnavigating cruising yachts continuing through to the Indian Ocean call on the Indonesian port of entry at Jayapura in northern Irian Jaya, the Indonesian western half of the island of New Guinea. The northern part of New Guinea is where the beautiful sailing is, and I strongly discourage going to Port Moresby to find a yacht heading west. This is because of the excessive crime in that city, and the fact that nearly all of the yachts there are engaged in a seasonal sail between the islands of the western Pacific and the ports of Australia. If you are trying to find passage west through Indonesia, most of the boats going there will check into Jayapura, and virtually all of the yachts you will find there already have a cruising permit and are going in your direction.

In northern Papua New Guinea, all yachts continuing on to the Philippines or Guam leave from Madang, but traffic is small. There is a great deal more traffic heading west through the Torres Strait to Bali or Darwin.

PHILIPPINES

The Philippines is more open than most countries, with little concern paid to cruisers. I recommend obtaining a three month visa ahead of time. Cruising permits are not required, and you will always be free to sail in, out and around the 7000 islands without telling a soul except immigration officials in some of the more established towns.

From the Philippines, the yachts pushing west head for Singapore predominantly, usually with stops in Borneo. When in the Philippines looking for passage, the best places to find yachts looking to sail long distances are in Manila and Subic Bay (to a lesser extent), but down south where island hopping is predominant, check the ports of entry at Iloilo on Panay Island, Cebu City, Puerto Galera on Mindoro, and Dabao, Zamboanga and Cagayan de Oro on Mindanao. You will have a good time along the way, especially if you take a snorkel.

BORNEO

If in Borneo, check Kota Kinabalu in Sabah, the harbor at Bandar Seri Behawan in Brunei and Kuching in southwest Sarawak for yachts ready to cross the South China Sea for Singapore. The best times to make this crossing is during the northeast monsoon, in the months of January to March. Although the typhoon season the rest of the year brings some nastiness to the region, serious storms rarely make it this far and boats, albeit few, will be sailing here all year.

INDONESIAN CRUISING PERMITS

One more note about Indonesia is that yachts sailing on a cruising permit (which is required) have on that permit a crew list which must be officially changed if you are to join the yacht at a later date. A crew change is usually a simple procedure and an agent at the port in which you join the boat can probably do it. Different ports treat it differently, but in my experience of voyaging through the archipelago, people can be taken aboard as 'guests' and others left in other places without so much as a raised eyebrow. Your biggest obstacle will be persuading the captain to let you on board as he will have a great deal more to lose if things turn sour. Just make sure that you officially check out of the country with immigration when sailing onward. You get a two-month visa if flying in but three months on a cruising permit, and extensions are not possible. The Indonesians are very friendly people in most places, and I have yet to encounter problems concerning such matters.

CHAPTER 8

PORTS IN THE PACIFIC

THE WEST COAST OF THE US

Considering that this book is intended to be a guide for voyaging primarily in tropical locales, I will focus most of my discussion on that region of the world. However, since it is also intended to give the reader information on traveling from the US, I have made it my primary concern to provide the information that will make it easy for him or her to find a yacht as close to home as possible. For this reason, I have provided guidance on locating yachts on all coasts of the continental US, but have concentrated on the more temperate harbors. I feel that if the reader wants to catch a yacht moving to the South Seas, he or she should aim for the southern shores of the continent, but if the coasts of Maine or Washington are at his or her doorstep, there is no reason to get too far away from home to find what is desired. With this, I begin my discussion on the coast of Washington and the Puget Sound.

WASHINGTON

SEATTLE AND THE PUGET SOUND

In **Seattle**, the biggest and best marine facility is located out of the way of the main commercial section of the harbor. Located off Seaview Ave. Just north of the Salmon Bay Waterway north of Seattle, it has about 800 slips and a boatyard with a travelift capable of hauling out yachts to 45 feet.

The best marine facility in the entire Puget Sound is located in the city of Everett about 25 miles north of Seattle. Called the **Port of Everett Marina**, it has room for more than 1500 yachts and a sizable boatyard is located on site.

Anacortes is another area of Puget Sound that has marina facilities. The town itself is located eighty miles north of Seattle at the gateway to the San Juan Islands, the islands that make the local yachting business practical. There are three marinas in Anacortes: Anacortes Marina, Cap Sante Marina and the Skyline Marina.

Skyline Marina is on Flounder bay west of Anacortes, it has full services available.

Anacortes Marina is located south of Cap Sante on the western shore of Fidalgo Bay. It accepts transients and has a wealth of facilities including haul-outs.

Boat Haven, or **Cap Sante Marina** is located just south of the Cap, has transient dockage close to the Harbormaster's office. There is also dry storage space for yachts.

La Conner town docks have some room for transients near pier 7 at the Swinomish Channel but only for boats that can get under the 75-foot bridge from the south.

In the Port of Bellingham, **Squalicum Harbor** has a fabulous transient area, and you must keep in mind that the harbor is really in two parts. It would be prudent to check them both. The older facility is to the west and has its transient dock adjacent to the harbormaster's office at the seawall. The newer harbor, just to the east and almost touching the older facility has its transient docks next to the harbor center alongside Roeder Avenue.

Port Townsend, across the water from Everett, has two notable marinas, one small and the other huge. The smaller is the **Point Hudson Harbor** right at Point Hudson, and although they accept transients, there are few services. The other facility is the **Boat Haven Marina,** about one mile to the southwest of the point mentioned above. They also accept transients, but it is best to check with the harbormaster first to look at the bulletin board. The berths are assigned to transients as they check into the port.

The **John Wayne Marina** is located in Sequim Bay, about ten miles west of Port Townsend, at Pitship Point off highway 101. At last check this marina was being expanded, and the current conditions are unknown. There are facilities and transient docks available.

Port Angeles, another twenty miles to the west, is the most likely spot to encounter Canadian yachts moving into US waters from the north. As Port Angeles is a port of entry and the closest sizable harbor to the entrance of the Straits of Juan de Fuca, the marina there is a great place to look for yachts moving south. There is a large transient dockage area there and several chandlers as well as a boatyard, marine hoist and a marine railway. It is a good place to find yachts moving into and out of the Puget Sound. The transient docks are located on the east side of the marina at the E and F docks adjacent to the boatyard. The marina itself is located on the north side of town, off Marine Drive.

At **Neah Bay,** at the southern tip of the entrance to the straits, there is a small harbor where transients will dock at one of a few floating docks or anchor in the bay.

GRAY'S HARBOR

Moving down the coast of Washington, the first place of interest for you is **Westhaven Cove** at Gray's Harbor. Located on the southern point of the harbor entrance, they provide berths for those transients moving along this rough coast looking for a long deserved rest, but there are few other services available.

COLUMBIA RIVER

In the Columbia River area there are two facilities close to the entrance that readily accept transients: Ilwaco and Astoria. **Ilwaco** is located on the inside of Cape Disappointment on the north point of the entrance to the River. Visit the harbormaster at the marina office and the transient docks at dock I. There is also a boatyard on the west side of the marina called Ilwaco Boat Works.

Astoria, at the southern end of the bridge of the same name, is the northernmost marina in Oregon. There, just west of the bridge is the West End Mooring Basin, the only facility in the area that will take in transients. There are no other services in the area.

THE COAST OF OREGON

Moving south along the Oregon Coast, there are two marinas with entrances of dubious quality, not recommended for any yacht. You will not likely find any traveling yachts visiting either **Tillimook** or **Depoe Bay,** as the bar is difficult to cross and requires intense local knowledge.

At the Yaquina Rivermouth in Newport, Oregon, you will find the first accessible harbor south of the Columbia River. On the southern shore of the entrance you will find the **Southbeach Marina,** used by recreational boaters both resident and visiting.

COOS BAY

The most used port on the coast between the Columbia River and San Francisco is Coos Bay. The **Charleston Boat Harbor** on the southern shore of the entrance is the place to find transient and resident yachts. The transients docks are the northernmost and southernmost docks of the outer harbor (docks B and F).

In **Chetco River**, at Brookings, Oregon, the northernmost marina is used by yachts although few brave the rough entrance to the river

NORTHERN CALIFORNIA

CRESCENT CITY

The most northern harbor in California is at Crescent City, which has a small craft harbor in town.

HUMBOLDT

In Humboldt Bay, most yachts head for the **Woodley Island Marina** north of the town of Eureka. If you get there, there is a large area for transients at the long flat pier to the west and at dock D.

BODEGA BAY

In the town of Bodega Bay, the Porto Bodega and Spud Point Marinas are used by yachtsmen living in the San Francisco Bay area to permanently dock their boats. The **Spud Point Marina** is a relatively new facility with 250 berths, a 70-ton travelift, and every other service needed. The **Porto Bodega Marina** has become a fishing marina in recent years since the other facility opened, but they do still accept transient sailors. If you are in Bodega Bay, this facility is definitely worth a visit as well.

THE SAN FRANCISCO BAY

There are many, many marinas in the San Francisco Bay area. I will start in Marin County and work my around to the east, then to the south and finally to the San Francisco waterfront before continuing the journey down the central coast. There is a fantastic magazine in the

San Francisco Bay area called **Latitude 38** that is set up for people such as you, and every April and October they host huge parties, usually at the **Corinthian Yacht Club** in Alameda, open to all interested. The purpose of the parties is to unite yacht owners with potential crew members, in April for the trip across to Hawaii and off to the South Pacific and in October to Mexico and points south. Pick up a copy of this magazine or call them at (415) 383-8200. They also have a section of their magazine dedicated to bringing crew and yachtspeople together. This section is called the crew list, and you can put yourself on the list with forms available in the January issue. The magazine also has a good classified section with a column devoted to yachts seeking crew.

SAUSALITO

Sausalito Yacht Harbor (415) 332-5000. 527 total berths, transient slips available occasionally, although they do not specialize in them. They also have a 25-ton marine hoist.

Sausalito YC (415) 332-7400. This club hosts the Sunset Series races every other Tuesday throughout the summer, and they will let you in if you show up.

Pelican Yacht Harbor (415) 332-0723.

Cass's Rental Marina (415) 332-6789. They run charters out of their marina and get involved with the Sausalito Cruising Club next door for Friday night barbecues after the race.

Sausalito Cruising Club (415) 332-9922.

Clipper Yacht Harbor (415) 332-3500. 700 total berths, all empty berths are available to transients. There is a marine hoist on the premises, run by Anderson's Marine, for yachts up to 120 feet long. They have no bulletin board, but West Marine close by has one.

TIBURON

San Francisco Yacht Club (Belvedere Cove) (415) 435-9133. They have no open races, but offer to place outsiders' names in their crew listing book at the club for yacht owners to reference.

Tiburon Yacht Club (415) 789-9889. They host Friday night races, and they say that somebody is always looking for crew. People gather in front of the yacht club around 5:30 pm.

Corinthian Yacht Club (415) 435-4771. They host Friday night races as well, also open to outsiders looking to crew. The members gather there around 6 pm.

Paradise Cay Yacht Harbor (415) 435-1652.

SAN RAFAEL

San Rafael Yacht Harbor (415) 456-1600.
San Rafael Yacht Club (415) 459-9828. They welcome people to leave their calling cards, and also have races on the weekends that outside crew members are welcome to join in on.
Loch Lomond Marina (415) 454-7228.
Loch Lomond Yacht Club (415) 459-9811.
Marin Yacht Club (415) 453-9366.
Marine hoists of 25 tons are in the yards of Harbor Boat Repair at 456-3660 and Roland's Boat Repair at 454-0528.

CARQUINEZ STRAITS AND THE EAST BAY.

Port Sonoma Marina (707) 778-8055.
Vallejo Municipal Marina (707) 648-4370. Over 500 slips available, and a 470-foot long transient dock. There are no bulletin boards and the docks are all locked. There is a 50-ton hoist at Yachtmasters next door.
Vallejo Yacht club (707) 648-9409. They host Wednesday night races, open for outsiders to crew. There are usually many opportunities for potential crew members.
Glen Cove Marina (707) 552-3236. 200 total slips, but many are covered (too low for sailboats).
Benicia Marina (707) 745-2628. 370 slips, plenty open to transients. The owner reports that there are a great deal of boats moving through between the bay and the delta at all times. He has the six-pack rule-- anybody who stands on the dock with a six pack and their thumb out is almost guaranteed a ride on a yacht.
Benicia Yacht Club (707) 746-6600. Thursday night races from April to October in a very active program. Plenty of room for outside crew members.
Martinez Marina (510) 372-3585. They have 400 total slips and three guest docks with plenty of room.
Martinez Yacht Club (510) 228-5450. They host regular races, but you must be a guest. The commodore suggests that a person coming in off the streets should try to meet up with a sailboat owner and ask him to sign him or her up as their guest. There is always room for crew members.
Crockett Marina (510) 787-1049. Very small marina with some transient berths and a 50-ton marine hoist.
Rodeo Marina (510) 799-4436.

RICHMOND

Point Richmond Yacht Harbor (510) 233-3224. Over 200 slips and a small bulletin board in the office.

Brickyard Cove Marina (510) 236-1933. 250 total slips and transient berths are always available. In addition, there are two accessible bulletin boards on the premises.

Richmond Yacht Club (510) 237-2821. They host beer can races every other Wednesday from May to October.

Richmond Marina (510) 236-1013.

Marine hoists, travelifts and boatyards at **Blue Bahia** 233-0804; **Cal Coast Marine** at 234-7960; **Stanford-Wood** at 236-6633

BERKELEY/ EMERYVILLE

Berkeley Marina (510) 644-6371. 925 total slips, 20 of which are set aside for transients. This marina is very open and friendly.

Berkeley Yacht Club (510) 540-9167. They host summer races on Friday nights and the last Saturday of each month in the winter, Fully open to outsiders with many opportunities for crew members.

Seabird Sailing Center (510) 548-3730. A good place to stop and talk to the people at the counter, they know about all the activities going on in the area yacht clubs.

Emeryville Marina (510) 653-3114. Room for 374 yachts, many open to transients when space permits.

Emery Cove Marina (510) 428-0505. Room for 430 boats, with room for transients most of the time.

OAKLAND

Visit the following marinas in Oakland: **Embarcadero cove Marina** (510) 532-6683; **5th Ave. Marina** (510) 834-9815; **Lani Kai Harbor** (510) 261-6532; **Jack London Marina** (510) 444-5858 **Portobello Marina** (510) 452-2987; **Seabreeze Marina** (510) 832-3951.

ALAMEDA

Alameda Marina (510) 521-1133. More than 500 slips, none set aside for transients, but they are welcome to occupy those that are vacant. They have a good bulletin board.

Ballena Isle Marina (510) 523-5528. 500-600 total slips, usually 100 or more open to transients. They have a bulletin board in front of each dock which can be accessed by visitors.

Fortman Marine (510) 522-9080. A marina with a great deal of ties with cruising yachtspeople, they are in constant touch with international cruisers. They have 496 total slips, a great bulletin board and are very friendly. They also have a 25-ton travelift.

Marina Village (510) 521-0905. With 750 slips, it makes this marina the largest private marina in northern California. They report a 95% occupancy rate. The bulletin boards can be used freely by outsiders.

Aeolian Yacht Club (510) 523-2586.
Encinal Yacht Club (510) 522-3272. They host the twilight series on Friday nights, very open to outsiders. They are a very active yacht club with lots of members.

SOUTH BAY

San Leandro Marina (510) 357-7447. The best looking marina in the bay, they have room for 450 yachts to 60 feet and lots of room for transients.
San Leandro Yacht Club (510) 351-9666.
Oyster Point Marina (415) 952-0808. 570 total slips, 70% occupancy rate. They have one bulletin board that gets plenty of attention.
Brisbaine Marina (415) 583-6975. 573 total berths, side ties for transients.
Oyster Point Yacht Club (415) 873-5166. Very, very friendly, very open to having guests join in their functions. Be honest with them about your quest and join in on the summer Friday night races.

SAN FRANCISCO

Gas House Cove Marina (415) 567-3695.
Pier 39 (415) 981-1796. 350 total berths. A great deal of international transients move through, especially in the summer. They have lots of bulletin boards that are open to outsiders wanting to post notices.
San Francisco Marina (415) 292-2013.
Golden Gate Yacht Club (415) 563-9716.
Saint Francis Yacht Club (415) 563-6363. Very exclusive club with excessive contact with international sailors. Unfortunately, they took down their bulletin board, and it is difficult to get in contact with them. Well worth a call, however.

THE CENTRAL CALIFORNIA COAST

HALF MOON BAY

There is only one marina in this bay, and it is called the **Pillar Point Harbor**, at (415) 726-5727. A popular spot to stop for those sailing between SF and Santa Cruz. It is a crowded marina in the summer. Check with the harbormaster at the foot of the dock.

SANTA CRUZ

The **small craft harbor of Santa Cruz** is another fantastic place for you to visit to find a yacht moving along the coast, as it is estimated that 50 yachts per day move in and out of this harbor on their trips up and down the coast. The harbor itself has room for nearly 1000 yachts, with most of the transients finding space at the ends of the piers. In the summer you will find them rafted up together at those locations. The harbormaster is located just east of the closest dock to the sea.

MOSS LANDING

This is not as popular as Santa Cruz, but you will find a sizable marina that is also filled with yachts in the summertime. Check with the harbormaster at the **Moss Landing Marina** south of the entrance. Also check the **Elkhorn Yacht Club** on the northern extreme.

MONTEREY

In Monterey, the **Municipal Marina** accepts transients along the docks on the inner side of the seawall. Check at the harbor office at the tracks. Also check the **Breakwater Cove Marina** at 373-7857. They accept transients as well.

MORRO BAY

Morro Bay represents the only protected harbor between Point Conception and Northern California. For this reason, the **Morro Bay Yacht Club** offers reciprocal privileges with other yacht clubs. They also have a dock for transients and a bulletin board. In the southern part of the bay is a small marina run by the **State Parks Department**, which offers nice, clean docking space to residents. No transients allowed are allowed there.

SANTA BARBARA

There is only one marina here, and it takes up the entire harbor. There is also an anchorage east of Stearns Wharf, but the transients mostly hang out in the protection of the harbor as rates are cheap and the surge is low. Check the harbormaster's office west of the dock and the yacht club between the harbormaster and the seawall.

VENTURA

Ventura has three marinas and at least one boatyard, but unlike the other harbors in the area, transients do not contact the harbormaster for transient slips, but instead tie up at his dock and make their own arrangements with the individual marinas. Check the **Ventura Yacht Club**, the **Ventura Isle Marina** on the west side of the harbor and the **Ventura West Marina** which, curiously, is on the east side of the harbor.

OXNARD

The Channel Islands Marina is aptly named because of its proximity to the Channel Islands. It has six marinas, five yacht clubs and two marine railways. From the entrance on the west side of the harbor, the first marina you are to encounter is the **Bahia Cabrillo Marina**, then the **Channel Islands Marina** and then the **Vintage Marina**. In the central Peninsula you will find the **Peninsula Yacht Anchorage** and on the east side is **Channel Islands Landing** and **Anacapa Isle Marina**. The harbormaster is located on the east side of the channel close to the marina entrance by the Coast Guard station. The municipal transient slips are in the east channel at the end, and on the western side of the peninsula. Also visit the **Islander Yacht Club** and the **Pacific Corinthian Y.C.** Port Hueneme has no recreational facilities.

LOS ANGELES AREA

MARINA DEL REY

The first in a line of excellent harbors you will find as you move into the Los Angeles area from the north, this harbor alone has room for 6000 yachts in its eight basins. There are 17 marinas and three yacht clubs there and many other services available for yachts, with docks set up specifically for transients. The space for transients is limited because of the long waiting list for residential docks and most of the space is allocated to them. Transient yachts are directed to basin H, the first they come to on the starboard side when entering the harbor. Visit the transient dock office in the center of Burton Chase Park at the end of Mindanao Way. Their number is (310) 305-9595. I have included the marinas in this discussion because they also make space for transients and offer better services than the municipal docks do.

If you are looking to crew on a yacht for initial experience, the harbor at Marina Del Rey is unfortunately not as open as other places in Southern California. The only yacht club that organizes regular weekly races is the **California Yacht Club**, which has what they call the Sunset Series on Wednesday Nights. This event is open to all wishing to sail and the atmosphere is very friendly.

Most of the repair facilities are located on the west side of the marina at the H and G basins on Bali and Mindanao Ways.

Following is a list of the individual marinas and clubs found in MDR, with information on each.

Admiralty (310) 821-4282.
Aggie Cal (310) 823-8964. 109 slips, not open to transients
Bar Harbor Marina (310) 823-4689. 400 slips, not open to transients.
Catalina Yacht Anchorage (310) 822-0669. Contact the dock master at 823-3684. 200 slips, not open to transients.
Deauville Marina (310) 823-4655. 490 slips, fully open to transient traffic.
Dolphin Marina (310) 823-4875.
Holiday Harbor Marina (310) 821-4582.
Islander Marina/ Pier 44 (310) 821-8881. Call the dock master at 823-4593. They have about 1500 slips collectively at their hotel and the Islander Marina, fully open to transients.
Marina City (310) 822-0611. Associated with an apartment complex, not open to transient traffic.
Marina Harbor (310) 823-8974. 700 slips, open to transients.
Mariner's Bay (310) 822-2001. About 300 slips, not open to transients.
Mariner's Village (310) 821-4461.
Neptune Marina (310) 823-4555. A marina and apartment complex, not open to transients. A total of 214 slips.
SMYC Marina (310) 823-2252.
Tahiti Marina (310) 823-4504. Call the dock master at 301-6535. 251 slips, open to transients.
Tradewinds Marina (310) 823-2026. 170 slips, marginally open to transients one night at a time.
Villa Del Mar (310) 823-4644. 201 slips, not open to transients.

And Yacht Clubs:

Windjammer's Yacht Club (310) 823-2345. Very stuffy, no weekly races.
California Yacht Club (310) 823-4567. Wednesday night races open for beginners, called the Sunset Series.
South Coast Corinthian Yacht Club (310) 306-2787.

KING HARBOR

Located in Redondo Beach, this harbor is quite small and does not have dedicated transient space, but the individual marinas offer space to transients when available. Otherwise, transients must anchor inside the breakwater with a stay limit of 3 days. The **King Harbor Yacht Club** has Thursday night races, open to all outsiders. The **King Harbor Marina** has a total of 850 slips, and they accept transient yachts. The other three marinas: the **Portafino**, the **Port Royal** and the **Redondo Beach Marina** all cater to powerboats and small yachts, but have transient yachts occupying their small marinas at times. Phone numbers: **King Harbor Yacht Club** (310) 376-2459; **King Harbor Marina** (310) 376-6926; **Redondo Beach Marina** (310) 374-3481; **Portafino Marina** (310) 376-8481; **Port Royal** (310) 376-0431.

LOS ANGELES/LONG BEACH/SAN PEDRO

There are ten marinas in the Los Angeles Channel, but for transient yachtsmen looking for a dock, there is really nothing available. The individual marinas have long waiting lists, and because of this lack of space all of the docks are allotted to residents. What this means for you is the opportunities for getting out on day sails is extremely good, but you will not likely find foreigners on temporary stays looking to sail onward. This is better served in the ports of San Diego, Long Beach and San Francisco. The sheer number of berths in this harbor (about 4000) will provide you with an excellent chance to get out for local sails to polish your sailing skills, and those yachts that are ready to pull out of the harbor after spending years as residents are numerous.

Just as Latitude 38 Magazine caters to the local racing and cruising community of Northern California, Santana is the Southern California sailing rag. Each spring they have a listing for crew looking for yachts for cruising and racing and a list of those skippers looking for crew. These lists are quite large, so there is probably a great variety of opportunities waiting for you between the pages. Santana keeps its hand on the pulse of the So. Cal sailing world, so it is well worth your while to pick up a free copy. Another good free publication is The Log, and in San Diego County the San Diego Log, which caters more for yacht owners but is a complete and resource-packed publication nonetheless.

One area that I don't cover in this book is Santa Catalina Island 26 miles off the coast of Long Beach. The yachts are numerous but they are out on moorings and difficult to approach, and those you will find there are out for a weekend sail only, but I ran across a social event that takes place there annually that should interest you. A man named Doug Owen puts together a cruising seminar/party weekend, free of charge, in the middle of October for cruisers sailing south at the end of the hurricane season. In the 1992-93 season 350 people on 150 yachts attended this seminar/party to tell stories, settle itineraries and match yachts with similar destinations. Up until now hitchhikers did not generally know about the seminar, but it sounds like a perfect weekend at the perfect setting to find a yacht setting south. Call the Catalina Harbor Department at (310) 510-2683 for details.

Long Beach is another huge yachting area and, like LA and Marina del Rey; it is stuffed with resident berths. They will allow yachts to stay a maximum of 15 days per month at their transient docks. The municipal harbors are the Downtown Marina and the Long Beach Marina. These and the private marinas total about 8000 berths. The marinas in Long Beach and Los Angeles are listed as follows:

Downtown Shoreline Marina (213) 437-0375 and **Alamitos Bay Marina** (213)594-0951 (administered by the City of Long Beach). 3800 slips total in the two marinas. Transients usually get spots at the end of the docks (end ties). Note that the bigger the yacht the closer to the mouth of the harbor it will be.

Cabrillo Boat & Yacht Basin, Inc. (310) 832-1907. Total of 115 slips/moorings,

Cerritos Yacht Anchorage (310) 834-4737. Total of 100 slips/moorings,

Colonial Yacht Anchorage (310) 830-1160. Total of 115 slips/moorings,

California Yacht Marina (310) 834-7916. Total of 260 slips/moorings,

Fletz Bros. (310) 832-0334. Total of 435 slips/moorings,

Holiday Marinas, Inc. (2 locations) (310) 833-4468 . Total of 200 slips/moorings in San Pedro, 165 in Wilmington.

Island Yacht Anchorages (2 locations) (310) 830-1111. Total of 145 slips/moorings at Henry Ford Road, Wilmington, 135 at Berth 200 in Wilmington.

Al Larson Boat Shop (310) 832-6404.

Al Larson Marina (310) 832-0526. Total of 125 slips/moorings,

Lighthouse Yacht Landing (310) 834-9595. Total of 90 slips/moorings

Los Angeles Yacht Club and Marina (310) 831-1203. Total of 100 slips/moorings

Pacific Yacht Landing (310) 830-0260. Total of 160 slips/moorings

Shelter Point Yachting Service (310) 832-7507. Total of 70 slips/moorings
Yacht Center Inc. (310) 834-5016. Total of 250 slips/moorings
Yacht Haven (310) 834-6892. Total of 250 slips/moorings
Leeward Bay Marina (310) 830-5621. Total of 189 slips/moorings
San Pedro Marina (310) 519-8177. Total of 96 slips/moorings
Cabrillo Marina (310) 519-3566. Total of 1180 slips/moorings
West Basin Marina (310) 519-8335

Yacht clubs in Long Beach and Los Angeles:

Alamitos Bay Yacht Club (310) 434-9955. A dinghy club, very small boats. Once or twice a month they have races and regattas.
Cabrillo Beach Yacht Club (310) 519-1694.
Hollywood Yacht Club. No phone at the club.
Huntington Harbour Yacht club (310) 592-2186. Smaller yachts are located in Huntington Harbor as discussed in the next paragraph. They host weekend races throughout the summer.
Little Ships Fleet of Long Beach (714) 846-7928. Very active racing club, they organize races with all of the area yacht clubs
Long Beach Yacht Club (310) 598-9401. They have a series of races called 'Wet Wednesdays', open to all who want to crew.
Los Angeles Yacht Club (310) 831-1203. No weekly races at this time, but friendly and open to outsiders.
Navy Yacht Club Long Beach (310) 519-9516. For DOD employees and retirees, they host Saturday races and regattas.
Seal Beach Yacht Club 431-9254. They host Thursday night races throughout the summer. Also, they have a good bulletin board for the public to use.
Shoreline Yacht Club of Long Beach (310) 435-4093. No regularly scheduled races, but open and friendly.
West Coast Yacht Club (818) 952-1856.
Westward Cruising Club (310) 833-9415.

HUNTINGTON HARBOR

You might as well forget about this marina for yachts, as there is a bridge at the entrance that has a clearance of only 23 feet, and only the smallest yachts can clear. The Huntington Harbor Yacht Club has regattas for smaller yachts and those with hinged masts. Their phone number is in the section above.

NEWPORT HARBOR

Newport Harbor is another yacht harbor full to the top with marinas; each marina is full of yachts with little extra room. There are also five guest docks by the Coast Guard office on the south side of the harbor entrance. Here is a list of the marinas and clubs and what they offer:

Lido Yacht Anchorage (714) 673-9330. 265 slips to 130 feet, open to transients throughout the year. Newport Harbor Ship Yard is on the premises.

Newport Dunes (714) 729-1100. 431 slips, open to transients most of the time. Very large, very busy, very friendly.

Bay Shores Marina, Balboa Marina and **Bayshore Marina** are all administered out of the same office at (714) 644-9730. They have 560 slips collectively, all open to transients when slips are available.

Balboa Yacht Basin (714) 673-1761. 172 slips, not open to transients at all.

28th Street Marina (714) 675-6538.

Newport Marina (714) 642-4644.

Yacht Clubs:

Bahia Corinthian Yacht Club (714) 644-9530. On Friday nights throughout the summer, they have the Summer Sun series, with all classes of yachts, and a big burger bash afterwards. Fully open to all.

Balboa Yacht Club (714) 673-3515. Twilight series on Wednesdays, beer can races on Thursdays. The twilight races are for small boats (dinghies), and the beer can races are for the bigger yachts. The yacht club doors are open to all during the races.

Newport Harbor Yacht Club (714) 673-7730. Send them a notice card with your phone number, and the boat owners will contact you if looking for crew.

Voyager Yacht Club (714) 644-4029.

DANA POINT

The Dana Point Harbor has two marinas and three yacht clubs. They offer guest docks and two anchorage areas for transients. Both anchorage areas are inside the breakwater, one all the way to the southeast end and one on the western end. The transient slips (guest docks) are on the eastern end of the island. The **Dana West Marina** has its office west of the Dana Point shopping area and constitutes the north half of the marina while the **Dana Point Marina** makes up the southern half with its office on the island. There is a boatyard adjacent to Doheny Park Road. It is interesting to note that the Dana West Marina offers slips to transients who are residents of the sister marinas of Harbor Island West in San Diego and Ventura West in Ventura. All told, the two marinas offer berths for about 2500 residents.

Dana Point Marina (714) 496-6137. End ties are available for transients.
Dana Point Yacht Club 496-2900. They host Thursday night races throughout the summer, open to all interested in crewing.
Dana West Marina 493-6222. Most of the larger yachts stay here, many end ties open for transients, a good bulletin board outside of the office.
Dana West Yacht Club 661-1185. Has Wednesday night races open to all interested in sailing, a good bulletin board outside the office.
Capistrano Bay Yacht Club 493-7102. Friday night yacht races all summer long for anybody looking to crew, extremely friendly. Will hold messages for those wanting to sail on other crew members' yachts.
Aventura Sailing Assoc. 493-9493. Sailing classes available for a price. A very good organization for those looking for structure.
Dana Point Ship Yard 661-1313. 50-ton marine hoist and a lot of yard space. easy access to the yachts in the yard.

OCEANSIDE

Oceanside Harbor has two marinas and a small boatyard, offering about 900 slips for residents and 50 for transients. The **Oceanside Harbor** at (619) 966-4580 administers all of the yachting traffic in the harbor and is the only marina. The **Oceanside Yacht Club** (619) 722-5751 has Wednesday night races through the summer. Show up at 5 pm and go upstairs; there are usually plenty of people looking for crew.

MISSION BAY

There are seven marinas in Mission Bay, only three that you would be interested in visiting. The reason for not spending much time talking about the rest is that there is a 38-foot fixed bridge that cuts it off from the ocean and its accommodations are limited to small resident craft and powerboats. The three marinas on the ocean side of the bridge are the **Mission Bay Marina,** the **Seaforth Marina** and the **Hyatt Islandia Marina**.

Mission Bay Marina (619) 223-5191. 200 slips, very open to transients, have 2 travelifts capable of hauling out yachts to 100 tons.
Seaforth Marina (619) 224-6807. 250 slips total, open to transients to 43 feet. They have a good bulletin board.
Islandia Hotel Marina (619) 224-1234.
Mission Bay Yacht Club (619) 488-0501. They have Thursday night racing throughout the summer, open to all interested. Located in Sail Bay.
Knight and Carver Boatyard (619) 222-6488. Very large boatyard, worthy of a visit.

SAN DIEGO BAY

The San Diego Bay has many yachting centers from Shelter Island to Chula Vista with 16 marinas, 9 yacht clubs and berthing for about 4000 boats. Your attraction to San Diego Bay is its location along the coast and the appeal it holds for yachtsmen from other countries and ports of colder climates. It is the biggest launching pad for transient sailors on the entire coast from Alaska to Costa Rica, being the spot for yachtsmen to provision and undergo repairs as they await November, the end of the hurricane season. For this reason the most important places for you to visit in these months are those marinas with lots of accommodations for transients and the boatyards. If you are in San Diego at the time of these yacht departures, be sure to pay a visit to **West Marine Products** on Rosecrans Blvd., **Downwind Marine** on Cannon St., **Pacific Marine Supply** and the **Kona Kai Yacht Club** for their annual cruisers' parties for those setting to head south. One of the reasons for the party is to match cruisers up with crew. The common time to have such parties is on Halloween weekend. The yachts that are pressed for time and are looking forward to a long sailing season in the Caribbean leave religiously in the first week of November. Don't disregard the value of visiting this yachting town for day sails as San Diego is one of the most popular sailing areas in the United States. Here is a list of facilities with the benefits of each from the North Bay to Chula Vista:

SHELTER ISLAND REPAIR FACILITIES
The Boatyard (619) 477-3991.
Eichenlaub Marine Boatyard (619) 222-9805.
Driscoll Boatyard (619) 224-3575.
Kettenburg Boatyard (619) 224-8211.
Shelter Island Yachtways (619) 222-0481.

Neilson Beaumont Marine (619) 222-4255.
Koehler Kraft Co. (619) 222-9051.

SHELTER ISLAND

Shelter Island Marina (619) 222-0561. 188 slips, many open for transients, one bulletin board.
Bay Club Marina (619) 222-0314. 154 slips, open to transients. A couple of bulletin boards scattered around.
Half Moon Anchorage (619) 224-3401. 180 slips to 50 feet, lots of transients move through in November on the way south. Bulletin boards available for use.
Kona Marina (619) 222-1191. Administered by the Kona Kai Marina, 252 slips to 50 feet. Accepts transients.
Kona Kai Marina (619) 222-1191. 264 slips and a guest dock. This is the spot for the large transients, docks to 90 feet and end ties for even larger yachts. One bulletin board.

COMMERCIAL BASIN

Shelter Cove Marina (619) 224-2471. 151 slips to 112 feet, transients accepted all year. One bulletin board in the office.
Sun Harbor Marina (619) 222-1167.

HARBOR ISLAND

Na-Ka-Oi Creative Services (619) 294-6655. Complete boat yard.
Harbor Island West (619) 291-6440. 690 slips, lots of room for transients all the time. Two bulletin boards, one in the deli.
Marina Cortez (619) 291-5985. 560 slips, transient slips when available. 2 bulletin boards.
Cabrillo Isle Marina (619) 297-6222. 420 slips, transient slips available. One bulletin board.
Sheraton Marina (619) 692-2249.
Sunroad Marina (619) 574-0736. 600 slips, room for transients most of the time. Two bulletin boards.

CORONADO AND DOWNTOWN

Glorietta Bay Marina (619) 435-5203. 102 docks, transients accepted sometimes.
Mariott Marina (619) 230-8995. 445 slips total, transient slips available. Located downtown.

CHULA VISTA

South Bay Marine Center (619) 427-6767.
California Yacht Marina (619) 422-2595. 300+ docks to 55 feet, transient slips available and a bulletin board.
Chula Vista Marina (619) 691-1860. 522 slips to 60 feet, transient slips and a bulletin board available.

YACHT CLUBS:

Chula Vista Yacht Club (619) 691-1860.
Coronado Cays Yacht Club (619) 429-0133. They sometimes have races on weekends, Wednesday night beer can races. They have a good bulletin board
Coronado Yacht Club (619) 435-1848. Wednesday night beer can races, open to all interested. Very friendly and a very good bulletin board out front.
Kona Kai Yacht Club (619) 222-1191. Home of the November Cruiser's party, a great place to be if wishing to go south.
Outboard Boating Club (619) 226-9155.
San Diego Yacht Club (619) 222-1103. Wednesday night beer can races, but you must be a member of another club
Silver Gate Yacht Club (619) 222-1214. No races, but they will post a note on the board for you.

MEXICO

BAJA CALIFORNIA

The problem with hitching rides in Mexico is that each yacht must declare their crews upon entry into Mexican waters, and then they must carry a crew list to all subsequent ports. Making changes to this list can be simple or difficult, depending upon the attitude and honesty of the port captain. To be certain of the current rules, call the consulate or **Romero's Mexican Service** in Newport Beach, Ca. at (714) 548-8931. Boatyards are at Ensenada, La Paz, Puerto Vallarta, Guaymas and Acapulco.

ENSENADA

The rugged coast of Baja is a difficult place to hook up with yachts, so if in doubt stay in San Diego. But if you are in a hurry to get on with it and don't mind the extra red tape, try the small and severely limited port of Ensenada for the passing transient. The yachts you are likely to find there are those on very limited budgets, getting repairs for bargain prices. The boatyard there is called the **Baja Naval** which has a small yard serviced by a 75-ton travelift. The docks belong to the **Ensenada Yacht Club**. Both can be reached by foot from Boulevard Costera. There is also word that there are a few Yankees setting up shop there to attract the big US dollars. The big race that brings yachts here every year is the Newport to Ensenada Yacht Race which happens in April.

CABO SAN LUCAS
The next place for yachts to find an available wharf along the Baja coast is about 900 miles south at the cape of the great peninsula, in Cabo San Lucas. Here, massive changes are constantly being made to the town and the wharf area; the most noticeable being the modern, newly constructed marina that sits at the end of the bay providing room for about 350 yachts. To be here around Christmas time is to be in one of the most enviable spots on earth for the hitchhiking sailor as its location in the northeast trades puts it in a slingshot position for the entire tropical Pacific and the Caribbean. Also, to visit this port or La Paz in May will put you at the starting blocks of the seasonal sail to Hawaii, with 20 days of downwind tropical sailing.

LA PAZ
La Paz, on the east coast of the peninsula, is a good spot to check, one of the best in Baja. The Sea of Cortez Sailing Week around the second week of April is the best time for you to plan your visit, as many cruisers do likewise. The attraction here is the excellent sport fishing, diving and tranquil waters of the Gulf of California. Although the quality of sailing is superb, those yachts you will find in the three marinas along the La Paz shore will not have long range goals in mind; they will have already found their destinations. The only exception is the fabulous boatyard here that services the entire Sea of Cortez and surroundings. It is called the **Marina de Don Jose Abaroa**, which has room for only 20 yachts, but it also has a 200-ton travelift and a boatyard. The importance of this boatyard is apparent when you consider that the nearest other haul-out facility of this

capacity is nearly 1000 miles away. The yachts stuffed in the Cabo marina that need repairs before their long crossing will have to do their work here, provided they can hobble around the cape and into La Paz Bay. The **Marina de La Paz**, with room for 90 vessels, is located at the end of 5 de Febrero Street. The third facility is the **Marina Palmira**, about a mile and a half north of town. This facility has room for about 50 yachts and provides other minor services.

PUERTO ESCONDIDO (BAJA)

On the trip north, Puerto Escondido has The Moorings charter fleet but little else for transiting yachts. The lagoon is a popular anchorage for cruisers, and there is a concrete pier and a dinghy dock, but your best bet is to get friendly with one of the charter customers and hope they are in need of a hand. Loredo, just to the north, is primarily a haven for the local sport fishing boats and sees few yachts pass through its waters, but those that do will usually stop at the municipal pier for a new supply of beer and a look around.

NORTHERN SEA OF CORTEZ

The port of **Mulege** is another fishing spot with little for yachts, and for the land traveler it is like the rest of Baja--another remote town on the most sparsely populated peninsula on God's green earth. **Puerto Santa Rosalia** has a marina capable of holding 12 yachts.

The rest of the towns along the eastern Baja peninsula are largely unvisited by those sailing the waters. **Bahia de Los Angeles** (LA Bay) and **San Felipe** are the only mentionables. You might find a yacht or two there, but don't hold your breath.

MAINLAND MEXICO

The winds along the coast of mainland Mexico are primarily northwest, as the northeast trades are bent by the adiabatic forces of the coast. For this reason, few yachts try to move north along the coast of Central America or Mexico from either the South Pacific or the Panama Canal, but instead make for the Hawaiian Islands or some far offshore spot. In the fall when the threat of hurricanes has diminished, however, you will find many yachts moving south along the coast bound for the canal or the southern departure points for the south Pacific.

SAN CARLOS/GUAYMAS

Along the coast of mainland Mexico heading south, the first worthy places to stop if you are looking to get onto a yacht are San Carlos and Guaymas, which are only a stone's throw from each other. San Carlos has a marina of good quality, with room for about 150 boats. It is also an excellent place to hide from storms. Guaymas has no marinas per se, but there is a waterfront where yachts can get what they need, and there are a couple of good boatyards in the harbor.

MAZATLAN

Mazatlan does not rival the yacht facilities further south along the Mexican west coast, but it serves as a popular landing spot for yachts crossing from Cabo San Lucas at the beginning of the year. In addition, those yachts crossing from the mainland of Mexico to the southern tip of the Baja Peninsula will head first to the northern port of Mazatlan to attain a more attractive wind direction for the crossing. From any farther south, it is nearly impossible to sail across with the predominantly northwesterly winds. From this point south, you will encounter southbound yachts quite regularly, but the harbors are far apart and only a few provide decent services for yachtsmen. Mazatlan is not one of the good ones, but it has a good, protected yacht anchorage and some services. Visit the port captain and the three or four chandler agencies on the eastern side of town along the channel. Incidentally, Mazatlan is the only harbor on the entire Pacific Mexican coast that is considered a hurricane refuge. If you are on this coast during the wet summer, this may be your spot.

SOUTH OF MAZATLAN

The ports to the south of Mazatlan see a great deal of yachts landing from a crossing of the Sea of Cortez. The most comfortable places to land from a distance and a wind point of view are San Blas and Puerto Vallarta, the latter being the one with the best services. Yachts sailing down the coast of Mexico with ambitious plans for longer cruises will also make the split in this area. Those making for the Panama Canal will continue along this coast, but those heading for the South Pacific islands depart the coast from either Puerto Vallarta or Manzanillo, since the shore takes a steep turn to the east from there. All that distance to the east must be recovered later in lighter winds if the South Pacific is the destination. Keep in mind, though, that in

November and December yachts will be making for the Caribbean, as the season is just starting there, while the South Pacific is in the thick of the hurricane season. Yachts sailing south in April or May will mostly be going to the south Pacific, as the storms will start brewing soon in the Caribbean.

SAN BLAS

San Blas is a small town with a few minor services; mostly the markets are the attraction for yachtsmen. There is a navy dock and a small boat basin, but the entrance limits larger yachts by virtue of its shallow depths. Most sailboats prefer to anchor in the large and scenic bay to the east, and taxi or walk the two miles or so to town. If you make it to this small harbor, don't ignore this bay, named **Matenchen Bay**. South of San Blas on the way to Puerto Vallarta lie many very beautiful anchorages and the small fishing port of **La Cruz**, but the scope of this book does not allow me to describe each in detail. Instead keep it in mind, and as you cover this coast by bus, keep an eye out for masts.

NUEVO VALLARTA AND PUERTO VALLARTA

About 15 miles north of Puerto Vallarta lies an ambitious real estate project called Nuevo Vallarta. It is the first of the fine marinas that line the coast and should be visited if in the area. It is a two-mile walk from the main highway turnoff about 12 miles north of Puerto Vallarta. At the present time it has accommodations for 350 yachts up to about eighty feet long, but there are talks of future expansion. Few other services are available at the present time.

Puerto Vallarta is the marina most frequented by the yachting world along this entire coast, and the facilities there support its popularity. A favored landing spot for those crossing the Sea of Cortez, the harbor is stuffed with stores for provisioning, chandlers, docks and even a boatyard. The boatyard is located on the southwest side of the harbor at **Opequimar Marine**; the public docks are at the **Club de Yates** at the end of the harbor, where there is room for 400 yachts. The other set of docks you will see is at Isla Iguana across the channel where the owners of the condos in the development there leave their yachts. I suggest you visit all three establishments as well as the harbormaster's office at the end of the harbor by the Marina Vallarta Hotel.

From Puerto Vallarta southward, there are few anchorages frequented by yachts, as the coast is steep and craggy, and you will not likely see sailboats hanging by anchor chain until you pass Chamela to the south. **Bahia de Chamela** is a very popular anchorage in season. A bit further south is **Club Med** in Careyes Bay, but it is not worth the trouble to invade.

MANZANILLO

Manzanillo is another great spot to have a look around, primarily for the development at Las Hadas (where they filmed "10"), but also the harbor in town is busy and the **Bahia de Santiago** to the north is a popular anchorage. The harbormaster is located at the north side of the town by the breakwater, and there have been reports of marina development there. **Las Hadas** is about four miles up the beach and has its own docks, and it seems to be the only place the yachties with money want to spend any time. It is a pleasant place to spend a few days.

In the stretch between Manzanillo and Acapulco, you will find nothing but fine sand beaches and a few rocky points, but few suitable places to anchor. The only places of refuge along this coast are **Lazaro Cardenas, Ixtapa/ Zihuatenejo** and a small jetty-protected port in the **Bahia de Tequepa**. The only real marina facility along this coast is one still being built in Zihuatanejo, which at this printing is probably complete. Regardless, if you are traveling this section of coast, Zihuatanejo is well worth a visit for its resorts and fine beaches, all being served by a common anchorage in the bay. There is another first class resort currently being built east of Ixtapa at Playa Palmar. Once complete, the cruising scene in south Mexico will be changed forever.

ACAPULCO

The next spot along this coast for yachts to tie up and take a walk ashore is one of the best in all of Mexico: the Bay of Acapulco. The western end of this magnificent natural harbor has the **Nuevo Club de Yates de Acapulco** (yates is Spanish for yachts), which has plenty of room, comes highly recommended for foreigners, but only for those who are members of other yacht clubs. The Yacht Club has repair facilities, including a 20-ton travelift, and a very good bar, but you might have difficulty getting in. There is a new marina in Acapulco, I'm told, and although it is not completely finished, it is open for business and is very luxurious. It has become the best place for a cruising hitchhiker to visit, but I don't have any information on it yet. There is also a 60-ton travelift in town that is a lot more reasonably priced than the one at the club.

PUERTO ESCONDIDO (MAINLAND)

South of Acapulco the only yachts that sail the coast are those on their way to the Panama Canal in the dead of winter, as the winds of the Gulf on Tehuantepec are extremely dangerous, unpredictable and impossible to avoid. The only good place along this southern coast all the way to the Guatemalan border is Puerto Escondido, a developing tourist destination and one of the best surfing areas in all of the eastern Pacific. Even in Puerto Escondido you will not find any services for yachtsmen, but in the the anchorage out in front of **Laguna Agua Dulce** south of town you are likely to find those yachts resting after the long passage from Acapulco.

EXTREME SOUTHERN MEXICO

Puerto Angel, Bahia Tangola Tangola, Salina Cruz and **Puerto Madero** are the only indentations in the coast south of Puerto Escondido, although they are rarely visited by cruising yachts. Puerto Madero, the last stop before entering the waters of the small Central American countries, is a decent spot for yachts to take on food, although it is expensive. It is best to stay in the areas to the north and avoid wasting a lot of time in these waters.

CENTRAL AMERICA

There is a complete lack of protected harbors along the west coast of Guatemala and because of the past political situations in El Salvador and Nicaragua and the instability of the governments, it is impossible to say what the conditions are with the bays and natural harbors in those countries. For these and other reasons, I will cover these three countries briefly and then do what the majority of cruising yachts do: concentrate on Costa Rica.

Puerto Quetzal is a small harbor on the Pacific coast of Guatemala with few services, but there are reports of a service area for yachts. El Salvador has two ports of entry--**Acajutla** and **Cutuco**, but few yachts get close to them. Honduras has only 70 miles of coast on the Pacific side; the ports of entry of San Lorenzo and Tela have no services for yachts. Nicaragua is not recommended for visiting at this time, as even provisioning is next to impossible in this country.

COSTA RICA

Costa Rica is a great destination for cruising yachts for a multitude of reasons, and although it is way more expensive than the other countries in Central America, it is very, very cheap by Western standards. The entire coast is pleasant for cruising as there are numerous bays and good anchorages from the border of Nicaragua to the border of Panama. The surfing is exceptional, the diving is good, the waters are clean and the people enthusiastically friendly. Unfortunately, there are no main yachting centers in the country except for the septic and smelly port of Puntarenas. **Golfito** has a good, protected anchorage and a dock with some services but it is difficult to get to by land. The anchorages frequented by yachtsmen are **Tamarindo** on the Nicoya Peninsula and the town of **Quepos** close to San Jose. There is no limit to the places you will find yachts anchored along the coast and in the bays.

The main service center is **Puntarenas** in the Gulf of Nicoya, and although there are many small yacht service yards, they change hands frequently. The best way to look for a yacht visiting this port town is to take a walk along the waterfront on the shore of El Estero on the north side of the peninsula.

PANAMA

The only place yachts visit on the Pacific coast of Panama is the vicinity of the entrance to the Panama Canal, more specifically at the dock of the **Balboa Yacht Club**. Until this year it had the reputation of being very unfriendly to foreign yachts, but now, in 1993, they are going through some major renovations which have added docks, 44 moorings, a marine railway and a repair yard; they improved service and renovated their bar and restaurant and now the only marina on the Pacific side of Panama is one of the best yacht clubs in the entire Pacific. About 600 yachts stop at this marina each year. See my chapter *Routes in the Atlantic* for a better description of the canal transit. The other spots for yachts to stay before either making their canal transit or the long crossing of the Pacific are the **Pedro Miguel Yacht Club** at the shore of Miraflores Lake and the anchorage off **Taboga Island** in the Bay of Panama. The Pedro Miguel Yacht Club is what is described as the do-it-yourself repair center of Panama, with a large portion of the active cruising fleet based there. You will find those dedicated shoestring sailors in a tight community getting their work done for long passages ahead. Taboga Island until recently was the friendly hang-out spot on the Pacific side of Panama, but since the Balboa Yacht Club changed its ways there might be no reason for cruisers to seek the refuge this island used to provide.

South of Panama on the Pacific side has nothing else to note.

SOUTH PACIFIC ISLANDS

Most of the South Pacific is comprised of prime cruising grounds, but there are very few good ports compared to the number of good anchorages. What this means is that you will have to hang out on the bigger islands and the more frequently visited port areas to seek berths cruising through these thousands of square miles of pristine reefs and islands. In addition, you will have to work hard to stay on good terms with those on board as it will be difficult for you to get off and find another yacht. As so few of the island groups have decent harbors, I will mention only those that do, and I do not encourage you to head out to the smaller islands with hitchhiking in mind. Most of the remote parts will only see a half dozen yachts per year or less, while the ports such as Suva, Fiji and Papeete, Tahiti will see several hundred annually. Obviously, your chances are much better in these bigger ports.

POLYNESIA

HAWAII

Within these islands, the general direction of travel is to the northwest, as the winds are more agreeable. The island of Hawaii is the most southeastern island in the Hawaiian chain and being the closest to California, the natural landfall after a sail across the Pacific. As the season wears on, the concentration of yachts moves to the northwest. The favored departure point for the return trip to the States is Kauai for its northern position in the chain, which is also the last island in the northwesterly journey. Try to follow the direction of the concentration of yachts as the season goes by to put yourself in the path of more yachtspeople. One thing to keep in mind is the paying schedule in these islands. The harbormasters usually allow transient yachts to anchor or tie up in their bays free for three days, but on the fourth day they charge them for all four days and then daily after that. This keeps transient yachts moving constantly. Here is a list of the annual races that occur in Hawaii or to Hawaii and the businesses that sponsor them:

March Sailing Regatta, Waikiki Yacht Club
April J-24 Regatta, Waikiki Yacht Club
May 21 Maritime Day Race Hawaii Yacht Club, Honolulu
May Around Oahu Race, Kaneohe Yacht Club
June Lipton Cup Challenge, Waikiki Yacht Club
June Long Beach to Nawiliwili Race, Long Beach Yacht Club, Ca.
June Victoria to Maui Race, Royal Vancouver Yacht Club
July 4 Pacific Cup Race, San Francisco to Oahu, West Marine Products, Santa Cruz
July J-24 State Championship, Waikiki Yacht Club
August Kenwood Cup, Royal Hawaiian Ocean Club, Honolulu
Sept. 1st Lahaina Race Week, Lahaina Yacht Club
Sept. Lahaina to Oahu Race, Hawaii Yacht Club, Honolulu
Oct. Duke Regatta, Waikiki Yacht Club

THE BIG ISLAND

One of the main ports of call in the Hawaiian islands is the **Port of Hilo**, on the island of Hawaii. It is primarily a commercial harbor, however, and the town is not all that well set up for tourism. **Radio Bay** is located where the rocky breakwater meets the land and is the location of the small boat harbor. There is no marina there, but the vast majority of yachts clearing into the state of Hawaii find this harbor convenient for their landfall primarily because of its proximity.

On the **Kona** side of this island, you have a couple of choices for spotting transient yachts. The harbor farthest to the north is **Kwaihae Harbor**, the second commercial harbor on the island. Compared to the rest of the leeward side of the island, Kwaihae is the most laid-back and quiet, and has the most room to swing at anchor. Within the harbor there is a small boat basin on the northern end across from the end of the breakwater, but it is usually filled to capacity with local small craft. Transients usually find more room in the southern end of the harbor. The sailors you will find here will be enjoying the only place on the big island to get some peace and quiet.

South from there is the small man-made shelter called **Honokohau Harbor**, which is administered by the harbormaster at Kailua-Kona. Honokohau is very small and crowded with lots of activity going on all the time, as tourists bring their fishing catches to the docks for weighing. It is one of the biggest land/water interfaces available for tourists, so naturally this harbor seldom sleeps. The inner basin has barely enough room for a large yacht to swing at anchor, and the docks are full most of the time with local boats. You might do better elsewhere. The only redeeming characteristic is the **Kona Marine Center** at the end of the inner harbor which has a travelift and small yard available for those who have just hobbled in from an eventful voyage.

Kailua-Kona is the main tourist magnet on the entire island, and the harbor, although having a crowded dock, is not the place for a transient yacht to go. The tourists that don't use the boats that sail out of Honokohau harbor use the boats that sail out of Kailua-Kona, which occupy most of what is available in this exposed harbor. The transient anchorage is outside of this harbor, exposed even more to the wind and the swell.

The small bays of **Keauhou** and **Kealakekua** to the south offer the only other respite from the elements, but are not much for services in their own right.

Important Phone Numbers:
   Port of Hilo (808) 935-4877
   Honokohau 329-4215
   Kawaihae 882-7565

The island of Maui has much more mileage of protected beach and much better harbors than Hawaii. The main harbors of refuge are Lahaina, Maalaea Bay and Kahului Bay, although there are a number of decent bays for yachts to anchor in peace.

The small boat harbor of **Maalaea** has room for 60 yachts, but is relatively unknown to the yachting community. The harbor is usually full in the summer season and fairly shallow. But owing to its proximity to the main tourist centers of Maui and its convenience for visiting by land, it should be checked if you are on the island.

Lahaina is the main port on the island of Maui, and although there is rarely room for transients, the harbormaster will give space to any yacht passing through. There is also a very good repair facility in the area. You will see many yachts at anchor in the harbor, although it is an uncomfortable squeeze and cannot be endured long. The Mala Wharf about a mile or so north will also be full with transient yachts at anchor.

Another good spot is Kahului Harbor on the northern shore of the isthmus of Maui. It is primarily a commercial harbor but has marine services for yachts as well.

Hana Bay is popular for its breathtaking beauty, but is on the windward end of the island, and, therefore, very rough and uncomfortable. It is well worth the long and winding drive that must be endured to reach the small harbor by land.

The only other notable anchorages around the island are in La Perouse Bay and Honolua bay.

Important Phone Numbers:
Lahaina Harbor (808) 661-3557
Maalaea Harbor (808) 244-7041

LANAI
The island of Lanai has Manele and Kaumalapau harbors; the only noteworthy is Manele. It has room for 24 yachts, all of them local yachts at their permanent docks. Not worth a visit at this time. Manele harbor (808) 877-5713.

MOLOKAI
The island of Molokai has only two harbors of interest, both located on the south shore of the island; only one is regularly used by transient yachts. That one is Kaunakakai Harbor which is set apart from the rest by the existence of civilization. If you are visiting Molokai, you will surely see this city, and the wharf is located within a healthy walk from the center of town. This meager wharf is located at the end of the half-mile long mole extending out on the reef.

The other notable is Komalo Harbor, about eight or so miles east of Kaunakakai. There is some room for anchoring in the space between the reefs and a dock at the end of a rocky pier. The only other safe places for yachts to anchor are **Lono** and **Pukoo** harbors, but they are not used much. **Kaunakakai Harbor** (808) 553-5105.

OAHU

The main course of your trip to Hawaii is on the island of Oahu, which should not surprise you.

Ala Wai is by far the largest marina in all of Hawaii. Most of it is run by the state and is therefore available to the public, and two yacht clubs control the other 40% of the space. The Basin has a total of 700 berths, which is very large by anybody's standard, and in Hawaii it means the state's sailing world is concentrated here. The docks of the **Hawaii Yacht Club** and the **Waikiki Yacht Club** are private, although you will find a number of slips being used by transients at the Hawaii Yacht Club. The Waikiki Yacht Club is usually full, so it would be unusual to find transients there. In the public docks and at the Hawaii Y.C. the prices are still very high, so you will not encounter many cruisers spending much time anywhere in Ala Wai. Be sure to visit the area set aside for transients and remember that there will be an almost constant turnover of yachts, so visit every day. For those yachts looking to get any work done, you will find them in the boatyard where Ala Moana Blvd. crosses Ala Moana Canal.

Kewalo Bay, just past Ala Mo, is the commercial launch pad for booze cruises and pay-to-sail adventures, so do not let the masts and the activity lure you into investigating. Proceed onward.

Those wishing to spend some time in the area and not wanting to endure the hassle and money drain of the Ala Moana basin anchor in the **Keehi Lagoon** at the far end of Honolulu Harbor. If you look for the masts it is not difficult to find, but by bus head north along the Nimitz Highway until you get to the Kapalama area near the airport. You will encounter many yachts at anchor and a few small marine facilities. For contacting the yachts at anchor, you must keep your eyes open for bulletin boards at the marine centers and look for the dinghy docks along the waterfront. These are your only interfaces with those yachts. A favorite dinghy dock in the past has been at the Keehi Marine Center, but these things change quickly. You should check the boat basins of the three marinas along this shoreline: the state run **Small Boat Harbor** (the largest), the **Keehi Marine Center** and the

La Mariana Sailing Club. The Keehi Center also has a small drydock and boatyard area.

Moving around the island in a clockwise direction, the first marina you will encounter is in the town of **Waianae**, at a basin of the same name. The basin is normally full of residents as with most other marinas in Hawaii, but **Pokai Bay** which is just outside the breakwater has lots of yachts at anchor in season.

Haleiwa Harbor is in the meat of the North Shore, surrounded by the giant North Shore surf and, even more intimidating, the giant North Shore surfers. In fact, the developers who planted this basin here faced fierce opposition from these heavy locals. The marina itself is not all that popular even in the summer months as so much wind has to be opposed to get here, but it is a very nice marina surrounded by some very nice beaches. Haleiwa Harbor does not have an excessive number of berths, but those it has are usually full nonetheless. Pay it a visit.

On the windward side of the island you will find the huge and picturesque **Kaneohe Bay**, fully exposed to the trades which generate swells that are totally smoothed by the barrier reef. There are three docking areas in this bay: the **Heeia Kea Boat Harbor**, the **Makaui Kai** condominium complex and the **Kaneohe Bay Yacht Club**, plus anchoring areas around the entire bay. The Heeia Kea Harbor is generally full with locals, the condo complex is completely closed to all outsiders but the Kaneohe Bay Yacht Club does allow transients to tie up for a period of two weeks at a nominal price. In the past they had limited their room for transients to just three docks, but things may have changed.

State Run Facilities:
Ala Wai Boat Harbor (808) 949-7749
Keehi Boat Harbor 841-6552
Waianae Harbor 696-6614
Haleiwa Boat Harbor 637-6090
Heeia Kea 637-6090
Kewalu basin 584-4158

Yacht Clubs and Private Marinas:
Hawaii Yacht Club 949-4622
Waikiki Yacht Club 949-7141
Kaneohe Yacht Club 247-4121

Makani Kai Marina 235-4416
Keehi Marine Center 845-6465
La Mariana 845-7738

Drydocks:
Ala Wai Marine 946-4213
Keehi Marine Cntr 845-6465
Kewalo Basin 537-2939

KAUAI

On the island of Kauai there are three harbors at the present time; the main one being Nawiliwili on the southeast coast by Lihui, Port Allen on the south coast and Hanalei Bay in the north which is the favored departure point for the mainland of the US.

In the harbor of **Nawiliwili,** you will find yachts at anchor all over: a main wharf for those taking on fuel and cargo and a small boat basin at the end of the inlet. There is only room for 15 yachts; some of which are permanent tourist attracters. Compare this to the 700 at Ala Mo on Oahu, and you can get a feel for the quaintness of this island.

On the south shore you will find Port Allen and Wahiawa Bay, both within four miles of each other. In **Wahiawa Bay** there are no facilities except a good anchorage. In **Port Allen**, actually inside of Hanapepe Bay, is located one of the best built small marinas in all of Hawaii. It has room for less than 30 boats, but there you might find a few transients during the season.

The last area I will mention in the Hawaiian Island chain is the last spot yachts usually stop before sailing back home, and that is in the beautiful **Hanalei Bay** on northern Kauai. There are no marinas or places to tie up here, but the anchorage is fairly comfortable. Yachtspeople usually use the river to the northeast corner of the bay to dock their dinghies. The alternate landing spot is beside the old pier. Help a yachtie load his groceries, and you might land yourself a free trip back to the mainland. **Nawiliwili Harbor** (808) 245-6996

THE MARQUESAS

The Marquesas are a very popular island destination for yachts because of their unbelievable beauty and rugged South Pacific charm. Unfortunately, they are devoid of yacht harbors and have no services available beyond simple provisions. The central port of these islands is **Baie Taiohae** on Nuku Hiva, where they reportedly have a boatyard and some new services for yachts. Be sure to visit the Keikahanua Inn. They seem to know what is going on in the Marquesas as far as yachts are concerned. The only other wharf on the islands is at **Atuona**, on Hiva Oa.

TAHITI

The islands that make up Tahiti, or the French Society Islands, used to have only one good yacht harbor regularly visited by yachts: **Papeete**, on the island of Tahiti. Its distinction as the cruiser's spot in the Tahitian Islands has now gone to Raiatea, as described below. In Papeete, however, there is a repair center in the eastern part of the port and a couple of boatyards in the north by **Motu-Uta**. You will find many yachts at anchor in the harbor and tied to the wharves.

The biggest yachting hangout in the Tahitian Islands is the place that caters solely to that crowd, brought upon by the opening of charter operations in **Raiatea**. Sun Yacht charters has their charter base there and a travelift, and the ATM charter fleet has recently moved there from Tahaa. **Apooiti Marina** is the location of The Moorings charter fleet and a group calling themselves Carnegage Services who store yachts through the hurricane season at very reasonable rates. This harbor is changing rapidly and is quickly becoming an important spot for yachts to hole up their yachts between the seasons.

Bora Bora also has a couple of wharves available to yachtsmen: one at the **Club Nautique** and one at the **Hotel Oa Oa**. Also check **Cook's Bay** in **Moorea**. The **Tahiti Yacht Club** in **Arue** has docks you might want to check. For an out of season visit, Port Phaeton on the island of Tahiti is the only harbor of refuge in all of the eastern Pacific islands.

THE COOK ISLANDS

The only real good place to chase down a yacht is in **Rarotonga**, simply because there is an international airport there and recent development has seen the building of facilities in **Avatiu** and **Avarua** harbors. If you find your way to this island, make for these two harbors, just a half a mile apart, where you can expect to find about a half dozen yachts at any time throughout the sailing season. There were reports that a marina was being built in Avatiu, but the plans were apparently abandoned because at this time yachts are still stern-tied to the quay. Across from the quay there is a run-down bar that the yachties use, called Tere's Bar, but the best bar in the area is closer to Avarua Harbor, called Jack's. Jack's is where the yachtsmen go when looking for a beer, so a visit to this bar should put you with the crowd you are after. Avarua is the commercial harbor, and it is doubtful that you will find any cruising yachts there.

SAMOA

American Samoa, being US territory, does not require a visa for Americans, so it is one place in the South Pacific where you can hang out indefinitely. The only port of call in American Samoa is **Pago Pago** on the island of Tutuila. For ten years or so there has been talk of building a marina there, but so far there is only a small quay and very little else. A popular cruising guide to the area reports that American Samoa saw about 300 visiting pleasure yachts call in 1990, so during the season you will see many yachts moving in and out of the harbor daily, anchoring in the harbor or tied end-to the quay. There is a boatyard in the harbor that does repairs on fishing boats, but they will accept work on yachts if the price is right. Also, there are about 50 yachts that sit out the hurricane season there each year. Another reason for visiting this US colony is for work. You can stay and earn some money if you have a skill in demand, such as computers or electronics, while waiting for your boat to show up

In Western Samoa, the only place to find yachts whose crews regularly come ashore is in **Apia Harbor** on Upolu Island. There are no wharves to tie up to there except at the harbormaster's dock, but many yachts hang at anchor in the harbor and dinghy ashore. There are regular flights to and from Pago Pago.

TONGA

Tonga has two harbors in its group: **Nuku'alofa** on the island of Tongatapu and **Neiafu** in the Vava'u group in the north. It is estimated that 150 yachts move through the Tonga group annually, due to its position between Australia/New Zealand and French Polynesia. Nuku'alofa has a new 100-ton slipway, many repair services and a long customs dock. You will also see a few yachts anchored along the town waterfront. Most yachts that visit Nuku'alofa tie up to the Faua jetty on the inner harbor. There is a yacht club there that caters to mostly locals, but the bar to visit is called the Waterfront Bar. In Neiafu, there are a couple of charter operations including The Moorings fleet, so there has been some recent development there as well. The harbor now hosts a 40-ton travelift and repair facilities, and you will see visiting yachts at anchor. It is also the only likely spot for yachts to hide out from the hurricanes that sweep through the islands each year.

MELANESIA

FIJI

Although Fiji does not have the reputation of being overly accommodating to cruising yachts, it has found itself with more of them than it can handle in recent years. My experiences have all been good with these people, but the officials are set in their ways and all regulations must be followed verbatim. Although the international airport is in **Nadi** (pronounced Nandi), **Suva** is the most important port on the island of Viti Levu, and the one with the most facilities. In Suva, most of the visiting yachts prefer to anchor in the bay, but there are moorings and soon there will be dock space available at the **Royal Suva Yacht Club**, located on the waterfront north of town. A better spot right now is at the **Tradewinds Hotel and Marina**, opposite the harbor from Suva in the Bay of Islands. Space is limited there but the bar on the premises is one of the greatest yachtie gathering places around. The **government shipyard** will do some yacht repairs, and an organization called **Yacht Help** has been set up recently that does just that, and they should know who needs what in and around Viti Levu. **Latouka**, on the western end of the island, has a newly-completed marina with a travelift. **Levuka**, on the island of Ovalau, is reported to be a gathering place for yachts and is a port of entry, but I have never seen yachts in that harbor.

VANUATU
There are two main ports in Vanuatu: Port-Vila on Efate Island and Santo in Loganville on Espiritu Santo Island. **Port-Vila** is the only secure harbor in the group, with the **Rossi Hotel** being the place for the yachtsmen to congregate. Also check **Yachting World** and the **Vanuatu Cruising Club,** located in Port Vila as well. Santo is where the only good boatyards exist, but the harbor is crawling with navigational dangers and is not used except for the boatyards and the bureaucracy. Around the corner from Santo is the fine anchorage of **Palikulo Bay,** which is where the foreign yachts seem to congregate once they have completed their clearance proceedings. Each hurricane season Vanuatu is almost assured of getting hit at least once, as they are in that unfortunate section of the Pacific. Otherwise it is a great place to visit, especially if you are a diver.

NEW CALEDONIA
Noumea is the port of entry in this country and a very busy and industrious commercial harbor, but not the place yachtsmen are looking to spend any real time when reaching this beautiful island. Instead, they proceed around the point to the south to the **Baie de Pecheurs** which has plenty of room to anchor and a 400-slip marina called the **Club Nautique** on the south side of the bay. There are two travelifts with capacities to 40 tons and a few other small marinas scattered around. There are reports of the construction of a large marina in the wharf area of the **Baie de la Moselle**, right in the commercial harbor.

THE SOLOMON ISLANDS
Despite the number of islands and the extent of fine cruising grounds in the Solomon chain, there are only three ports in which you might make the acquaintance of traveling yachtsmen. The first is **Honiara** on Guadacanal Island which has the **Point Cruz Yacht Club** and a fuel dock, but most yachts leave from there after a rest at the club to anchor in **Tulagi Harbor** across the water to the north. Honiara has good provisioning and the yacht club can arrange limited services. In Tulagi Harbor, which is the repair center for the islands, there is a slip for putting yachts up for repair. When in the area, visit **Taroaniara Shipyard** on Florida Island. In the Port of **Gizo** on the

island of the same name, there are good stores for yachts to provision and another haul-out facility for yachts to 40 feet.

PAPUA NEW GUINEA

The Country of Papua New Guinea makes up the eastern half of the island of New Guinea. The other half, Irian Jaya, belongs to Indonesia. Papua New Guinea is an extremely diverse country with many beautiful islands, beaches, mountains and rivers; the people and the villages are among the most primitive and culturally intact of those from any piece of land on earth. The only thing missing is the development you would expect to find with a land so rich in resources, but that is what has kept the culture so intact. There are only a small handful of ports in which any development for yachtsmen has been undertaken, but the cruising grounds go on forever. Many yachtsmen consider this section of the world the best cruising area on earth, and all who have cruised it will agree that it cannot be satisfactorily covered even in years of constant cruising. The main port is **Port Moresby**, a modern city on the south side of the main island, which has a great deal of yachting development, but the crime makes it dangerous even in daylight. The other ports seem to be very friendly, not sharing the Port Moresby attitude. One of the main attractions (or distractions) you will notice is the seasonal journeys many Australians make to this country, as it is quite close to their northern Great Barrier Reef ports and affords them some genuine adventure close to home. I will cover the major ports in the order of their importance in the yachtsman's eye.

Port Moresby: The obvious place to head to first is the **Royal Papua Yacht Club** on the city waterfront. The visiting yachts moor stern-to the jetty on the south side of the harbor, and there is an area where the smaller yachts can move in at high tide and work on their hulls on low tide, as there is a great tidal range. For those yachtsmen with more money, there are a couple of slipways down on the end of the peninsula that are expensive but complete. You might even find a yacht or two tied up to the city wharf downtown. Be sure to read the local guidebooks to bring yourself up to date on the dangers in Port Moresby. It has a nasty reputation.

Samarai: Although this tiny island is difficult to get to for the boatless wanderer, it is convenient to the cruising yachtsman because it is the southernmost port of entry in Papua New Guinea waters. Those Australians not wanting to go out of their way to clear in at Port

Moresby will all be here at the end of the cyclone season in May and then clearing out of the country here at the end of the year. Realize that almost all of the seasonal visitors to this country will be heading for the north coast and to the islands, and a detour to Port Moresby would be too time consuming. Besides the government offices, there is really not much in Samarai as far as services are concerned, but there is a great boatyard across the strait on the mainland called the **Belesana Slipway**. The seasonal sailors use this slipway quite often.

Rabaul: On the northeastern end of the island of New Britain sits the **Simpson Harbor**, beside the city of Rabaul. This is the most protected harbor in all of the Pacific, and one of the best suited for yacht repair as well. The protection of this harbor makes it a popular place for yachtsmen to hole up for the hurricane season, and being the only major Pacific harbor of refuge north of the hurricane belt, it affords a tremendous alternative to sailing as far as New Zealand or Australia to await the safety of May. For this reason Rabaul is the best spot in all of New Guinea to visit in the off-season. Although the harbor lacks chandlers and facilities familiar with yacht repair, it has slipways large enough for any size yachts and great provisioning. There is also a good yacht club at the east end of the waterfront.

Besides Port Moresby, the only other good harbor on the mainland is at the town of **Madang**. The waterfront at the north end of town has a yacht club and a great deal of commercial activity, while the south end of town in **Binnen Harbor** has the dedicated yacht facilities, including a marina and slipway. The marina is the focal point for the yachtsmen visiting this harbor, as it has a good restaurant and bar, a ship chandler and assorted services. The slipways have good repair shops around them. In addition, Madang Harbor is fairly well protected and a few yachts hole up there for the hurricane season.

PORTS OF MICRONESIA

There are no harbors in the entire Marshall Island chain, but the Federal States of Micronesia has a few. The region is more commonly known as the Caroline Islands. Farther to the west is the group called the Marianas, of which only Guam and Saipan are significant.

THE CAROLINES

There is a large commercial harbor on the eastern end of **Kosrae Island** in the Lehu Harbor, one of the three harbors on the island but the only one ever visited by yachtsmen. There are no facilities. **Ponape Island** has very meager facilities as well, but a number of yachts visit this island for the fabulous scuba diving. Visit **Sohens Harbor** in the north of the island near Kolonia. The inner harbor will have two or three foreign yachts at any given time outside of the hurricane season, and there have been recent reports of a new marina. In **Truk Lagoon**, the only life ashore for yachties is at the east end of **Moen Island** at the public harbor. There are a couple of wharves but few supplies. The yachts visiting this harbor have only one thing in mind: dive. The **Continental Hotel** is the only place resembling life for yachties.

In **Yap**, visit the small and incomplete harbors of **Colonia** and **Ulithi**. It is unlikely you will find many yachts hanging out for more than a few hours even in the busy season, but it is said that **Yap Fisheries** now has a 70-ton marine railway.

Palau, another fine example of dense tropical vegetation surrounded by fringing reefs of superb diving quality, has only one area for yachts to group and find the limited services they need. That is in the area of **Koror** and **Malakal** harbors on the western end of Koror Island. There is a 100-ton boatyard and little else, but the cruising permits are divvied out there and only there. It is clearly the only place on the island to go.

THE MARIANAS

The most recognized island of all of Micronesia is **Guam**, and although quite small, it has the most modern facilities for yachtsmen. A very good harbor in the center of the island's length called **Port Apra** has a US Navy installation and a commercial port. Facilities for yachtsmen exist, as one could expect. The most important anchorage is offshore of the **Marianas Yacht Club** on Cabras Island on the north side of the harbor. In all of the harbors in Micronesia, this is the one you will see the most yachts; a close second is the **Agana boat basin** in Agana Bay. This is a fairly new marina that has room for 42 yachts up to 45 feet long. One other place to check is at the **Dillingham Shipyard** a few miles east of the Marianas yacht club.

The other port worth mentioning in the Marianas is the **Saipan Harbor** about 70 miles north. There is a crane for hauling boats out of the water and the **Over the Reef Yacht Club**, but to find a yacht sitting in the yard would be extremely lucky. This and the other islands in the Northern Marianas are very seldom visited by yachts, except for those making their ways to Japan or Hawaii from Guam.

NEW ZEALAND

The North Island of New Zealand is one of the best spots in all of the Pacific and perhaps all of the world to start your journey. A multitude of yachts sail for the South Pacific islands from May until September, and even in the Pacific hurricane season there are boats moving off to Australia. The North Island has many very good harbors dotted around its perimeter, but the superiority of **Auckland** will give you all the reason you need to ignore the rest. If you have the inclination to visit the other harbors on the North Island, you will not be disappointed. The stretch between the Bay of Islands and Tauranga along the north coast of the North Island is by far the best cruising area, visited by hundreds of foreign and countless local yachts each year, and for the most part the rest of the New Zealand coastline is ignored. The reason is obvious once you set your eyes on the shorelines and notice that the majority of deep and calm bays lie along this coast. The majority of yachts with impending or continuing international journeys leave out of Auckland, many stopping in the Bay of Islands on their way to or from the South Pacific. In addition, New Zealand must be the easiest place on earth to hitch a ride on land.

In the Bay of Islands on the northern tip of New Zealand, you will find some good harbors and a greater number of good anchorages filled with southward-sailing yachts in November, northward-sailing yachts around April and yachts sitting out the hurricane season in between. The rest of the year sees yachts moving in all directions, and the small bays in this area are sometimes filled to capacity. Visit the bays at **Russell** and **Opua**, place your ad on the local boards and keep your eyes open for the ads from yachts looking for crew. Opua has a couple of fine boatyards, but you'll have to do some walking around the waterfront to see who is high and dry. Most small yachts take advantage of the extreme tides in the area and put their boats on the drying grids in **Opua** and **Whangarei** and do their hull work at low tide to save money. Also visit the **Bay of Islands Yacht Club** just north of Paihia at the mouth of the river. Whangarei is a bit south of the Bay of Islands, and it seems a bit too far inland to be an important spot for yachts, but in the northern peninsula of the north island it has the best repair facilities and the only good marina. Check the yachts at the city wharf and the jetties and the boatyards on both sides of the channel. Go to **Oram's Marina** first as it is accompanied by a good boatyard. Check also **WECO** and **Smith's** who are boat builders also.

All three are capable of hauling out yachts to 100 tons. The first thing you will notice when reaching the Bay of Islands by land is that the hundreds of inlets and bays yield endless possibilities for yachts to take refuge from civilization, and you will probably find it difficult to pick out the places you will want to include in your search. Go no further than Opua, Russell, Whangarei and the yacht club north of Paihia.

Auckland is one of the yachting capitals of the world, according to any New Zealander you will ever meet. One statistic to support this claim is that Auckland Harbor has more yachts per resident of the city than any other city on earth. This means that it is a fantastic spot for you to catch a ride for a day, a week, a year or two. Because the local yachts are so abundant, the marinas and supporting industries have been extensively developed, which in turn has been attracting long-term cruisers from all over the world. The harbor has recently undergone extensive upgrading to the point that every square foot is now taken up by slips. As a result, there are so many yachts hanging out in the marinas and in the repair facilities that there is little reason to go elsewhere in the country to find a yacht preparing for a trip abroad. Furthermore, most of the facilities are within a mile of the center of town, so in an afternoon you should be able to cover all of the marinas, chandlers and boatyards. Put together a good advertisement with a phone number or some other contact. For example, talk to someone in a local business and ask if they can hold messages for you.

The obvious place to look is at the West Haven Marina on the south end of the Harbor Bridge, a mammoth marina full to capacity with yachts most of the year. To the east of that basin lie many wharves that hold the lines of the largest visiting yachts, those willing to pay the money to be at the city's waterfront, but most of the time these docks are occupied by commercial craft of one sort or another. On the waterfront north of the bridge you will see a lot more moorings than slips, although that will change soon.

PACIFIC AUSTRALIA

Queensland sees a tropical hurricane about once a year, but when there is no severe meterological activity it is quite a nice place to sail. Since New South Wales is so far south, it is rarely touched by these storms and provides a sufficient refuge to those escaping the South Pacific for the southern hemisphere summer. Nevertheless, the pleasant sailing season for this entire coast is considered to be in the months of May to October, but you will find yachts cruising all year.

NEW SOUTH WALES

The obvious place to start out on the Australian east coast is the giant harbor at **Sydney**. The best time to be there is around Christmas time as the most popular race in that part of the world, the Sydney to Hobart, usually leaves this coast on the day after Christmas. If you intend to visit this region, make for The Spit, Point Piper, Kirribilli, Mosman and Rushcutter's Bay yacht clubs and the marinas in and around **Manly** and **Middle Harbour**. The cruising center of Sydney is concentrated in Rushcutter's Bay in the huge marina there and at the Cruising Yacht Club of Australia. The Cruising Club should not be missed. In the Botany Bay area, visit the yacht clubs and facilities at Kogarah Bay. In **Broken Bay**, make for **Pittwater** and the seven yacht clubs there. **Lake Macquarie** is also a cruiser's haven; the Belmont Bay area seems to be the best. Despite the marina and wharves at Thorsby Bay, Newcastle is more of a commercial harbor than a cruiser's mecca, and the ports to the south will better serve your needs.

As you travel north along the coast, you will find little to attract cruising yachts besides the small wharves and anchorages for as far as Coff's Harbor, 250 miles north of Sydney. There, you will find a good marina on the north side of the small harbor. A limited boat harbor can be found at **Yamba**.

QUEENSLAND

Queensland has a lot more for yachtsmen than NSW, with warmer waters and more interesting cruising from Surfer's Paradise and the Gold Coast all the way up to the northern extent of the Great Barrier Reef. The southern end of Queensland has a fabulous bay with complete marine facilities; unfortunately, the shallow depth of the harbor prohibits most cruising yachts from reaching them. Nevertheless, visit the harbors at **Southport** and **Runaway Bay** if you are visiting the Surfer's Paradise area. In the **Brisbane** and **Moreton Bay** areas, make for Scarborough, Manly and Brisbane harbors and the facilities at Doboy Creek. **Mooloolaba Harbor** is also a great spot to find yachties moving north for the season. There are many facilities in the area of the yacht club on the west side of the entrance and at Lawries marina to the south. North along the coast, you will find yachts at the marina at **Tin Can Creek**, at the Maryborough Sailing Club at **Mary River**, and at the small marina in **Bundaberg**. North of there the next spot to visit is at the boat harbor at **Gladstone** with its 50 or so berths for cruising yachts. **Rosslyn Bay** has a marina on the north side of Double Head, and although the facilities are limited, it is the last accessible harbor for northbound yachts to stop before heading into the beautiful cruising grounds of the southern Great Barrier Reef. There are no other harbors along the coast all the way to Mackay.

Mackay itself is a popular place for yachties to visit before, during or after a sail to the **Whitsunday Islands**. It has an excellent harbor bustling with activity all year long. **Hamilton Island**, in the Whitsunday group, has one of the finest harbors on the entire east coast of Australia, and it is a fantastic spot to link up with long-term or short-term sailors. The marina has 400 slips and the price is high, so most of those staying there are just passing through. Hamilton Island also has the largest charter company in Queensland. It is well worth the trip out by ferry from Mackay. **Shute Harbour** has a marina in the planning stages to accommodate the excessive cruising traffic in the area, but at the time of this writing, there is not much there but a small wharf. There are also small marinas at **Airley Beach** and **Bowen**.

In recent years there has been a great deal of marine development in both Cairns and Townsville harbors, each struggling to win the affections of the cruising community. With the recent downturn in maritime trade along this coast, both cities have found the cruising dollars increasingly important. Along the north Queensland coast, these two harbors should be the focus of your search. In **Townsville** visit the Ross Creek and Breakwater marinas and the Townsville Yacht Club. In **Cairns**, at the west side of the Trinity Inlet, you will find a marina and the Cairns Sailing Club; on Smiths Creek you will find most of the activity associated with repair and long-term berths. By far the best is the Northern Queensland Engineering Assoc., which has extensive yacht storage and commercial repair capabilities. Keep in mind that virtually all of the yachts sailing in the barrier reef region will make at least one stop in Cairns. There is a small wharf at **Cooktown**, but nothing else of interest for you all the way to Cape York.

Thursday Island is in a strategic spot on the road from the Pacific to the Indian Ocean, unfortunately there is not much there to recommend it for cruising sailors. The facilities are the bare minimum, the anchorage is not sheltered from prevailing winds, the officials are not friendly and things are very pricey. A trip there, to the

Torres Strait, will put you in the path of nearly all of the circumnavigators of both the world and of Australia, but so will a trip to Darwin, and Darwin is a much more interesting spot to hang out. Darwin is detailed in the next chapter.

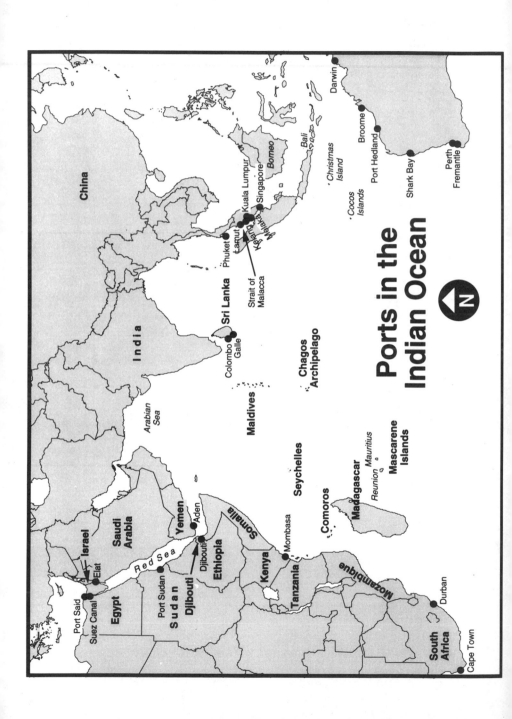

Ports in the
Indian Ocean

N

CHAPTER 9
THE INDIAN OCEAN AND THE RED SEA

THE INDIAN OCEAN

When stepping off one of the Indian Ocean's fringing continents onto a sailboat for a transoceanic journey, one is moving from one great adventure to another. The coasts that border this ocean are largely foreign to Western tourists as are the beautiful islands in between. The Indian Ocean and the Red Sea are geographically and culturally separated from the rest of the sailing world, and with the exception of Western Australia, is not close or convenient enough for a seasonal sail away from home. This means that when compared to the Atlantic and Pacific, this vast expanse of water is strange to Western yachtsmen, and most of the sailors found here are engaged in circumnavigating the world. Even with the Suez Canal and the Red Sea joining this body of water to the Mediterranean, the reputed red tape and piracy keeps many yachts from cruising there. For you it provides a huge classroom to learn open water navigation, local weather forecasting and other skills in open ocean seamanship, as well as giving you an adventure unequaled worldwide. Although the islands separating the East African Coast, the subcontinent of India and the northwest shores of Australia are among the most beautiful islands on earth, the long distances between them make mass tourism impractical. When approaching a sailor preparing to go for a long distance voyage across the Indian Ocean, one is greeted friendlier than in other oceans and has a better chance of getting aboard a given yacht. Although few yachts sail here, fewer crew members walk the docks seeking passage, and the hitchhiker is usually in for a long trip. Most captains will see him or her as a precious commodity and will be reluctant to let go of a good hand as there are no reliable ports for crew reshuffling. In addition, there are few places on earth where you can find the cultural diversity and geographic beauty that you can find in the Indian Ocean.

THE MONSOONS

Ideal cruising routes and sunny days are not always compatible in this part of the world, but the weather patterns of the monsoons dictate them both. There is a phenomenon that occurs locally every place in the world where the land meets the sea, called the adiabatic wind. As the land mass heats up, the air above it does too. It rises and the wind over the water blows in to take its place so that all during the day one will find a sea breeze, or onshore wind. Now try to imagine this effect occurring on a much larger scale, affecting an entire continent and lasting an entire season. Take a look at a world map and note the positions of the Pacific, Atlantic and Indian Oceans. Remember that all global weather is affected by the interfaces of land and sea, coupled with the spin of the earth, known as the Coreolis Effect. The Indian Ocean, with respect to land masses, is vastly different from the other two oceans in that it is cut off in the north by the Asian continent around the Tropic of Cancer whereas the Pacific and Atlantic are exclusively water almost pole to pole. It is no wonder that the continent of Asia inhales deeply for almost six months as the sun beats down overhead and exhales when the sun retreats to sea. That vast inhalation occurs in the summer months of the northern hemisphere, bringing marine moisture and rain into India and Southeast Asia for half the year.

The winds that make up what is commonly known as the southwest monsoon originate around Australia, actually blowing from the southeast until they cross the equator where the Coreolis Effect bends them to the right, and they proceed blowing from the southwest. The months between April and October are the time that people call the southwest or the southeast monsoon, depending upon where they are. As the wind reverses in October it drags the dry, hot air back off the land mass and out to sea, where it picks up more moisture and dumps it on the southern ocean and the northern Australian continent. During these months from October to April, the wind blows from the north and the season is called the northeast monsoon in the northern hemisphere and the northwest monsoon in the southern hemisphere, the Coreolis Effect bending the winds to the left as they cross the equator.

The wind patterns of the monsoons are well known by meteorologists and farmers of the affected land masses, and the seasonal changes can be predicted almost to the day. Once the reversal is complete and the winds are set, they can be depended upon to deliver breezes constantly and steadily over night and day for months at a time. It is when these weather changes occur and the winds are in the process of changing direction that the nasty storms and cyclones happen, but the months of these anomalies are well known and with the right information, can be avoided with almost complete certainty. For you, it is only necessary to remember that the wind in any given season blows towards the sun, and the destination of the wind is where the rain is. In other words, the winter season of the given area is always the best time to sail, the only exception being South Africa, which is affected more by the Atlantic weather system than the monsoon. As sailors only like sailing in warm and dry weather with favorable winds, the best sailing times are fairly well defined in the Indian Ocean and the Red Sea, and it is very easy to get anywhere you want to go by looking at a pilot chart and figuring out your route. Poor planning can make this ocean an uncomfortable place to sail.

SAILING ROUTES FROM AUSTRALIA

Upon leaving the Pacific, most boats continue their voyage through the Torres Strait. The port of call there is Thursday Island which sees many yachts moving in both directions, but like the South Pacific it experiences tropical storms in the summer months and is preferably avoided from December to March. The best time for yachts to make their way west is from May to October, those having sailed the Pacific Islands during the season making their onward passages in October; while those that preferred to summer in New Zealand or Australia (a much more popular alternative) sail through when the chances of cyclones are over and the weather is much better beyond. As an alternative to making your way to the South Pacific in May, go to Perth or Fremantle at this time and search for a yacht sailing west as the Indian Ocean enjoys its best weather. May and early June are the best times to sail from western Australia, but June and July are the best times to leave Thursday Island or Darwin. Sailing across the southern Indian Ocean can be done any time from May through October; the southeast trades blow this entire time but peak in the months of July and August. The other months of the year usher in the cyclone season and should be avoided.

Some yachts sail north for a more direct route to the Red Sea by way of Cocos Keeling and Sri Lanka and wait until around August to leave Western Australia. They usually plan to make their final landfall in late September at the end of the favorable winds of the southwest monsoons.

When a yachtsman engaged in a circumnavigation makes his way through the Torres Strait, he knows which way he is going to go to get around Africa. The choices are clear, and this is where he takes departure of the common route. If he decides the Red Sea is his path, he will probably sail north to Bali, then to Singapore and up through the Straits of Malacca to Thailand, across the Andaman Sea and into Sri Lanka and then to the Red Sea. If the southern route is chosen, a lengthy crossing is required to the Mascarene Islands (Mauritius and Reunion) or Madagascar, then around the Cape of Good Hope into the Atlantic Ocean. Most boats choose the Red Sea route because of the short hops and the safety of company, but the southern route has its fascination as well.

SAILING ACROSS THE SOUTHERN INDIAN

When crossing the Indian Ocean to South Africa, one should keep in mind that virtually all yachts bound for the Cape make their final passage to Durban only in October and November. The window of fine sailing is broad in the southern ocean as the southeast trades blow from the month of May until late October, with the winds blowing uncomfortably strong in the middle of this range. The final crossing to South Africa should be done around October when the chance of gales has gone down. The majority of yachts wait until the first week in November for the crossing from Mauritius or Reunion to Durban, South Africa, when the gales have calmed sufficiently and the cyclone season has not yet arrived. The most popular route goes from the departure points in Australia to Cocos Keeling or Christmas Island, then off to Reunion or Mauritius directly or by way of Chagos. With this in mind, one can plan a trip to arrive in South Africa in late November. If one wants to spend much time exploring the Indian Ocean, it would be prudent to leave the area of Northern Australia in May or June or for a rushed trip search for a yacht sailing in a more direct route in the months of August or September. Remember that the season of the SE trades corresponds with the dead of winter in that hemisphere, and though the trades are at their strongest, the southern swells from winter storms can make the trip very uncomfortable.

The islands in the southern Indian Ocean have little to offer cruising yachts as far as facilities are concerned, but the attractions of these islands for yachts has little to do with development. The places to visit if in the Mascarene Islands are Port Mathurin on Rodriguez, Port Louis and Grand Baie on Mauritius and Saint Paul, Réunion.

SAILING ACROSS THE NORTHERN INDIAN

The northern route is much more popular for circumnavigators of the world not only because of the attraction of the Mediterranean Sea, but for the scenery as well. This path is more defined than the southern route, but the specific stopping points and lengths of stay vary more as there are more to choose from.

The most common path is via Bali, Indonesia and/or Singapore when the Southeast monsoon is strongly set in June, July and August. The majority of yachts leave Darwin and Thursday Island in June and July bound for the islands or shores of Southeast Asia and the Straits of Malacca, but to get into Indonesia a cruising permit is required. If the yacht already has the required permit and your name is not on it, you might encounter problems with the Indonesian officials. However, since that permit is so elusive, the great majority of yachtsmen avoid Indonesia entirely.

AUSTRALIA

Darwin, which has the best facilities by far in this part of the world, greets traveling sailors from all over the world and provides for them a place to catch up with much needed repairs and a rest. The popularity of the cruising club there gives them somebody to talk to about the past crossing, future crossing, or cruising possibilities along the coast. For those cruising through the Torres Strait directly from a crossing of the Pacific, Darwin is the first stop in nearly ten thousand miles for any real work to get done.

There is a marina in Darwin, although the restrictions are heavy and most cruising yachts are not accepted for dockage. The commercial port is a lot more forgiving, and in the recommended cruising months there is ample room for yachts to use the moorings that belong to the shrimp boats that call Darwin their home, as they are out shrimping most of that time. The Darwin Sailing Club, based in Fannie Bay, is the premier lounging ground for traveling yachtsmen and is very friendly to cruisers, but you might have some trouble getting in. The last time I was there, I went in looking for an old friend of mine who I heard was visiting the area, and the Commodore threw me out three consecutive days. My tactic was to be honest and open, but it didn't work. I wish you better luck. The Dinah Beach Cruising Yacht Association is a less formal club, located in Frances Bay. They are reported to be very friendly. The Cruising Yacht Association of the Northern Territory should be consulted for their local contacts. They are the group responsible for organizing the annual Darwin to Ambon race which sees about sixty yachts sailing towards eastern Indonesia each year. Frances Bay has the repair facilities, and when you get there it will be obvious where the yachts are. Visit Frances Bay Slipway and Sadgrove's Quay.

In the northern part of Western Australia there is very little in the way of facilities for cruising yachts. In fact, there are only three decent wharves and marinas along this entire coast from Darwin all the way to North West Cape. The first is at Entrance Point in Broome, but the incredible tides make tying up at the wharf or even anchoring a nightmare. Port Hedland also has a tidal problem, of course, but there is a marina with floating docks to alleviate these difficulties. There is also a Port Hedland Yacht Club. Damper and the Hampton Harbor Yacht Club and Marina provide a fantastic resting place for yachts cruising this long coast going to or from the islands of Indonesia and the Indian Ocean, and is probably the favored spot for cruising yachts along this entire coast. On North West Cape the Exmouth Yacht Club serves those using the marginal anchorage there.

In the Shark Bay area, Carnarvon is the last good harbor yachtsmen encounter while traveling north, and is frequently used as a jump-off port for long distance voyages. They have a marina, a yacht club and full repair facilities.

On the southern shore of Western Australia one will find every facility needed at Geraldton including a marina and full repair facilities. There is also a good harbor at Port Denison, a new marina at Jurien Bay and an outstanding little marina at Two Rocks. South from there you will find the now famous marinas at Perth and Fremantle, site of the 1987 America's Cup. Visit Hillary's Boat Harbor in Perth and the Challenger Harbour, Fishing Boat Harbour and the Success Boat Harbour in Fremantle. There are ten yacht clubs in Fremantle and a few more in Cockburn Sound, although I will not list them here.

BALI

The island of Bali, which is part of Indonesia, has a reputation of being very accommodating to foreign yachtsmen and many decide to pull into Benoa Harbor without a cruising permit for a bit of a rest.

The officials will usually grant a two or three day stay. The yachts that have cruising permits can have them changed more easily here than in any other island in Indonesia, so if you find a yacht that would like to take you for a journey along the Indonesian Archipelago, this would be the place to have yourself added to that permit. For these reasons as well as its great central location, I rate Bali among the best spots for hitching a ride in all the Indian Ocean. In Bali, contact Made Gerip, an old friend of mine who is the only person around who can straighten out cruising permit problems efficiently. If there is a yacht looking for crew, Made will know. He can be found in Benoa Harbor, everybody knows who he is.

Yachts sail out of Bali in all directions for the greater part of the Southwest Monsoons from May to October. The later part of this span is the time to find Australian boats sailing home before the weather turns ugly, and it is also likely you can find yachts in September making the late departure directly for Sri Lanka before the northeast monsoon sets in.

SOUTHEAST ASIA

Perhaps the most popular meeting place in this part of the world is Singapore, where a relatively low number of boats sailing south from the Far East meet a high number of boats cruising up from the Torres Strait area and Northern Australia to join the Christmas voyage up through the Straits of Malacca. About three hundred yachts call into Singapore annually, most making their way west during the northeast monsoon. Although very few yachts progress in the other direction, they cross during the other season, when the southwest monsoon is firmly rooted in June, July and August. Because of the infrequency of yachts heading into Singapore from the Malacca Straits and beyond, I advise against waiting there at that time for a boat unless you just want to see Singapore in the driest season (when it only rains half the time) or are passing through. Yachts heading eastward into the South China Sea depart Singapore in December as well.

In Singapore, the place most yachties usually aim for when looking for a place to tie up and rest is the Changi Sailing Club on the eastern tip of Singapore Island. Word is going around that a huge marina, called the Raffles Marina, is being built on the western end of the island at Tuas and should be complete by the time of this printing. When this marina is operational the cruising face of Singapore will be forever changed. The other spot on the west coast is the Singapore

Yacht Club on the Selat Pandan River. There is a 40-ton travelift at the Yacht Solutions Boatyard in Loyang Bay and a 70-ton travelift at Keppel Marine Services in Bukit Chermin. Both yards are swarming with yachties most of the year, since the greatest attraction of Singapore is the repair possibilities.

THE MALAY PENINSULA

The most popular departure points along the west coast of the Malay Peninsula (including Thailand) are Phuket, Penang Island, Lumut (30 miles north of Ipoh), Malacca and Kelang, with the best repair facilities in Kelang and Singapore. Kelang, the port of Kuala Lumpur, has the Royal Selangor Yacht Club and a small boatyard that sees yachts moving in both directions during the season. The Selangor Yacht Club organizes the Raja Muda Cruising Rally which takes place in late November. The town of Butterworth, which is only on the map because of its proximity to Penang Island, is a place to visit for those yachts clearing in or out of Malaysia. The season to leave is December to April with most boats sailing out in January and February and a few cruising through before December to spend extra time in Phuket. Visit the boatyards to secure passage from here and make your best effort to get along well with those on board as it gets more difficult to find passage westbound the further you get from Singapore. In May and June the only direction yachts sail is eastward, and the most alluring place in southeast Asia is Singapore. At that time the routes fan out across the South China Sea bound for Borneo, the Philippines, Japan and Hong Kong, but almost all of those will spend some time in Singapore for repairs. Again, the possibilities are severely limited with only an estimated half dozen annually making that eastbound passage. Two or three months later the northbound yachts begin landing in Singapore to await the northeast monsoon to continue their northbound passage. I suggest you wait.

PHUKET

As stated above, most of the yachts that leave early spend some time in the islands off the west coast of Thailand. Phang Na Bay, known as the Bay of Phuket, is one of the most beautifully intriguing sailing locations in the world. If you have the opportunity to sail these fairy tale waters by all means do so. You will be able to set anchor beneath jungle clad overhangings of massive rock towering hundreds of feet overhead beside white sand beaches and warm waters swarming with fish. Phuket is a great place to sail during the northeast monsoon, and many sailors will spend the early part of that season there before making their way to Sri Lanka in January and February to get into the Red Sea in the spring and sail the Mediterranean in the summer. Specifically, Nai Harn Bay on Phuket Island is the main anchorage and is the home of the Phuket Yacht Club, although until recently has not been as much of a yacht club as it has been a resort. The Ao Chalong Cruising Club, whose office is at the Latitude 8 Restaurant in Chalong Bay, is your best contact. The club is run by expatriated sailors who keep in constant touch with the yachts moving through the area and will know about any available bunks. Quantum Marine, run by John Batt, is another good contact point close by. Also located on Phuket Island is Phuket Marine, which has a 40-ton marine hoist and good contact with cruisers. Other boatyards of dubious quality are Phuket Yacht Services and Ratanchai Slipway. About eighty miles south of Phuket is the port of Kantang, which has good repair services and should be checked if time permits. At least this town will not be crawling with international travelers, a condition which is becoming an ever-increasing annoyance in Phuket.

SRI LANKA

From the departure points of Southeast Asia, almost every yacht cruising westbound makes a Sri Lanka stop at the harbor of Galle on the southern tip of that island. In Galle, visit Windsor Yacht Services, as they keep abreast of yacht movement through Sri Lanka in person and by radio. Don Windsor, who died last year, kept a log book of all yachts that visited his abode, and he let anybody remotely related to yachting into his home. I hope his family is carrying on the tradition. There is now a navy shipyard in Galle and repairs are available there. The northern part of the country has been politically unstable for many years and is not a particularly safe place for yachts. Colombo has a few yachts now and then, but Sinhalese attacks on Tamils and Tamil attacks on Sinhalese have kept it unsafe. When I sailed into Colombo Harbor in 1985, the acting American Ambassador warned us not to leave the boat at all for a few days, and bombing could be heard throughout the days and nights. Galle is a more pleasant place to be anyway and so far has been untouched by civil violence. Between 90 and 100 yachts touch base there each year, about 80% of them heading west during the northeast monsoon, some heading east during the southwest monsoon and some just hanging out for the winter season. The best time to be there is from January to March when yachts are making their way towards the Red Sea. If you find yourself in India at any time of the year, a better bet is to head south to Sri Lanka as few yachts sail into India. The red tape involved, the minefields of fishing traps along the coasts and the unfavorable winds during the northeast monsoon make India a treacherous destination for yachts. A few do call in at Cochin, Goa and Bombay along the west coast during these winter months, but visiting any port in India is usually pointless.

THE ISLANDS OF THE NORTH INDIAN OCEAN

From Galle, some yachts sail south into the Maldives in January and February with the wind at their backs as some of the best scuba diving in the world lies before them. The hundreds of paradise islands that ring the atolls of this island chain are surrounded by underwater cliffs of dense marine vegetation and clear tropical waters with temperatures in the eighties. The exclusive resorts that sit on some of these cays charge their patrons a couple of hundred dollars per day to dive just their own local reefs, but the cruiser has the priceless access to them all.

The next stop is one of the most sensational places I have ever visited: the Chagos group. In the center of the Indian Ocean is an uninhabited tropical fantasy, everything you have ever dreamed of in an island paradise without the people. One group of islands, called the Salomons, is a tiny group of cays on an atoll about eleven miles across. The small band of islets was used by the British military in the fifties, then abandoned suddenly leaving a library full of books, a tank full of water, poultry gone wild, fruit trees and a vegetable bonanza. The center of the atoll is a harbor protected from all swells and has become a favorite place for yachts to hang out for months. It is a place to see and spend some time, but one can only hope that nobody gets to feel too much at home there. The monsoons do not affect Chagos much, so yachts are there nearly all year, in transit across the North and the South halves of the Ocean. Neither the Maldives nor Chagos would be a very practical place to go looking for passage, but it would behoove you to get there on a yacht from another part of the ocean.

The other notable group of islands in the North Indian Ocean, the Seychelles, is worthy of a visit for this type of quest. Located one thousand miles off the coast of Kenya, I rate it the most beautiful group of islands in the world. With its story book history of French pirates and African slaves, the people are full of stories of lost treasure and ghosts and visions coming to them in dreams. What makes the Seychelles so visually appealing is its unique topography made of granite instead of the usual coral or volcano. Some people consider this small group of islands the eighth continent for this reason, and the sight of huge granite boulders lining the beautiful tropical beaches attracts thousand of photographers here each year. The Seychelles are very popular with international sailors for these reasons and more, and the weather is ideal from May to October. The time to be in the Seychelles is in May as yachts leave to cross in all directions. The other monsoon transition period is the alternate time to visit, with the most yachts setting sail for the Red Sea in late September. The entire Southwest Monsoon has yachts crossing to the islands to the south including the Comoros and west to the coasts of Kenya and Tanzania, but consider where the yachts are going from there before you decide to go. From the Comoros Islands, most yachts head to Durban in October and from the east coast of Africa they head up to the Red Sea in May or September.

SAILING FROM AFRICA

Along the coast of Africa the only places you are likely to find foreign yachting activity are in Kenya, Tanzania, South Africa and, recently, Mozambique. From Kenya and Tanzania, yachts sail only in the months of the southeast trades, which fortunately correspond with the dry and pleasant weather from April to October. During this season, the currents run north at a clip of three or four knots, so the yachts are ever moving northward. From Kenya, it is advisable to seek out passage towards the Red Sea at the start or the end of the southwest monsoon season, as the winds are a bit too forceful in the core of the summer. That would put the best time to skirt this continent at around April or May, and again in September and October. The earlier time would likely see more boats heading in that direction because of the possibility of catching the summer in the Mediterranean, whereas the September departure will put the boats in the Red Sea for six months before ideal weather in southern Europe arrives. Boats also leave for Sri Lanka in the late summer around August and some sail for the Seychelles in January, February and March. The cruising yachts you will find in the southern portions of eastern Africa will be sailing for Durban and Cape Town in October and November between the end of the winter gales and the start of the summer cyclones.

The last area I will discuss in this section is the last Indian Ocean country many circumnavigating sailors see, that being South Africa. Durban is a respectable port with little room for foreigners, but the Point Yacht Club is friendly and yachts find room to tie up at the International jetty. Richard's Bay, which has the Zululand Yacht Club, is also a popular stop for those moving through in October and November, as is Port Elizabeth to the southwest. The biggest departure point for the Atlantic crossing is, of course, Cape Town. Most of the cruising yachts in Cape Town hang out at the marina and the Royal Cape Yacht Club, which has about fifty berths and a boatyard. Most of the pre-transatlantic work is done in this yard. The Hout Bay Yacht Club in its namesake bay to the south has a similarly sized marina, but is not nearly as popular.

THE RED SEA

It is clear to me that the only real reason to visit Egypt by yacht is to get through the Suez Canal or provision to go somewhere else. After battling the swarms of intruders that climb aboard at all hours and in all places to ask for handouts or to take anything that isn't locked down, yachtsmen cannot wait to get out of the Canal or the harbors that border it. I have a friend who actually had to wash a group of them off the side of his tugboat with a fire hose and chop off their lines with a fire ax. I remember at least fifteen boats getting in our way as we made a passage of the Canal, forcing us to stop so that they could ask us for a package of cigarettes or a bottle of whiskey. With the bribes to officials and the gratuities to the pilots, I can understand Egypt's lack of popularity with the cruising world. In my first trip through the canal, our cook got locked up for buying food without a permit, I contracted hepatitis and we blew out of the harbor in the middle of the night to avoid the red tape of officially clearing port. Then we had a group of drunken Egyptian soldiers open fire on us in the deep of the night from behind a sand dune and our kidnapped dog was returned to us accompanied by an under-the-table bill of many, many Egyptian Pounds. In retrospect, however, I remember the finest diving I have ever done, the clear, warm water and the reefs so packed with fish and soft corals of every color, the hundreds of shipwrecks that have never been dived on before, riding the backs of giant Manta Rays over breathtaking reefs, and I know all of the hassles were well worth it. Except the hepatitis. As far as the Suez Canal is concerned, though, I think I would take my chances with the Cape of Africa.

As an introduction to the Red Sea, Egypt has no sense of welcome. But as bad as Egypt is, the rest of the Red Sea is worse. Or so the books say. Saudi Arabia cannot be approached by the sea under any circumstances by threat of confiscation of the boat. That is one threat I would take seriously, since it does happen once in a while. The other countries along the Red Sea are benign as far as anchoring and beach landings are concerned, if any offense is taken they will let you off with just a warning. We were boarded several times by officials to check our papers, and we never encountered problems other than in the Suez Canal. Every story of a Red Sea crossing is different, some being worse than mine, but a good attitude can mollify these obstacles.

In the southern Red Sea there are no ports that I would recommend visiting for your pursuit, as the restrictions are too strangling. Instead, find a yacht in the Seychelles or on the African east coast to sail north through the Red Sea.

Saudi Arabia can be sailed and visited as long as the yacht has clearance, but permission is difficult. Ethiopia is not a cruising destination as yet, but the government may open its doors soon. The long coastline and the superb diving in Ethiopia will make this a fabulous place to sail once they begin welcoming sailors. Oman is beginning to welcome Western sailors, but it is still not at all practical for a quest such as yours. Somalia is strictly forbidden to everybody. The rest of the countries lining the shores of the Red Sea are explained below. The only fleet of charter yachts is owned by The Moorings and is based in Hurghada, Egypt, although Eilat, Israel has some private crewed charters that are mostly dive boats.

WEATHER AND THE ROUTES
The predominant winds in the Red Sea blow from the northwest all year, only the very southern extreme being the exception. Since northbound voyages are more frequently made than southbound voyages, the dominant winds add to the frustration sailors face in this sea. In the spring the northwest winds are not as strong as they are the rest of the year, and at times the northeast monsoon finds its way into the straits of Bab el Mandeb, counteracting the prevailing northwest winds to give sailors some downwind sailing for the beginning of their

journey. Fortunately, this is also the most popular time for yachts to transit this sea from the south as the northeast monsoon in the Indian Ocean carries them to the Gates of Sorrow (the Straits of Bab el Mandeb) and the Mediterranean beckons them for the season. The Red Sea has no well-defined season of its own and the winds fluctuate very little, so the sailors that make this northward voyage will be battling head winds most of the way at any time of year.

For those heading south, the winds are much more favorable and with the exception of the spring months, they carry through almost the entire Red Sea. With the monsoonal effect explained above, yachtsmen will encounter a head wind in the southern extreme in the months of February and March, but as the Red Sea provides the most pleasant weather during the spring, this is easily endured. Most cruising yachts move through to the south in these months because of the weather and the wind directions beyond. The eastbound passage of the Indian Ocean is more practical in the late spring with the southwest monsoon not yet at its peak.

In summary, the Red Sea sees most yachts moving in both directions in the months of February and March, but it is not uncommon to find them all year. The dominant head winds present little more than a minor obstacle if the navigator is confident and vigilant. This sea is not quite as narrow as it appears on a world map.

EGYPT

Unfortunately, Egypt must be endured for a passage in either direction, giving rise to bitter feelings and some callusing of the nerves. As for the harbors, no yachtsmen spend any time just hanging out and your only bet is to visit these ports to gain passage through the Canal. The exceptions are the tiny port of Hurghada south of Suez, and the port of Sharm el Sheikh on the southern tip of the Sinai Peninsula. The attraction of both Hurghada and Sharm el Sheikh is the superb diving close by, and with the Sheraton Hotel, the Moorings fleet and the Club Med in Hurghada, supplies and provisions are at hand.

ISRAEL

The only port in Israel that touches the Red Sea is Eilat with only a few miles of coastline, but what a port it is. To cruising yachtsmen and tourists alike it provides the only touch of Western comforts in the entire Red Sea, and it has the great advantage of being close to the superb diving grounds of Râs Muhammad and the surrounding reefs. Among the local dive boats hanging on the moorings and tied to the docks, there exists a small cruising community. It is a tight-knit group of happy people who are easy to approach and will know about any crew vacancies in the area. For a southbound voyage this small port should be visited, it being the best spot to find passage in the entire Red Sea. If you are looking to sail north, it is better to go directly to the Mediterranean to avoid the Suez Canal. Eilat has no facilities besides its moorings and a few piers.

SUDAN

The only spot to visit is Port Sudan, which is a place to take on fresh veggies and not much else. Port Sudan is a very important commercial harbor that has the usual facilities for large ships and can provide emergency repairs to yachts, but don't count on finding yachts there.

DJIBOUTI

Since the requirements for visiting this small country are stringent, I will not advise arriving by air. If the traveler has no yacht set up to visit in this port, the red tape is prohibitive and only a ten day visa is granted. However, if you are already there and are looking to change yachts, you will find yourself in a fantastic place to do so, as there are many yachts that call into this port during their passage. The Club Nautique de Djibouti is the only facility worthy of mention, as at any one time during the spring there are usually twenty or thirty transient yachts anchored in front, all of which use the facilities. There are also some repairs that sailors can accomplish at the naval base, although they will all be using the yacht club during their stay.

YEMEN

Yemen, which now encompasses both the previous boundaries of Yemen and South Yemen, has little for visiting yachts except for a sailing club in Aden to rest at and take a shower. There is also a naval dockyard in the port of Aden that might sometimes do some work on yachts. All other ports along the long coast of Yemen are strictly forbidden to foreigners. As with Djibouti, I do not recommend visiting this country as the entrance requirements are very forbidding for airline passengers.

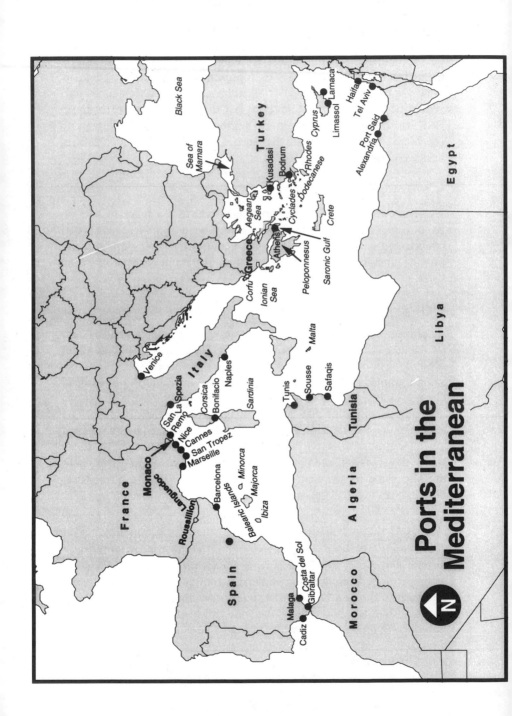

Ports in the Mediterranean

Black Sea

Sea of Mamara

Turkey

Kusadasi
Bodrum

Larnaca
Haifa
Tel Aviv
Limassol
Cyprus
Rhodes
Dodecanese
Port Said
Alexandria

Egypt

Aegean Sea

Cyclades

Crete

Greece

Athens

Peloponnesus

Saronic Gulf

Corfu

Ionian Sea

Venice

Italy

La Spezia
San Remo
Corsica
Bonifacio
Naples
Sardinia

Malta

Tunis
Sousse
Safaqis

Libya

Tunisia

Nice
Cannes
San Tropez
Marseille

Monaco

Languedoc

Roussillon

France

Barcelona
Balearic Islands
Minorca
Majorca
Ibiza

Algeria

Malaga
Costa del Sol
Gibraltar
Cadiz

Spain

Morocco

N

CHAPTER 10
PORTS AND ROUTES IN THE MEDITERRANEAN

THE SPOTS

One of the biggest cruising destinations on earth, the Mediterranean enjoys a reputation of warm weather, steady winds and a long cruising season with a great variety of things to see and do. The entry requirements for Americans are very lax in Europe, and it is possible to stay about as long as you want. Every country with a coastline that touches the sea generally requires only a passport for US citizens; the only countries that will not allow you a visit without a pre-arranged visa are Albania, Syria, Libya and Algeria, which are countries that you will probably not want to visit anyway. Egypt will issue a visa upon arrival.

The tone of the yachting community is different in the Mediterranean than elsewhere in the world and harder to penetrate. For the most part, those cruising yachts encountered in this sea will be hopping from port to port along the European coasts of the Western Mediterranean or island hopping in the Aegean Sea, and with the crews not being faced with long crossings and with guests usually aboard for the ride, the yacht owners are less apt to sign on crew from the docks. The bars and restaurants along the way are not usually yachtie hangouts as much as those in the South Pacific and the Caribbean, but are more likely to have overland travelers, wealthy Europeans, Americans and tourists of all description with a few cruising sailors here and there. When striking up a conversation with the owner or captain of a cruising yacht along the Riviera, you will be looked upon more as a traveling salesman than a potential crew member or a potential friend. Don't expect visiting American yachties to be happy to talk to a fellow American here. There are a great deal of Americans visiting the Mediterranean all season long, and they will see you as just another one of the great multitudes of tourists. A better way is to visit the repair facilities throughout the Mediterranean and offer a hand to the captain or engineer, work up a conversation and slowly let your quest be known. Another way is to place cards on the bulletin boards of the marinas or search for the social activities such as the Sunday barbecues in Larnaca, Cyprus. In places away from the confusion of the Riviera, such as in the outer islands of Greece, points of land in Turkey and the ports of Cyprus, Egypt, Israel and Tunisia, you will find yachts more apt to pay attention to you. If you can be there in the spring, the wintering spots will be your best bet for latching up with long-distance voyagers. With the exception of Tunisia and Egypt, few yachts visit Mediterranean Africa at all, nor do they visit Syria, Lebanon or the Southeastern Coast of Turkey. The State Department now forbids American yachts from visiting the waters of Yugoslavia. As for the rest of the countries, I will describe cruising routes and ports of call in detail from the Straits of Gibraltar to the coast of Israel.

The most popular wintering places for yachts awaiting the fine weather of the spring include the entire Spanish and French coasts and parts of Italy, particularly on Sardinia; the marinas of Greece near Athens; Kusadasi, Turkey; Larnaca, Cyprus; Manoel island on Malta and Tunisia.

CRUISING DIRECTIONS AND ROUTES

The prevailing flow of yachts in the Mediterranean is from west to east along the Spanish, French and Italian Rivieras as most yachts enter the sea at Gibraltar and travel with the currents and winds at their backs. World cruising yachts, however, move in the opposite direction, entering the Mediterranean from the Red Sea via the Suez Canal, bucking the flow of the prevailing winds and currents the entire way. But the winds are as diverse as the cultures in this section of the world, and it is not difficult to plan a passage under sail in any direction, provided the sailor is in possession of the right information. As a result, yachts move in all directions here, but the predominant flow is to the east along the coast in the spring and early summer and the reverse direction in the late summer and fall in large steps. Approximately 1000 yachts annually make their way back to the mouth of the Mediterranean for their Atlantic crossings to the Caribbean, stopping as infrequently as practical along the way.

SPAIN

The Mediterranean coast of Spain is literally stuffed with marinas and each marina is stuffed with boats. There are so many marinas, in fact, that just to see the big ones is quite a chore and a couple of days' work, so I suggest you find a place in the sun with a pen and a pile of 3x5 cards, write an advertisement of your availability, and cruise the coast by bus or train, posting your add at the more than fifty sizable marinas you will encounter. Put on it the phone number of your residence and a brief description of your better qualities, then sit back and enjoy your vacation in Spain.

Here is a brief list with the generalities of each of the major marinas along the Spanish coast, giving a quick run down of each harbor and what can be expected. I will start at the Portuguese coast and move along to the east, skipping Gibraltar (it is covered after Spain) and continuing along the Mediterranean all the way to the French coast. Be advised that the yacht clubs in Spain are generally closed to outsiders, so the public bulletin boards at the marinas and the boatyards and repair facilities are your best places to go. The most popular wintering destinations are at Puerto Sherry, Puerto Banus, La Duquesa, Benalmadena, Al Merimar, Alicante and Puerto de Calpe.

ANDALUCIA

The Andalucian coast of Spain, located between the Portuguese border and Gibraltar, is not as much visited by voyaging yachts as one would imagine, although the facilities can be as good as those found along the Mediterranean coast of Spain. The notable spots are in Cadiz and Puerto Sherry. In Cadiz, there is a yacht club filled with local yachts and a fishing harbor with room for anchoring. There are also two small boatyards that cater to yachts. Puerto Sherry has an 800-berth marina and a boatyard with a 50-ton travelift which gives it the distinction of being the finest harbor for yachts in all of Andalucia.

COSTA DEL SOL AND THE COAST TO THE EAST

The coast from Gibraltar to Aguadulce is generally known as the Costa Del Sol, one that is extremely popular with cruising yachts all year. The ports along the Costa del Sol, as I describe in more detail than the rest of Spain, are popular for yachts landing after long

Atlantic crossings because of a technicality prohibiting those making first stops in Gibraltar (a British possession), from landing successively in Spain. Those yachts that do stop in Gibraltar first usually visit the Spanish coasts anyway, but those yachts unfamiliar with sailing customs in the Mediterranean prefer not to take the chance.

Sotogrande, which is soon to become the destination of choice for the wealthy cruisers, has a crane that can haul out boats to 150 tons for maintenance in its large boatyard. La Duquesa, which is a port of entry, is quieter and a lot cheaper, a place for boats to spend their winters. Estepona has a small marina with limited facilities, but Puerto Banus further along the coast is absolutely giant. Marbella Marina in Marbella and the new marina at Cabopino, ten miles farther, are much smaller but have good facilities and many yachts. The Fuengirola Marina, halfway from Marbella to Malaga, is a quiet, inexpensive place with good repair facilities. Next along the coast is Benalmadena, another giant marina for cruising yachts. Skip the harbor at Marbella, which is really just a commercial port, but visit the Real Club Mediterraneo, which is a local yacht club and Marina filled with local yachts. From there stop by Torre del Mar, with its limited facilities, then the fishing harbor and yacht club at Motril. Next, go to the huge marina at Puesto de Almerimar, which is the largest marina on this entire coast. It is also a very popular spot for cruisers to depart the coast for trips to the eastern countries and to the Balearic Islands, and to return from such trips. Also check the marina at Aguadulce, which is also very large.

From there things get a bit more sparse, but still you will find a good supply of marinas. Check the harbors at Almeria, Cartagena, Alicante, Denia, Valencia, Terragona, Barcelona, and Falmados. The biggest repair facilities outside of the Costa del Sol are in Barcelona.

THE BALAERIC ISLANDS

The hub of the Spanish sailing world has to be Palma, Mallorca, in the Balearic Islands. There are ferries running directly from Valencia, Denia and Barcelona, but they cost about $14 US for a third class ticket from Valencia one way, so you might want to weigh the advantages of paying them a visit (or hitching a ride out). Palma and other Balearic ports are the favorite wintering spots of Spain; Mahon on Menorca is the port of choice for boats on long-distance transits between Spain and spots farther to the east. The other marinas around the Balearics include Andraitx and Alcudia, both on Mallorca, and the port of Ibiza on the island of the same name, which is a very popular party spot with one of the biggest discos on Earth, and a much younger crowd than in other spots in the Mediterranean.

GIBRALTAR

The port of Gibraltar is one of the biggest and most important ports for yachts sailing in this part of the world, especially those who intend to avoid the Riviera. When entering the Mediterranean, most yachts have a well-defined destination, and likely reservations at one of the large Spanish marinas. Those yachts will miss Gibraltar as their destinations are right around the corner. The sailors who intend to continue to Italy or beyond without a stop in Spain will provision in Gibraltar and spend a few days resting. At the present, this port sees as many as 5000 yachts each year from 50 foreign countries. Gibraltar provides the best opportunity for provisioning for a long crossing to the Aegean Sea; it is a port of choice for wintering and it is a great landing spot for transatlantic yachts which may or may not stop in Bermuda or the Azores. This means that Gibraltar is a great port for crew changes and good place to rest. Captains and crew will be ready for a beer on solid land and conversations with new faces. If you do sign on, experience is not important because the other crew members will have all the experience needed. In addition, many yachts staying in Spain use Gibraltar as their repair center.

The main marina center of Gibraltar is located south of the airport among the facilities of the main harbor. Sheppard's Marina, which has a boatyard for 50 yachts, a 40-ton travelift and a 120-slip marina, is by far the transient center of the port. The staff tries to discourage long-term residents, keeping most of its slips open to those moving through, but a few have made it their home. The chandler there is full of salesmen who know the yachting community well, so a visit there and a chat with the proprietor will give you valuable insight. The newer Marina Bay Marina has more room than Sheppard's, about 200 berths, and sees about 300 yachts annually. There is talk about two more marinas being planned in the near future, one called the Queensway Quay, with room for 300 yachts, and one at Rosia Bay south of the main harbor. It is likely that both of those will be complete by the time of this printing. The Gun Wharf Yacht Center is one of the most important repair facilities in the entire Mediterranean and is outfitted for the huge yachts that the Mediterranean is famous for. This repair center has six railways for yachts up to 200 tons, but for the smaller yachts trying to get by on a shoestring, the price there can be prohibitive. There are numerous other repair businesses in Gibraltar that cater to this crowd, notably the Gib Yacht Center near Sheppard's, and Sheppard's itself. The Royal Gibraltar Yacht Club is one of the world's oldest yacht clubs and extends a welcome to transiting yachtsmen from around the world. Visit this club if you can, but be on your best behavior.

FRANCE

The Mediterranean shore of France is in many ways similar that of Spain, as you can literally hop from marina to marina along its entire coast. The main reason most yachts visit this chunk of high priced real estate is so that their owners can drink and bump elbows with other yachties in these very expensive and sophisticated marinas. It can be an uncomfortable place for those who are not accustomed to wearing jewelry and drinking champagne, and it is easy to feel out of place in its cafés and night clubs. It is also a place where there is very little adventure. It is locked into a corner of the Mediterranean Sea and the coast is fully developed, so if you were to find a berth on one of the tens of thousands of yachts sailing there in season, it is a good wager that you won't do a whole lot of sailing in any direction. I have met crews of yachts here and on the adjoining coast of Italy who have told me that they have never seen their yachts journey more than thirty miles from their home ports. It is reported that ninety percent of the yachts found in the marinas along this coast rarely leave the harbor. The position of the French Riviera does not make it convenient for a yacht moving through the Mediterranean to stop for a quick bite and refuel and be on its way. It is clearly well out of line of the long distance routes, and the reputation of its prices makes the extra distance traveled unrealistic.

However, a good way to find a berth is to visit this coast in the spring and look for a yacht that is wintering there, ready to move on when the season opens its doors. There are a great number of giant marinas along the entire coast, primarily along the Cote d' Azur and the French Riviera, which is also the step off spot for yachts sailing on to Corsica. The Languedoc-Roussillon Coast west of the Rhône stretching to the Spanish border is also dotted with new, giant marinas with every service imaginable; many being built or planned right now. From Marseilles east to the Italian border there is also a lot of building going on, but there are more established facilities and more well-known marinas that cruising yachts will be familiar with. The coast east of the Rhône, primary between St. Tropez and the Italian border (known as the Cote d' Azur) is more compressed and hosts a much higher concentration of boat basins and harbor facilities, probably the most in the entire Mediterranean. In addition, a train runs along this rugged and mountainous coast, making it relatively easy to move from marina to marina by land. The roving masses of travelers along this route make accommodation in the cheaper places nearly impossible to obtain in the season, so I suggest you find a nice place to stay off the beaten path, get your advertisement cards out and make a journey of it.

This list is how the southern coast of France sits now, but the marine development in this part of the world is a dynamic thing, and it is difficult to say what tomorrow will bring.

MARSEILLE TO ST. TROPEZ

From Marseilles to the east, you will need several days to cover the marinas. It may look as if the possibilities are endless, but don't let the crowds of yachts lull you into thinking you will have hundreds of responses. In Marseilles, visit the Marseilles, L'Estaque and Pointe Rouge marinas. Visit Cassis, La Ciotat, Saint Cyr Les Lecques, Bandol, Sanary and St. Pierre les Embiez ports. In Toulon, go to the Yacht Port du Toulon, Port de la Seyne, Saint Mandrier and Port Pin Rolland marinas. From there, pay a visit to Hyères, Port de la Londa, Bormes les Mimosas, Le Lavandou and Cavalaire harbors. The islands offshore in this area also are crammed with yachts, primarily at Port Cros, Porquerolles and Port du Frioul. There are boatyards in Marseilles, Toulon and Hyères.

THE FRENCH RIVIERA

The next major cruising area encountered when traveling along the coast to the east begins at St. Tropez, and runs all the way to the Italian border with only an occasional stretch of coast without a marina. In St. Tropez, there is a sizable marina and a boatyard, and in the western extent of the bay lie marinas and boatyards in Grimaud and Cogolin. In the northern part of the bay lies the Port de Sainte Maxime with its two boatyards and another big marina. From there, stop by the marinas at Frèjus, St. Raphaël, Santa Lucia, La Galère,

Port de Thèoule, La Rague and La Napoule. Of these, the St. Raphaël area has the largest marinas, possibly even the largest in the entire Mediterranean.

In Cannes, there has been much development in recent years, and now there are five marinas and a boatyard in Cannes Bay. Also visit Port Public Vallauris, Port Camile Royan and Port Gallice in the bay east of Cannes, and the giant marina and the two boatyards in Antibes. St. Laurent du Var, on the right bank of the mouth of the River Var, also has a marina and boatyard worthy of a visit. The marinas and boatyards at Beaulieu and Cap Ferrat, west of Nice, Villefranche, the Port of Monaco and Menton, against the Italian border should be visited just for the sheer number of yachts found here, in the center of the cruising world known as the French Riviera.

CORSICA

Corsica is a beautiful place to sail but not altogether packed with marinas. The biggest and best are in Ajaccio and Bastia and Banifacio in the South. If you are to travel through that region looking for a place on a yacht, I suggest you instead make for the northeast coast of Sardinia.

ITALY

The Italian Riviera is appropriately named as it is the place in Italy where people vacation and where the yachts settle, much like its French counterpart. However, the difference between the two is staggering; with less recent development and more natural scenery, it is a much nicer place to travel. Like the Riviera in France, the train runs along the coast, and with a Eurail pass you can get off at every coastal town from the border to La Spezia and have a look at the harbors and the chain of marinas. Among those that are the biggest are San Remo, Santa Margherita and Lavagna, next to Chiavari. South of La Spezia the marinas get a bit more sparse, but one harbor that is stuffed with foreign yachts in transit is Naples. South of there small fishing villages are the norm and few good yacht harbors stand out.

The eastern coast of Italy is more plain and is not sailed much, and with the Yugoslavian coast across the Adriatic Sea being much more attractive to sailors, the east coast of Italy has been underdeveloped over the years. The exception is in the Gulf of Venice, with ten marinas within just a few miles of each other. The rest of the coast has not been developed, but we might see more coastal yachting development the longer Yugoslavia stays in civil unrest .

One of the better places to find a yacht engaged in traveling large distances is on the Costa Smeralda of northeast Sardinia. The ferry runs directly to Olbia from Civitavechia and Genoa. In Costa Smeralda the trains are awful, so rent a moped and visit the harbors that dot this coast.

MALTA

Yachts that are in a hurry to move east to Greece, Turkey or the Suez Canal and those later in the season sailing back must make a decision whether to sail north or south around Sicily. Those that choose the southern route usually stop in Malta before embarking on their long trips to the far eastern end of the Mediterranean or to Crete. If Greece is the destination, yachts usually choose the northern route, stopping instead on the coast of Italy. Sailing back to Gibraltar from the northeastern Mediterranean, it is sensible for cruising yachts to make the trip through the Straits of Messina, missing Malta altogether. Those sailing directly from Crete, Cyprus or Egypt for the eastern Mediterranean stop in Malta to rest and provision. In addition to being an excellent place to find passage to distant shores, Malta has a reputation as a supreme wintering spot with excellent repair facilities, a beautifully natural harbor with good marinas and lots of room, with warm and clear water the entire year. It is almost 500 miles south of the Italian Riviera so it sees more sun, and it has a good international airport linking it to the world.

The best place to go on Malta is the huge complex in Marsamxett harbor. Around the northern part of the harbor you can find boat yards in Marza and Gzira and particularly on Manoel Island, the best being the Manoel Island Yacht Yard. Stop by the Royal Malta Yacht Club also on that island. The Msida Marina is where the big boats tie up, and there is quite a bit of activity there all year. They are currently building two more marinas there and the repair facilities are constantly being expanded, so there will be even more activity as time goes by.

TUNISIA

The entire Mediterranean coast of Africa west of Egypt has remained relatively free of cruising yachts over the years as red tape, crime and prohibitive governments have kept development to a minimum. The only significant exception is Tunisia. Although there are a lot fewer yachts along this coast than in other parts of the Mediterranean, the facilities are good and, like Malta, those well traveled sailors of the west have discovered its warmth and safe harbors for wintering. For this reason, it warrants a visit at the end of the winter season when last minute repairs are being done and the cruising life comes alive. It is virtually impossible to find a yacht in Europe that is heading for Tunisia, but after a trip across the African north, the ports of Tunisia provide excellent portals to Europe or to Malta which is not far offshore.

There are at least four marinas in Tunisia and more are in various stages of planning and construction. Two marinas, in La Goulette and Sidi Bou Said, are within ten miles of Tunis. Both of these have good repair facilities; Sidi Bou Said has the best in the country. In the southern end of the Gulf of Hamamet there are two more marinas: Port Kantaoui which is ten miles north of Sousse, and another at Monastir. Monastir has a dry dock as does the harbor af Sfax. Five more marinas that are in planning are at Tabarka, Ghar El Melh, Korbous, Hamamet and on the northern point of Jerba Island. You will find the wintering yachts at La Goulette, El Kantaoui and Monastir. Note that Tunisia, unlike Malta, does not fall into position as being a normal long distance harbor for boats in transit. But in April, May and June, it is an excellent spot to seek out passage to the Spanish, French and Italian Rivieras.

GREECE

The Greek Islands are among the most popular in the world for the tourist and sailor alike, and bring hundreds of private yachts to their waters annually. Several charter firms have opened operations in these islands in the last few years, and they never have a problem filling their yachts with charter customers. The islands have their own brand of beauty, recognized worldwide, and have more history than any touring scholar would ever want to see. Luckily, the main port in the region is centrally located and has the international airport close by. For the person looking to get onto a yacht heading out to the Greek Islands, there is really no other place to search than Athens and Piraeus. The number of marinas is unmatched in the eastern Mediterranean and is rivaled only by the mammoth facilities in

France, Spain and Italy. I will discuss briefly each large yacht facility in these neighboring cities, and outline some of the other marinas and wharves in the outlying areas. The primary cruising routes through Greece run from Corfu in the northwest down around either side of Cephalonia and into the Gulf of Patras, through the Corinth Cut and into the Saronic Sea. From there most boats spend time in the islands of the Cyclades and the Dodecanese as far east as Rhodes. Few yachts find reason to wander far from that narrow path, except to get away from the other cruisers. These areas are where I intend to concentrate my discussion.

ATHENS AND PIRAEUS

First of all, don't go to the main harbor looking for yacht clubs and marinas full of yachts; they are all located south (and east) of the commercial harbor. The commercial harbor is used only for shipping traffic. Fortunately, the finest harbor in all of Greece (finest for you, but dreary, dirty and loud for its patrons) is also the closest to the city of Athens. It is called Zea Marina. The reasons that it is the best place for you to go is that it is crammed with foreign yachts in the season; it is a port of entry and has every facility conceivable including haul-outs. There is transportation from there to all other areas of Greece including ferry service to the islands in the Saronic Gulf. There is also a subway to Athens. This harbor provides wintering to foreigners and has many slips open to transients. All official business can be handled on site, and the services available to the traveling yachtsman are spelled out in the local cruising guides and they recommend this harbor above all others. In other words, it is crowded and busy, so I recommend it highly. Zea Marina is located on the point of land south of Athens, around the corner to the east of Piraeus harbor.

Farther to the east of Zea is the Mounichas Marina, but it is mostly closed to all but the most elegant foreign yachts, and even they must make arrangements ahead of time to use the harbor. I do not recommend visiting this marina. This is also the case with Faliron Marina, farther east.

Kalamaki Marina is the second most popular harbor in the Athens area for visiting yachts, but it is a bit farther out of town. This is a brand new marina that was an overflow for the other crowded marinas in the area, but has filled up quickly. It is very friendly to the transient sailor and has repair facilities on the grounds. In addition, Kalamaki is a holding area for boats awaiting the passage through the Corinth Cut.

The Gilfada Marinas are the next in line down the coast, and although they are not overly accommodating to foreign yachts, there are reports that they are currently being redone and in a year or two they will be the largest and most complete marinas in all of Greece. These marinas are in the path of the arriving jets at the international airport, and the sound keeps many yachts away.

Vouliagmeni Marina near the town of the same name south of Athens on the coast is a friendly facility welcoming transiting yachts when room is available. It is comfortable and provides many services to those who patronize it, but keep in mind that it is one of the more expensive marinas in the area and will be the place to find the more elegant yachts.

On the west side of Athens proper lie the boatyards that service the area. There are several in the town of Perama, three miles west of Piraeus, capable of hauling out large yachts. If Zea Marina is unable to provide you with a berth on a yacht, it would be worth your while to see who is in the yards.

THE GULF OF PETALI

Just around the corner to the east of the southern cape of the Greek mainland (Cape Sounion) is the port of entry of Gaidouromandra. The boatyard is responsible for most of its popularity, as it provides an opportunity for yachts to spend the winter or undergo repairs. Farther north where the mainland almost meets the island of Evia is the port of Khalkis. This is a port busy only with those yachts accessing the northern Aegean Sea. There is a bridge that connects the island to the mainland, and many yachts must wait for many hours for this bridge to open. This makes this port one of the most visited in the area. There is also a boatyard in the harbor.

THE SOUTHERN PELOPONNESUS

The Argolic Gulf on the southeast corner of the Peloponnesus is fairly popular with yachtsmen, but does not warrant a trip to seek out passage on a yacht. If you find yourself there, check Navplion, Astros, Poulithra and the island of Spetsai.

THE CYCLADES

This group is the most popular in all of Greece, and the cruising sailors spend a great deal of time roaming around the 30 or so islands, but on none in particular. There is only one sophisticated harbor in this entire group: Ermoupolis on Siros, which is the only port of entry. I will attempt to give you the places the yachts frequent, but realize you will see yachts at anchor everywhere, but few tied up to a quay. It will be very difficult to find a yacht to catch a ride on for the following reason: these islands are stuffed with backpacking travelers, and the yachtsmen will be looking to avoid them whenever possible. Remember, you are one of them.

Siros has a small shipyard, some floating docks and services available. Ayios Nikolaos on Kea is a very popular anchorage in the summer, and Gaviron on Andros has room for yachts to tie stern-to the quay. Tinos has a harbor and room for a few yachts in addition to providing the best drinking water in all of Greece. Mykonos is one of the most picturesque islands in Greece and very popular with yachtsmen, tourists and backpacking travelers. There are dozens of great bars and restaurants there, and quite a few yachts. Livadhi, on the island of Serifos, is another good place to find yachts at anchor and a few at the quay. Paros has a good inner harbor at Paroikia where you will likely find a few yachts tied up and in various states of repair There is a small quay at Ios Harbor on the island of Ios, and also at the port of Thera (Santorini). Thera is another beautiful island popular with Westerners, and has a rich geological and archeological history, and many yachts tie up at the quay or anchor off in the deep water of the bay to spend time in the town at the top of the cliff. It is quite a sight.

THE AEGEAN SEA

Volos, on the Greek mainland, has a recently developed yacht area on the southeast end of the harbor, and all repairs are available including haul-outs. Thessaloniki, on the gulf of Thermai, also on the mainland, has a yacht club on the south end of the harbor. Porto Carras Marina near Nea Marmara on the Khalkidhiki Peninsula has a marina and is a popular place for yachts to winter. Kavala and Alexandroupolis are also worthy of a visit if in the area. Khios, in the eastern Sporades, is the yachting center in the eastern part of the Aegean Sea and perhaps should be visited if you are nearby. The other spots to visit in this area are Mirina, on Limnos, and Pithagorion on the island of Samos. Pithagorion is particularly worthy of a visit because of its accessibility to Kusadasi, Turkey. The port itself is sparse for yachts even in season, as are most of the Sporades.

THE DODECANESE ISLANDS

Simi, Kos and Kalimnos all have good facilities; Kalimnos has the best provisioning while Kos has the greatest number of foreign visitors. The best place to visit in all of the Greek islands is Rhodes, complete with its astonishing history. It has a very crowded harbor with boats from all over the world. There is a very large and complete boatyard and a marina for large yachts, an international airport and ferry service to Turkey and other islands in Greece. If you find yourself in southern Greece or southwestern Turkey, you should not miss this harbor.

CRETE

If you are on Crete looking for a yacht in season, you are in a good place. Not only is it a fantastic island to visit and to find yachts doing the slow cruise through the Greek islands, but it is one of the best places in all of Greece to catch international sailors just passing through. Many yachts have also found Crete a great spot for wintering. Head for the north coast, particularly the harbors of Chania, Iraklion and Ayios Nikolaos. Chania and Ayios Nikolaos are particularly fine harbors, but most yachtsmen will prefer the services available at Iraklion which has a boatyard, a sufficient marina and great provisioning.

CORFU AND THE IONIAN SEA

Corfu is a very popular place to visit for tourists and yachties all over the world, and despite all of this, has retained its charm. A beautiful island with its own brand of Greek history and scenery in stark contrast to the rest of Greece, it stands firmly as a place to see when moving through the Mediterranean, even without its popularity for yachts. The town you will unquestionably visit first is Corfu, which is also the finest place to look for foreign yachts. It is crowded in summer (especially in the old harbor); it is the most likely place in the entire Ionian for yachts to clear into Greece; it has a lot of room for yachts and a good boatyard and many cheap dormitory-style hotels in town. The second place to check is the port of Gouvia, just a few miles up the coast, which has services of all sorts and is a popular place to winter. The only other port worth mentioning in Corfu is Palaeokastrita, which has a respectable marina but little else.

Preveza is another good site to visit and is a lot closer to Athens, but it is primarily a commercial harbor. There is a good marina beside the Fort Ay Andreas, with many services but no boatyard. Levkas, just a few miles to the south on the island of the same name, is a bit more suited for yachts. The group to contact there is Contract Yacht Services, as they arrange all repairs for yachtsmen and get them set up for wintering. Farther south on the east coast of Levkas is the port of Vlikho, which has two boatyards capable of hauling out large yachts. Also check Vassiliki Harbor on the southern end of the island.

If you are on Cephalonia, check out Argostoli, as there is more yachting activity here than anywhere else on the island. There are a couple of yacht repair shops, but no real boatyards.

TURKEY

Turkey, being a large charter destination, is often ignored by the cruising crowd, who have no idea what they are missing. In my opinion, Turkey has some of the finest cruising grounds on earth, and certainly some of the most unique. The craggy southern coast is filled with bays and very small municipal docks, making it a poor place for a hitchhiker to travel overland seeking water-bound transit, but it is one coast that should be sailed along if the opportunity arises. The best harbors to visit when looking to sail along the southern coast of Turkey are Bodrum, Marmaris, Fethiye and Antalya. Also, despite the unfriendliness that Turkey and Greece hold for each other, Rhodes has the largest harbor in the area and you will have a great chance of finding a yacht heading for the southern coast of Turkey from there.

Along this coast, Bodrum has the best waterfront with the most room, great provisioning and a few local workshops. Marmaris, a few miles to the east, also has some room for yachts, but the harbor gets cramped rather quickly. Both of these harbors have marinas used for wintering. Datça (south of Bodrum), Fethiye, Kas, Kemer and Antalya all have marinas that have recently been built, although I have not seen any reports of their quality.

Kusadasi (pronounced *KOOSH-ODYSSEY)*, on the western shore south of Izmir, has a number of charter fleets and a surprisingly modern marina complex, and has become the premier cruising destination on the western coast of Turkey. There is light yachting activity at Ayvalik, east of the island of Lesvos (and a new marina

202 The Seagoing Hitchhiker's Handbook

there), in the Gulf of Marmaris and in the Bosphorus Straits at Istanbul, although nothing really stands out.

CYPRUS

The island of Cyprus is split by two bitter factions: the south sympathetic to Greece and the north sympathetic to Turkey. So bitter are the two halves that there is a UN peacekeeping force patrolling the border, which a visitor must not attempt to cross. That is unfortunate when considering that a trip into the interior will only yield a visit to part of this beautiful island, but not so much of a drawback when you realize that the perimeter of the island lacks good anchorages and coastal cruising is not recommended. Instead, Cyprus is one of those places for wintering yachts, parking it for trips inland or provisioning. As a result, Cyprus presents a fantastic opportunity for finding yachts sailing away for distant shores at the end of the winter season. Circumnavigating sailors, having recently run the gamut called the Suez Canal, favor the mild climate of Cyprus for the winter before sailing off to the west in the spring. Cyprus also has very good provisioning: as good as anywhere in the western Mediterranean and a far cry better than the surrounding countries. For this reason, many charter boat companies choose this island for purchasing their unperishable food items and supplies. There are also good repair facilities in three main ports of the southern portion.

Northern Cyprus is very rarely visited by yachts as the lack of harbors would suggest. In the southern part of the island, officially named Cyprus, there are three harbors; the most notable is Larnaca. This harbor has the Larnaca Marina which is a large port stuffed each winter with slumbering yachts, a boatyard with a 40-ton travelift and dry storage for 150 yachts, good supermarkets and a variety of parts stores unmatched in the eastern Mediterranean. The Larnaca Marina seems to be the social center of the entire island where cruising is concerned, playing host to the citizens (or ex-citizens) of dozens of countries at any one time. The culmination of this social scene is found at the world famous barbecues that take place every Sunday at the marina. The marina itself has room for about 600 yachts afloat, with the owners of the marina in touch with many more by ham radio. If a spare bunk opens up on a yacht sailing in the eastern Mediterranean, the staff there would know about it. In addition, the owners of the marina also organize a cruising regatta each spring.

Limassol, while not quite as massive as Larnaca, has a marina and some municipal docks as well as a small travelift and modest boatyard. Paphos has very little for traveling yachts beyond a protected anchorage.

ISRAEL

Israel does not have extensive foreign involvement in its sailing activities, due to its security restrictions and its lack of enticing coastline. Sailors that are interested in visiting Israel usually leave their yachts elsewhere, although the Mediterranean ports of this country are perfectly suitable for transiting yachts.

The Mediterranean coast of Israel has two good ports: Tel Aviv and Haifa. Tel Aviv has the main body of the indigenous sailing population and the best facilities. Visit the Atarim Marina and the boatyard close by. In Haifa, visit the Haifa Yacht Club and the repair facilities there. There are also marinas at Jaffa, near Tel Aviv and at Akko, by Haifa. The rest of Israel is ignored by the foreign cruising crowd. Just remember that the clearance requirements are stringent in Israel and you must have things in order if you plan to leave the country by yacht. Be prepared to be searched and to be asked a great deal of questions.

EGYPT

In Port Said, visit the Port Said Yacht Club, which is where the yachts awaiting a canal crossing moor or tie up to the dock. The yachts waiting to cross the Canal usually are required to sit two to four days for the permit to be processed, giving you time to get to know the crew. There is a small boatyard in Port Said, and the provisioning there is reasonable, but groceries are usually delivered to the yacht club.

In Alexandria there is the Yacht Club of Egypt, which is dirty and corrupt. The only cruising yachts that you will find there are those who do not know any better, and chances are once they see the club's obsession with separating the clients from their money, they will be in a hurry to get out fast. Regardless, it is reported that Alexandria has the best repair facilities in all of Egypt, with a few small boatyards and workshops.

EPILOGUE

To those of you who wish to report to me any changes to any of the ports you have visited, or you find your accounts to be different than mine, please send them to me via *High Adventure Publishing* at the address on the title page. Leave me your phone number and I will contact you to discuss possible changes in later editions. If you have any special requests or you need special information of this nature, please write me a letter, and I will answer it if I am able.

This concludes your vicarious tour of the world, and with that I leave you to your resources. Good luck.

APPENDIX 1
WORLD CHARTERS

CHARTERS IN THE ATLANTIC

Sun Days Worldwide Charters, Canary Islands 011-44-822-853375.
Yachting International Ireland, Canary Islands 011-353-61-333206.
Char-Ten, Canary Islands (800) 423-4460.
Florida Yacht Charters (800) 537-0050.

CHARTERS IN THE CARIBBEAN:

A-B Sea Sailboat Charters (800) 227-5127. 14 yachts to 35 feet located in Tampa Bay.

Eleuthera-Bahamas Charters (800) 548-9684. 25 yachts to 45 feet, located in Hatchet Bay, Eleuthera, Bahamas.

Bahamas Yachting Services (800) 327-2276. 21 yachts to 40 feet located in Marsh Harbor, Abaco, Bahamas; 19 yachts to 52 feet located in Philipsberg, St. Maarten.

Southwest Florida Yachts (800) 262-7939. 30 yachts to 37 feet in Fort Myers, Fl.

St. Petersberg Yacht Charters (813) 823-2555. 11 yachts to 41 feet, located in St. Petersberg, Fl.

ATM Yachts (800) 227-5317. 45 yachts to 45 feet, located in Guadeloupe and Martinique; 4 yachts to 50 feet in Ance Marcel, Saint Martin.

Abaco Bahamas Charters (800) 626-5690. 14 yachts to 44 feet located in Hope Town, Abaco, Bahamas

Bimini Yachting Vacations (800) 444-3996. 10 yachts to 47 feet in St. Maarten; 27 yachts to 47 feet located in St. Thomas, USVI; 8 yachts to 47 feet located in St. Vincent, Grenadines.

Bitter End Yacht Club (800) 872-2392. 11 yachts to 30 feet located in Virgin Gorda, BVI.

Brittish Virgin Islands Charters (800) 533-2842. 10 yachts to 44 feet located in Nanny Cay, Tortola, BVI.

Caribbean Sailing Charters (800) 824-1331. 18 yachts to 50 feet located in St. Thomas, USVI.

Caribbean Sailing Yachts (800) 631-1593. 35 yachts to 51 feet located in Tortola and St. Vincent, BVI.

Caribbean Yacht Charters (800) 225-2520. 44 yachts to 52 feet located in St. Thomas, USVI.

Discovery Yacht Charters, Inc. (416) 891-1999. 6 yachts to 42 feet located in Tortola, BVI

Go Vacations (416) 674-1880. 8 yachts to 45 feet, located in Grenada; 7 yachts to 38 feet located in Simpson Bay, St. Maarten

Hinckley Charters Caribbean (809) 776-6256. 16 yachts to 51 feet located in Caneel bay, St. John, USVI.

La Vida Charters (800) 524-2550. 23 yachts to 47 feet, located in St. Thomas, USVI; 31 yachts to 51 feet located in St Martin

MIRA Swan Charter (800) 833-7926. 17 yachts to 46 feet located in St Maarten.

Misty Isle Yacht Charters (800) 668-7727. 18 yachts to 41 feet located in Virgin Gorda, BVI

North South Yacht Vacations (800) 387-4964. 28 yachts to 39 feet located in BVI.

Privilege Charters Inc. (302) 655-1405. 13 yachts to 45 feet located in St. Martin, Guadeloupe.

Russel Yacht Charters (800) 635-8895. 24 yachts to 52 feet located in Fort de France, Martinique, Grenadines.

St. Maarten Bluewater Cruising (416) 845-7007. 6 yachts to 40 feet located in Phillipsburg, St. Maarten.

Sun Yacht Charters (800) 772-3500. 40 yachts to 47 feet located in Oyster Pond, St. Martin; 15 yachts to 53 feet located in Ance Marcel, St. Martin; 25 yachts to 47 feet located in Crabb's Peninsula, Antigua.

Sunsail Stevens (800) 638-7044. 45 yachts to 47 feet located in Tortola, BVI and St Lucia.

The Moorings (800) 535-7289. 41 yachts to 50 feet in St. Lucia; 12 yachts to 50 feet located in Granada; 138 yachts to 50 feet located in Tortola, BVI; 22 yachts to 50 feet located in St. Martin; 23 yachts to 50 feet located in Guadeloupe

Tropic Island Yacht Management, Ltd (809) 494-2450. 30 yachts to 50 feet located in Maya Cove, BVI.

Via Carib Yacht Charters (514) 982-6649. 10 yachts to 43 feet located in St. Lucia.

CHARTERS IN THE PACIFIC.

Alaska Wilderness Sailing Safaris (907) 835-5175. 5 yachts in Whittier, Ak. 40-foot yachts are crewed for sailing in the Prince William Sound.

Alaska Sailing Adventures (907) 835-5175. Fleet located in Valdez, Ak.

Wind Works Sailing School Rentals and Charters (206) 784-9386. 7 yachts to 40 feet, located at Shilshole Bay Marina of Puget Sound.

Marina Sailing of Channel Islands (805) 985-5219. Based in Channel Harbor, Ca. with 25 yachts to 43 feet for sailing to the Channel Islands.

Sailing Center of Santa Barbara (800) 350-9090. 40 yachts to 50 feet sailing along the Santa Barbara coast and the Channel Islands.

San Diego Yacht Charters (619) 297-4555. 20 yachts to 42 feet.

The Moorings (800) 535-7289. 11 yachts to 50 feet located in the Sea of Cortez Baja base of Puerto Escondido; 11 yachts to 50 feet located in Tonga; 22 yachts to 50 feet located in the Leeward islands of Tahiti.

ATM Yachts South Pacific (800) 227-5317. 18 yachts to 50 feet, located in Faaroa Bay, Raiata, Tahiti.

Sun Yacht Charters (800) 772-3500. New fleet in Tahiti.

Charter Link New Zealand 649-09-5358710. 17 yachts to 45 feet, located in Auckland, NZ.
Rainbow Yacht Charters 649-09-3780719. Fleet in Auckland, NZ; fleet in Vava'u in Tonga and in Fiji.
Queensland Yacht Charters (008) 075 013. Fleet location: Airlie Beach, Queensland, Australia.
Whitsunday Yacht Charters (079) 469 512. Fleet located in Whitsunday Islands, Queensland, Australia.

CHARTERS IN THE MED

GPSC Charters Ltd. (800) 732-6786. 264 yachts to 55 feet, spread out all over the Mediterranean in Athens; Marmaris, Turkey; Palma De Mallorca, Spain; Sardinia, Italy; Split, Yugoslavia.
Russel Yacht Charters (800) 635-8895. 98 yachts to 52 feet located in Athens, Corfu, Salonika, Rhodes and Lesvos, Greece.
Alpha Yachting, Piraeus, Greece 4164642-4525602
The Moorings (800) 535-7289. Extensive fleet in Greece out of Athens, Corfu, Porto Carras, Rhodes and Kos; in Turkey out of Marmaris and Finike; in France out of Hyèrs, Juan-les-Pins and the Corsican ports of Ajaccio and Maccinaggio; and in the ports of Palma, Mallorca and Ibiza in the Balearic Islands of Spain.

CREWED CHARTER COMPANIES

A Windward Mark (800) 633-7900. Camden, Me

Albatross (800) 922-4864

Anacortes Yacht Charters (206) 293-4355 Washington State.

Ann-Wallis White (301) 263-6366 Maryland.

ATM Yachts (800) 634-8822

Avery's Boathouse (809) 776-0113 USVI, Caribbean.

Bay Breeze Yacht Charters (616) 941-0535

Bay Island Yacht Charters (800) 421-2492

Blackbeard Charters (800) 327-9600. Miami, Fl.

Burr Yacht Charters (313) 463-8629.

Burr Yacht Charters (800) 445-6592

BVI Bareboats (800) 648-7240

Cape Yacht Charters (800) 345-5395.

Caribbean Sailing Charters (800) 824-1331

Carolina Wind Yacht Charters (800) 334-7671.

Cruzan Yacht Charters (800) 628-0745. Florida

CYOA (800) 524-2073. St. Thomas, USVI

Dolphin Yachting (800) 524-8292. St. Thomas, USVI, Caribbean.

Eagle Yacht Charters (516) 944-6760

Easy Sailing (800) 780-4001

Ed Hamilton and Co. (800) 621-7855

Educational Cruising (805) 967-4700

Ela Yachting (613) 234-3360

Florida Yacht Charters (800) 537-0500

Fraser Charters (619) 225-0588

Fun in the Sun (800) 327-0228

GPSC Ltd. (800) 732-6786

Hinckley Charters Caribbean (809) 776-6257. USVI, Caribbean

Hinckley Crewed Charters (207) 224-5531

Honolulu Sailing Co. (800) 829-0114

International Charter Connection, (800) 366-6532.

Island Yachts (800) 524-2019

JAC Worldwide Yacht Charters (800)662-2628. Antibes, France.

Jet Sea USA (305) 467-6600

Jubilee Yacht Charters (800) 922-4871

Landfall Charters (800) 255-1840. Florida

Le Boat (800) 922-0291

Lynn Jachney Charters (800) 223-2050

Mckibben Sailing Vacations (800) 845-0028

Mystic Yacht Charters (800) 873-2692

Nicholsen Yacht Charters (800) 662-6066

North-South Yacht Vacations (800) 387-4964

Ocean Charters (800) 922-4833

Privilege Charters (800) 262-0309. Florida

Proper Yachts (809) 776-6256.USVI.

Seabreeze Yacht Charters (800) 388-6224.

Seven Seas Yacht Charters (800) 346-5355

Southwest Florida Yachts (800) 262-SWFY

St. Petersberg Yacht Charters (813) 823-2555

Sun Yacht Charters (207) 236-9611

Sunsail (800) 327-2276.

The Moorings (800) 437-7880.

Thomas Sailing (800) 258-8753

Trade Wind Yachts (800) 825-7245

Tropic Island Yacht Management (809) 494-2450. BVI.

Vacation Yachts (800) 833-7926

Valef Yachts USA (800) 223-3845

Whitney Yacht Charters (800) 223-1426

For a more complete list, see the annual August charter issue of Cruising World Magazine.

Bibliography

A Cruising Guide to the Caribbean, Stone, William T. and Hays, Anne M., G. B. Putnam's Sons, New York, 1990

A Cruising Guide to the Caribbean and the Bahamas, Hart, Jeremy and Stone, William, T., G. B. Putnam's Sons, New York, 1982

Belize and Mexico's Caribbean Coast, Rauscher, Freya, Wescott Cove, Stamford, CT., 1991

Belize Handbook, Mallan, Chicki, Moon Publications, California, 1991

Best Sailing Spots Worldwide, Robinson, Bill, William Morrow and Co., NY, 1991

Carribbean Island Hopping, Bellamy, Frank, Gentry Books Ltd, Great Brittian, 1979

Chapman's Piloting, Maloney, Elbert, S., Hearst Marine Books, NY, 1989

Charlie's Charts of the Hawaiian Islands, Wood, Charles E., Charlie's Charts, Canada, 1986

Charlie's Charts of the US Pacific Coast, Wood, Charles E., Charlie's Charts, Canada, 1988

Charlie's Charts of the West Coast of Mexico, Wood, Charles E., Charlie's Charts, Canada, 1990

Circumnavigating Australia's Coastline -2-, Toghill, Jeff, Reed Books Pty Ltd, NSW, 1988

Cruising Guide to Eastern Florida, Young, Clayborne S., Pelican Publishing Co., Gretna, Louisiana, 1990

Cruising Guide to Tahiti and the French Society Islands, Davock, Marcia. Wescott Cove, Stamford, Ct. 1985

Cruising Guide to the Northern Gulf Coast, Young, Clayborne S., Pelican Publishing Co., Gretna, Louisiana, 1991

Cruising Guide to the Northwest Caribben, Calder, Nigel, Tab Books, Camden, Maine, 1991

Cruising Guide to the Virgin Islands, Doyle, Chris, Cruising Guide Publications, Inc., Clearwater, Florida, 1992

Cruising Guide to Western Florida, Young, Clayborne S., Pelican Publishing Co., Gretna, Louisiana, 1992

Cruising the Pacific Coast, West, Jack and Carolyn, Pacific Search Press, Seattle, Wa., 1984

Cruising World Magazine articles by Nigel Calder, *A New Day Dawnin' in the DR,* July, 93, pp. 30-32; Jimmy Cornell, *Another Side of Egypt,* Sep. 92, pp. 77-80, *Asian Crossroads,* April 92, pp. 81-82, *The Azores,* Nov. 91, pp. 48-55, *Bali High,* March 92, pp. 91-93, *Central St. Lucia,* Aug. 92, pp. 93-95, *The Columbus Coast,* Dec. 92, pp. 76-77, *Convenient Costa Del Sol,* Nov. 92, pp. 85-86, *Darwin: Indian Ocean Getaway,* Feb. 92, pp. 68-70, *Destination: Indian Ocean,* Jan. 92, pp. 38-42, *Heart of the Riviera,* Mar. 93, pp. 79-81, *Islands of Eternal Spring,* June 89, pp. 26-29, *Landfall: Gibraltar,* Feb. 89, pp. 22-23, *The Malacca Road to Phuket,* May 92, pp. 81-83, *Mediterranean Stepping Stones,* Dec. 92, pp. 76-78, *Popular Province,* May 93, pp. 85-87, *Portals to the Red Sea,* July 92, pp. 71-72, *The Rambunctious Red Sea,* Aug. 92, pp. 61-64, *The Riviera Rundown,* Feb. 93, pp. 91-93, *Run Up the Welcome Flag,* Oct. 90, pp. 23-25, *Sri Lanka Make and Mend,* June 92, pp. 77-79, *Tranquil Venice Lagoon,* Jan. 93, pp. 93-95, *Trans-Atlantic Stepping Stones,* Aug. 90, pp. 21-22, *West to San Tropez,* Apr. 93, pp. 109-111, *Winter Hideaways,* June 90, pp. 20-22, Articles by Earl Hinz *Avoiding Tropical Cyclones,* Nov. 90, pp. 19-21, *Destination: Hawaii,* Mar. 88, pp. 79-89, *Destination: Micronesia,* June 90, pp. 42-49, *Getting Along in Fiji,* May 91, pp. 35-36, Mar. 91, p. 45; *Tahiti's Leeward*

Islands, March 89, pp. 26-27, *Two Samoas, A World Apart*, Mar. 90, p. 29, Kellogg Flemming, *Basking in the Balearics*, Feb. 89, pp. 62-65, *Cyprus*, Apr. 88, pp. 22-25, *More Than a Canal*, Mar. 93, pp. 42-46; George Day, *Passage to the Pacific*, Dec. 91, pp. 51-55, *Tamure, Tamure*, May 92, pp. 56-61; Bob Duke, *Destination Ensinada*, Feb. 89, pp. 93-97; Ron Gray, *Cruising Mexico's Gold Coast*, Nov. 92, pp. 58-62; Danny Greene, *Islands Beyond the Stream*, Apr. 92, pp. 62-63; Tristan Jones *An Island Between Two Worlds* July 88, pp. 18-23; Katherine Knight, *New Scene at Balboa Y. C.*, May 93, p. 13; Frank Papy, *Destination: Florida Keys*, Jan. 89, pp. 97-103; Tor Pinney, *Agua Dulce, Guatemala*, Oct. 92, pp. 64-67; John Raines, *Transiting the Canal*, Mar. 93, pp. 47-49; Bill Robinson, *Phuket*, Mar. 90, pp. 114-117; Don Street, *An Atlantic Outpost*, Feb. 88, pp. 59-62; Simon-Craig Van Collie, *The People's Race to Hawaii*, Feb. 91, pp. 27-28; Cruising World's Editorial Staff, *Cruising World's Sailing Vacation Guide*, Aug. 93, pp. 37-68.

Dollarwise Guide to the Bahamas, Frommers, Porter, Darwin, Prentice Hall, NY, 1988

Fieldings 1989 Caribbean, Zellers, Margaret, William Morrow and Co., NY, 1989

Fodor's Cancun, Cozumel, Yucatan, Fodors Travel Publications, Inc., NY, 1991

Fodor's Caribbean, Fodors Travel Publications, Inc., NY, 1992

Fodor's Jamica, Fodors Travel Publications, Inc., NY, 1992

Fodor's Pocket Puerto Rico, Fodors Travel Publications, Inc., NY, 1991

Fodor's Virgin Islands, Fodors Travel Publications, Inc., NY, 1991

Greek Waters Pilot, Heikell, Rod; Imray, Laurie, Norie and Wilson Ltd, Cambridgeshire, England, 1990

Landfalls of Paradise, Hinz, Earl, R., Western Marine Enterprises, Inc., California, 1986

Let's Go Mexico, Harvard Student Agencies, Inc., NY, 1991

Los Angeles Times *Cruisers Soak Up Salty Stories*, Shearlean Duke, page E2, October 6, 1993.

Sail Magazine Articles by Kent Brokenshire, *Down and Out in Antigua and Barbuda*, Apr. 91, pp. 110-113; Frank Rosenow, *For a Season, Home*, Dec. 90, pp. 61-62; Bob Paine, *Where Columbus Slept*, Dec. 90, pp. 43-47; Amy Ullrich, *Under a Mythic Spell*, Sept. 90, pp. 81-85; Nancy Schwalbe Zydler, *An Island For Every Day*, Oct. 90, pp. 60-63;

Sailors Guide to the Leeward Islands, Doyle, Chris, Cruising Guide Publications, Clearwater, Florida, 1991

Sailors Guide to the Windward Islands, Doyle, Chris, Cruising Guide Publications, Clearwater, Florida, 1986

Sea of Cortez Guide, Brown, Dix, Western Marine Enterprises, Inc., Ventura, Ca., 1982

The Traveller's Handbook, Shales, Melissa, The Globe Pequot press, UK, 1988

The Weather Book, Williams, Jack; Vintage Books, NY, 1992

Waterway Guide, Northern Edition 1991, Edited by Judith Powers, CCI, Hilton Head, SC, 1991

Waterway Guide, Mid-Atlantic Edition, 1989, Edited by Judith Powers, CCI, Hilton Head, SC, 1989

Waterway Guide, Southern Edition 1992, Edited by Judith Powers, CCI, Hilton Head, SC, 1992

World Cruising Handbook, Cornell, Jimmy, Tab Books, Camden, Maine, 1991

World Cruising Routes, Cornell, Jimmy, Tab Books, Camden, Maine, 1990

World Cruising Survey, Cornell, Jimmy, Tab Books, Camden, Maine, 1989

Yachtsman's Guide to the Bahamas, Fields, Meredith Helleberg, Tropic Isle Pub., Inc., No, Miami Florida, 1988

Yachtsman's Guide to the Virgin Islands, Fields, Meredith Helleberg, Tropic Isle Pub., Inc., No, Miami Florida, 1990

Index